HANDBOOK KEY

LOGICAL COMPLETENESS

45	46	47	48	49
Sentence Unity	Faulty Co-ordination	Faulty Subordination	Overloaded Sentences	Choppy Style
50	**51**			
Comparisons	Words Left Out			

CLEARNESS AND ORDER

52	53	54	55	56
Awkwardness Obscurity	Proper Arrangement	Dangling Modifiers	Reference of Pronouns	Parallelism Correlatives
57	**58**	**59**	**60**	
Shift in Point of View	Mixed Constructions	Mixed Imagery	Transitions	

EFFECTIVENESS

61	62	63	64	65
Emphasis by Position	Repetition	Balance	Climax	Weak Passive Voice
66	**67**			
Conciseness	Variety			

THE PARAGRAPH

68	69	70	71	72
Topic Sentence	Length	Unity	Arrangement	Use of Details
73				
Transitions				

STYLE

74	75	76		
Tone	Maturity	Concreteness		
77				
Glossary				

The Macmillan Handbook of English

THE MACMILLAN COMPANY
NEW YORK · BOSTON · CHICAGO · DALLAS
ATLANTA · SAN FRANCISCO

MACMILLAN AND CO., Limited
LONDON · BOMBAY · CALCUTTA · MADRAS
MELBOURNE

THE MACMILLAN COMPANY
OF CANADA, Limited
TORONTO

THE MACMILLAN
HANDBOOK
OF ENGLISH

by John M. Kierzek
Professor of English, Oregon State College

THE MACMILLAN COMPANY
NEW YORK

Published January, 1939
Eighth Printing January, 1946

Set up and electrotyped by T. Morey & Son
Printed in the United States of America

PREFACE

The Macmillan Handbook of English is designed for use in college courses in English composition. The technique of using a handbook, either as a basic text in the classroom or as a reference book, is so well known that nothing more need be said about it here. The author of a new handbook, however, should be permitted to call attention to certain special features in it.

This book is a rhetoric and a handbook combined. It may be used as either or as both. The first part of the book attempts to give the beginner the sort of helpful, common-sense advice about writing that he needs the most when he is a beginner. This section is followed by chapters on grammar as a tool of effective writing, on the building of good sentences, on paragraph structure, and on the writing of the research paper. The material of the second part of the book—the handbook itself—is organized under seventy-seven rules. An index and a theme-correction chart help both the student and the teacher to find any rule easily and quickly.

It is most difficult for any author to speak of his own work with appropriate objectivity. If this book has merits, the students and the teachers who use it will find them soon enough. What I can say here will not add to their total. Yet I wish to explain a point of view which I have tried to keep throughout the book. I have tried to treat the student as a mature person. I have tried to speak to him as one learner would speak to another. A learner must be guided by rules until he knows enough about writing to be superior to rules. If I were learning to skate, or to dance, or to play tennis, I should submit myself to a discipline, knowing well that there is a freedom beyond rules. There is a freedom in writing which comes as a result of discipline. The student will understand, I trust, that although every rule in the book is based on strictly contemporary usage, this usage has been interpreted with discretion and a reasonable conservatism. The rules are the discipline of learning.

But the student should also see that scattered throughout the book there are numerous references to more comprehensive and scholarly discussions of English usage. These are the invitations to the student to investigate for himself and to decide for himself. These are the open doors through which he may walk—and discover, perhaps, some lifelong interests.

To Professor Oscar Cargill, of Washington Square College, New York University, my most hearty thanks for his helpful criticism of the book in manuscript and in proof.

J. M. K.

CORVALLIS, ORE.
December, 1938

CONTENTS

CONTENTS

CONTENTS

CONTENTS

CONTENTS

CONTENTS

PART III: APPENDIX

Part I: The Expression and Communication of Thought

Writing is like pulling the trigger of a gun: if you are not loaded, nothing happens.—Henry Seidel Canby.

THE THEME

You have attended the first meeting of the English composition class. Like most first meetings, it was a solemn affair, somewhat terrifying—to your instructor as well as to you. Sitting there, feeling curious and awed, depressed or amused, or even comfortably superior, you dutifully recorded in your notebook the instructor's name and his office hours, listened to his explanation of the nature of the course, heard a familiar phrase, "The object of all writing is the communication of ideas or impressions from one mind to another," and then—

"For our next meeting I shall ask each of you to write a theme—" ("How many words, please?" "Oh, something between five hundred and a thousand will do.") "—a theme out of the material of your own experience and observation."

"What kind of theme? . . . What shall we write about? . . . Does it have to be true? . . . May we write a story? . . . I haven't anything to write about! . . . Won't you please assign us a subject?"

"Just write about yourself," continued the unruffled voice of your instructor. "Tell me where you have lived, what work you have done, what hobbies you have been interested in. Tell me about your education, your friends, your sports, your ambitions, your disappointments. If you wish, tell me what brought you to college, what your religion is, what your philosophy of life is. Write about something that means much to you. I want to get acquainted with you as quickly as I can. I want to know you as individuals, as persons, not as a class in English composition. The better I know you, the more I can help you with your problems in writing."

"Just write about yourself—" Troubled and vaguely disturbed, you left the classroom, confronted at the start with all the fundamental problems of writing. You knew you had something to say, for you had lived, you had gone to school, you had thought about your friends, about your education, your hobbies, your sports. You had read books and magazines. You had ideas about politics, marriage, dictators, unemployment, dancing, baseball, motion pictures. You actually had too much to write about. Your real problem was how to select one out of the thousand interesting subjects you could write about, how to organize your material, how to present it to your reader so that it would mean to him what it meant to you. You had to catch your reader's attention and hold his interest until he had finished reading what you had written.

You had expected to be taught how to write—if you are an exceptional student, you may even have thought of education as the process of learning instead of being taught—but you did not expect to produce a theme day after day, or three times a week, or once a week, before you had made your own the magic power of laying words end to end in such a way that they would come alive before the eyes of your instructor. You are told to learn to write by writing. And your common sense tells you that this is a reasonable method. In fact, there is no other way. We must all learn to write by writing.

The first few pages of this little book have been written to help you with your problems at the beginning of the course in English composition.

WHAT TO WRITE ABOUT

If you honestly feel that you have nothing to write about, the best thing for you to do is to write a theme explaining to your instructor just why you have nothing to write about. You have never been outside of your own dull, prosaic, conventional town, where nothing ever happens. You have never read anything. You do not dislike hobbies; you are just not interested in them. Sports are a dreadful bore. You have no friends. Your parents just happened to you. You did not come to college; you were sent here. You have often wondered why you are so different from other persons of your age. In short, you are a monstrosity, incredible, an amazing *lusus naturae*—but, of course, that is all utter nonsense.

Actually you are a normal young person of college age, and your native good sense tells you that you can save yourself much fretful wasting of time by immediately taking stock of your resources. You can begin to organize and classify your experiences. Let us start this process of taking stock with a list of general subjects about which every college student has something to say:

1. Occupations	6. Sports	11. Friends
2. Hobbies	7. Morals	12. Nature
3. Reading	8. Manners	13. Pets
4. Travel	9. Customs	14. Organizations
5. Education	10. Home	15. Amusements

Now let us take each of these large divisions and draw up a list of possible theme subjects. And, by the way, let us not confuse subjects and titles. These are *not* titles.

Occupations

1. Applying for a job	5. The work of a life guard
2. The lure of aviation	6. How hops are picked
3. Why I want to teach	7. Running a paper route
4. Washing dishes in a sorority house	8. The waitress at a summer resort

9. Growing prize-winning roses
10. Why I want to be an engineer
11. With the night crew
12. Delivering groceries
13. I want to be a country doctor
14. My job is keeping house
15. I know a plant hybridizer
16. A clerk in a department store
17. Marriage as a career
18. I caddie at the country club
19. The work of a football coach
20. Does society owe me a job?

Some of these subjects you know nothing about. Others you could discuss intelligently. Check these for future use. Now think about the work that you have done and the work that you plan to do after you leave college. Consider the various aspects of your job, occupation, profession, or career—whichever it is to you—analyze it in terms of your qualifications, the opportunities it offers, the spiritual and material returns you expect from it. Then proceed to add twenty more theme topics to this list. Record these in your notebook.

If you question the value of a theme of this sort, glance through some of the popular magazines, like *Harper's Magazine*, *Scribner's Magazine*, or *The Saturday Evening Post*, and notice how frequent are the essays or articles discussing either an occupation or the relations of men and women to the work they do.

Hobbies

1. What is a hobby?
2. What is philately?
3. Indian relics
4. Collecting first editions
5. Strange hobbies I have observed
6. Hunting with bow and arrow
7. Semiprecious stones
8. Building model airships
9. Wood carving
10. Mother collects antiques
11. Hunting with a camera
12. Making enlargements
13. Building birdhouses
14. Hobbies for profit
15. Grooming a prize-winning calf
16. What I know about guns
17. Tying trout flies
18. Collecting sunrises
19. My short-wave set
20. What my hobby has done for me

WHAT TO WRITE ABOUT

Reading

1. What I read for recreation
2. Books that have influenced me
3. Why I prefer biographies
4. Censoring my mother's reading
5. How I read the daily paper
6. The pulp magazines
7. Beauty-shop magazines
8. The typical true-confession story
9. Why adventure appeals to me
10. My favorite character from fiction
11. Here is a book you should read
12. Books for a hermit on a desert island
13. Outguessing the author
14. Great detectives of fiction
15. I should like to be an author
16. Newsstand magazines
17. Books my English teacher recommends
18. Books my English teacher should read
19. What is a classic?
20. Why I like poetry

Travel

1. Seeing America first
2. Travel as an education
3. Exploring in a canoe
4. Tourist camps
5. Walking tours
6. Passports and visas
7. A trip to England
8. Touring with a trailer
9. The perfect vacation
10. Glacier Park trails
11. Visiting the national parks
12. The impossible traveling companion
13. A trip to Japan
14. What to take on a horseback trip
15. Camping in the Sierras
16. Travel by airplane
17. I like to meet people
18. The discomforts of travel
19. Travel in Russia
20. Traveling with a camera

Education

1. Why English?
2. The popular teacher
3. College or a job
4. Learning from experience
5. What is a practical education?
6. Educating the emotions
7. Learning or being taught
8. The education my father had
9. Does business want honor students?

10. The value of honor societies
11. What every dentist ought to know
12. What is a college?
13. My ideal university
14. College students I could do without
15. College professors who bore me

16. Aptitude tests
17. The value of a course in the arts
18. Youth is the time for experiments
19. The lecture course
20. Education for leisure

Sports

1. What is sportsmanship?
2. Learning how to take defeat
3. Strategy in tennis
4. The quarterback calls the plays
5. How to dribble in basketball
6. Bicycle clubs
7. How to sail a boat
8. What is a good coach?
9. Trout fishing
10. How to use a fly rod
11. Why Americans like baseball

12. Sports for the tired business man
13. What to watch in a football game
14. The fun of polo
15. Archery as a sport for women
16. How to hunt rattlesnakes
17. Fishing for salmon
18. Taking care of a trap line
19. To die for dear old Siwash!
20. The fastest game on earth

Morals

1. Changing conceptions of morality
2. Negative goodness
3. My religion
4. My philosophy of life
5. Is " necking " immoral?
6. The morals of business
7. Honesty—a virtue or a policy
8. Are chaperones necessary?
9. Cheating in examinations
10. An honor system (code)
11. Respect for the law

12. Gambling
13. Playing the slot machines
14. Borrowing
15. Going to church
16. What college has done to my religion
17. Self-reliance
18. Is cheating justified?
19. College students and drinking
20. It's all right if no one finds out

Manners

1. Manners in a sorority house
2. Are good manners important?
3. This modern freedom
4. Neglected courtesies
5. Manners in the home
6. When life was more formal
7. Joe College meets Jane Co-ed
8. Is college making us civilized?
9. What is gracious living?
10. At a formal dance
11. The type of college girl I like
12. The type of college man I like
13. Manners and personality
14. What is a gentleman?
15. There are no more ladies!
16. Etiquette for a "date"
17. "Don'ts" for the popular girl
18. One man I should like to remake
19. Be yourself
20. Politeness is frozen kindness

Customs

1. Family prayers
2. Wearing green caps
3. The fraternity initiation
4. Strange customs
5. Why do we shake hands?
6. We salute the flag
7. Cowboy ballads
8. Baptism by immersion
9. Ladies wear hats in church
10. Hog-calling contests
11. The woman does not pay
12. White ties and tails
13. Told to me by my grandmother
14. The snake dance of the Hopi Indians
15. A Polish wedding
16. The Pendleton Roundup
17. The new dances
18. Survivals of old pagan customs
19. The Saturday night bath
20. Rice and old shoes

Home

1. What makes a home?
2. A freshman son to his father
3. Sister falls in love
4. Planning a new house
5. Uses of structural glass
6. The outdoor living room
7. My mother
8. Home-making as a profession
9. The well-planned kitchen

10. Father comes home at night
11. The house of charm
12. The fireplace
13. I am an only child
14. Planning a small dinner party
15. Heating and air-conditioning systems
16. Antiques and good taste
17. Getting acquainted with father
18. I live in an apartment house
19. Financing a new home
20. Taking care of the baby

Friends

1. My dog is my best friend
2. What is friendship?
3. Mary is a fair-weather friend
4. To have a friend you must be one
5. The uses of friendship
6. Friends for different moods
7. Hysterical Helen
8. Shop-worn friends
9. The ethics of our gang
10. A shoulder to weep on
11. Friends I never miss
12. He didn't have what it takes
13. My roommate
14. She was always in trouble
15. We speak the same language
16. Friends I have almost forgotten
17. Girls I have known
18. The art of friendship
19. A boy's best friend is his motor
20. What older women have taught me

Nature

1. I want to be a naturalist
2. Making wild-flower collections
3. Transplanting wild flowers
4. The glass-bowl garden
5. Sunrises I have seen
6. On the lake in a storm
7. My favorite trout stream
8. Vacationing in the Cascades
9. I know an interesting swamp
10. Bird songs
11. How to photograph flowers
12. How to photograph lightning
13. Feeding birds in winter
14. Climbing a mountain
15. Nature and the farmer
16. The window garden
17. Miracles that nature never thought of
18. The work of plant hybridizers
19. Flowers of the desert
20. The passenger pigeon

WHAT TO WRITE ABOUT

Pets

1. Every boy should have a dog
2. The intelligence of cats
3. The one-man dog
4. The loyalty of a dog
5. Cats are independent
6. Strange pets I have heard about
7. Skunks make charming pets
8. My pet snake
9. How to take care of a horse
10. My pet won the blue ribbon
11. How to tame a chipmunk
12. Feeding stations for humming birds
13. We adopted a goat
14. My mother takes in stray cats
15. How to take care of a canary
16. Taming a coyote
17. A dog for an apartment house
18. My favorite breed of dogs
19. He was just a mongrel
20. The more I know men—

Organizations

1. Life in a fraternity house
2. How to direct a Camp Fire group
3. The Girl Scouts
4. Why I am a Republican
5. I belong to no party
6. Educated in a sorority house
7. Work of the Boy Scouts
8. Secret societies in high school
9. Why secret?
10. Rituals and ceremonies
11. What church membership means to me
12. Training for citizenship
13. The art club
14. A meeting of the writers' club
15. Learning to co-operate
16. The nonconformist
17. Too many clubs
18. Why I am a joiner
19. Loyalty or individualism
20. The American Student Union

Amusements

1. Chess, the perfect game
2. Do you read the comics?
3. How to enjoy a college dance
4. I play bridge by ear
5. Games for an informal party
6. Games for a beach picnic
7. Football as a spectacle
8. How to amuse a younger brother
9. Reading for recreation
10. Just loafing

11. How to entertain a chaperone
12. Playing football for fun
13. The play instinct
14. Coffee and conversation
15. A friendly game of poker

16. My idea of a perfect evening
17. Tears in the theater
18. The formal reception
19. Our neighbors drop in
20. Parlor games

Here are three hundred topics. Like the sensible, provident student that you are, you will explore this collection of topics, ready to mark the ones that touch something in your own experience. Underline them at once. Better still, copy them in your notebook. Add to your list a few topics of your own that this list will undoubtedly suggest to you.

THEMES OF PERSONAL EXPERIENCE

To a certain extent, all your writing must come from your own experience. What you write must come out of your head. If you are asked to use material that you have found by read-ing, or by asking questions, or by listening to the talk of an-other person, you must still assimilate your material, organize it, make it your own, before you can give it to others. If you quote, you must give credit for the quotation. To use the ideas or words of another without giving due credit is plagia-rism or literary stealing.

At the start you may be puzzled by hearing your instructor announce that your theme must be "expository." Most freshman composition courses stress exposition more than they do the other forms of writing: narration, description, and argument. But do not be disturbed. You have been using exposition all your life. Exposition is explanation. Through exposition you may make clear an idea, convey a fact or a re-lated series of facts, explain a process or a method, an organization or a system. You write exposition when you explain what you mean by a practical education, when you interpret a poem, when you tell how to make a contour map, when you make clear the organization of a CCC unit. All these are examples of themes from material of your own living, thinking, and observation. The range of subjects is almost infinite.

The following classification of types of expository writing is neither systematic nor comprehensive. It is to be taken simply as a preliminary survey, a rough map, which you will use until you can move about without the use of a map.

THE DEFINITION

Vote for the conservative candidate . . . he is a radical . . . he has no religion . . . he is not a gentleman . . . that is a communistic principle . . . she is utterly without a sense of loyalty—you hear these words thrown about as if pinning a label on a person settled anything. What do you mean by conservative, radical, religion, gentleman, communistic, or loyalty? To you a conservative may be a dignified statesman who radiates good sense and virtue; to me he may be a troglodyte who believes that nothing should ever be done for the first time. You see the need of exact definitions, so that you and your reader will be using words in the same sense. The writing of definition is, also, a valuable self-discipline, a check against fuzzy thinking.

In the formal, or scientific, definition, you put the term to be defined in a class or *genus* and then differentiate it from the other members of the class. In the informal definition you will also try to classify and differentiate, but you will have more freedom of method. Let us suppose that you indulge in a bit of analysis: just what do you mean when you speak of a man's religion? Is religion an attitude, a system of morals, an emotion, a set of rites and ceremonies? How does it differ from theology, from going to church, from a philosophy of life? What is essential? What is incidental or extraneous? State your ideas and then support them by concrete examples. What is a religious man? How does religion reveal itself in his daily living? What is a man without religion? How does he differ from a man with religion? You see what a theme of definition is—classifying, naming of essential qualities or attributes, telling what the term or object is and is like, telling what it is not, and clarifying every step by concrete instances.

THE PROCESS THEME

If you explain how to do something or how to make something, you are writing an exposition of a process. How to construct a mole trap, how to apply for a job, how to bud a rose, how to organize a camping party—these are all subjects for process themes. The method of writing them is simple. Arrange your material in the order of happening. Explain each step of the process clearly, taking care to give more space to that which is important, or difficult of understanding, less space to that which is less important. You may fictionize your material, that is, introduce a character who goes through the process you are explaining. Stewart Edward White, in explaining how to make camp, uses an interesting variation of this method. His fictional character first commits every mistake against which the author wants to warn his reader. Then by direct exposition the author explains how an experienced woodsman makes a camp.

Keep your reader in mind as you write. Explain so clearly that he cannot misunderstand you.

THE THEME OF FACTS AND IDEAS

Most of your themes will deal with facts and ideas in some form or other. A definition deals with facts. So does a process theme. But each calls for a special technique, which may be easily learned. The usual theme of facts calls for no special technique in arranging and presenting information. The writing of it is best approached from the point of view of an imagined reader. "Tell me why I should study architecture," he says to you. "Explain philately to me. Just what started the civil war in Spain? How does socialism differ from communism? How do you justify honor societies?" Your answer to any of these questions will constitute a theme of facts and ideas.

Let us suppose that your instructor has asked you to write about the causes of the civil war in Spain. "Hum-m-m," you ponder. "Just what do I know about this civil war in Spain? I haven't been there to observe. This, then, must be an invitation to find out by reading, to organize, simplify, and clarify the information, and then to present it in my own words." Precisely so. First get your facts. Then organize and simplify. How many causes were there? About fifteen? How many were really significant? About three or four. Then concentrate on three or four. Discuss each one in turn, and, if you think it necessary, mention the less important causes briefly in passing. If one cause is more important than the rest, use it at the end of your theme and give it more space.

As you plan and write, keep your reader in mind. You are writing for him. You are writing in order to give him information that is interesting to him, that is sifted out and arranged for his convenience, that is properly evaluated.

THE THEME OF OPINION

You may be asked to express your opinions on various subjects—books, fraternity initiations, subsidized football, lecture courses, traditions, modern music, or ancient dictators. It is well, for you and for the nation, that you have opinions, that you try to think for yourself. Thinking is occasionally painful, often dangerous, but always exhilarating. Opinions are judgment in the making. Do not be afraid to have opinions—nor to change them when you find that they are wrong. Above all, be honest in what you say. "Speak what you think now in hard words," wrote Emerson, "and tomorrow speak what tomorrow thinks in hard words again, though it contradict everything you said today." The world will probably see to it that you do not abuse your privilege.

In organizing the theme of opinion, remember again that in expository writing any order is better than no order at all. Select and group your ideas. Aim at your target—the reader. You think, for example, that college football players should be paid according to their value to the team. Your reader asks, "Why do you think so?" If you must explain in five hundred words, or eight hundred words, give him three or four good reasons. Support each reason by explanation, by examples, and by concrete details.

THE ASSIGNED SUBJECT

An assigned subject may call for material either from experience or from reading. A subject assigned to a whole class is usually a general one, which each student must limit to fit his own resources and point of view. For example, an instructor may say, "For your next theme, analyze yourself in terms of the job or profession for which you are preparing. Determine the qualities of personality or character which your profession demands. Analyze your own characteristics. Then try to explain how college is, or is not, preparing you for your chosen profession." An assignment like this is a legitimate task in thinking, analysis, and organization. Every theme in the class will be different, and yet all themes will be similar in purpose and to some extent in organization, for the assignment gives you the form to use. Or your instructor may ask you to write about football or fraternities. You cannot, it is plain, write all you know about football or fraternities. You proceed to narrow your subject; you select one topic out of many possible topics. In eight hundred words you cannot give the history of football or tell how to play it, but you can tell your reader how to watch the blockers clear the path in front of a quarterback running for a touchdown. You cannot give all the arguments for or against fraternities, but you can tell how your experience with one has made a civilized citizen out of an inhibited egotist.

If your instructor tells you to write a paper on the TVA, or the hero of *Paradise Lost*, or the discovery of insulin, your first step is to get the necessary information from the reference library. What phase of the subject you select will depend on what you think is significant and interesting.

HOW TO PLAN THE THEME

In planning your theme, let us repeat, you must limit your subject to fit the space you have, you must aim at your reader, and you must organize your material. In doing this you observe the rhetorical principles of unity, coherence, emphasis, and interest. All effective expository writing observes these principles—whether by intention or by accident does not matter.

After you have narrowed your subject, you should give your theme direction by deciding upon an objective. Let us make this clear by two examples. Your general subject is "Antiques." You decide to concentrate upon one idea—that a piece of antique furniture is worthless unless it possesses a functional beauty which would make it desirable even if it were not an antique. Or you choose to write on "How to take care of a horse." You do not intend to write about horses in general —farm horses, cavalry horses, draft horses. You write for a college girl who has been given a saddle horse, and you tell her how to feed and groom it. To make doubly sure that you are aiming at a target, try to express your theme idea in a single declarative sentence.

The outline for a short theme should be short. Your first impulse will be to attempt too much and to plan too elaborately. You may write your outline on a piece of paper or you may carry it in your head. An experienced writer will seldom make a written outline for a paper of a thousand words; he will plan, nevertheless, as carefully as you do.

Since most expository writing proceeds by topics, your first outline will consist of the topics which you must discuss in order to make your theme idea clear and interesting to your reader. Summarize in a single sentence what you intend to say about each topic, and you have the sentence outline. That is as far as you need to go. If an outline is to simplify a subject, it must be simple in itself. Do not clutter it with details. Save these for your finished theme. The fearful labyrinths which some students construct for outlines are worse than a waste of time.

HOW TO PLAN THE THEME

The following are examples of adequate outlines prepared by students in writing thousand-word themes:

Three More Laps to Go
(Outline)

1. My reasons for coming to college:
    a. To learn a trade
    b. To learn how to live
2. My reasons for wanting to learn a trade
3. My progress in secretarial science
4. My progress in culture and discipline:
    a. To find an ideal of beauty and culture
    b. To learn mental discipline
    c. To find my relation to the world I live in

The second outline is for a thousand-word process theme dealing with artificial pollination of corn:

More Bushels
(Outline)

1. Natural pollination by air
2. Importance of cross-pollination
3. Artificial pollination:
    a. Daily inspection of corn field
    b. Placing glycine bags over new shoots
    c. Observation of shoots through glycine
    d. Use of paper bags to catch pollen
    e. Shaking pollen over the corn silk
    f. Keeping records of pollination
4. Fixing a strain by "selfing"

The third is an outline for a process theme in which the writer decided to use the narrative method:

How to Sell Magazines
(Outline)

1. Scene on a rainy afternoon after a day of no sales
2. Conference with my guide and partner over my failures
3. My partner planning a test case of his methods:
   a. Not to refer to the magazines
   b. To talk about my own troubles
   c. To establish an atmosphere of sympathy
4. My return, with no sales, after being forced to listen to my customer's troubles
5. My partner making the sale
6. My partner explaining that he got the order by suggesting marriage to the prospect

HOW TO BEGIN

"The best way to begin is to begin. Do not write introductions. Just plunge in." All this is sound advice but meaningless to the beginner. One might as well tell him to learn how to dance by plunging in—some persons do dance that way—or to play contract, or to swim. After all, one must know what he is to do after he plunges in. Here are a few suggestions that may prove helpful. Other ways of plunging in are possible, and if you are really curious, you can find them for yourself by studying essays and articles in current magazines.

1. Begin by specifying the phase or aspect of the subject to which you intend to limit your discussion.

I have chosen to discuss what to me appears the most vital and, as it happens, also the most deadly issue of the day: war as a menace to our immediate future.

> —Bronislaw Malinowski, "The Deadly Issue," *The Atlantic Monthly*, vol. 158, p. 659 (December, 1936). Reprinted by permission.

HOW TO BEGIN

Here in America we have talked about the "depression" until most of us are heartily sick of the topic. In spite of all the talk, however, I have not heard much discussion of the third of the three crises through which we are passing simultaneously—the economic and political crises and the crisis in character.

> —James Truslow Adams, "The Crisis in Character," *Harper's Magazine*, vol. 167, p. 257 (August, 1933). Reprinted by permission.

2. Begin with an incident, real or imagined, out of which the discussion arises, or which illustrates the point of the discussion.

One day in the early weeks of 1931 two men were sitting with Lord Cecil in the British Foreign Office, in the so-called "cabinet room."

> —Philip Noel Baker, "The Drift toward War," *The Yale Review*, vol. 23, p. 662 (Summer, 1934). Reprinted by permission.

A long time ago—all of three years, perhaps longer—I saw a fleeting item in a periodical to the effect that 41 per cent of our national wealth is controlled by women, and that the percentage is rising.

> —Albert Jay Nock, "A Word to Women," *The Atlantic Monthly*, vol. 148, p. 545 (November, 1931). Reprinted by permission.

3. Begin with a question or a series of questions, the answers to which will constitute the essay.

Visiting a television studio gives the impression of looking directly into the future. The newest and most shining gadget of science—breathtaking in its implications—is about to emerge into everyday reality. What forms will television entertainment take? What new crafts and skills will it require in writing, acting, costuming, scene designing, lighting and directing? How will it relate itself to the other arts of the theatre—from which will it draw and upon which improve?

> —T. R. Carskadon, "Report on Television," *Theatre Arts Monthly*, vol. 21, p. 465 (June, 1937). Reprinted by permission.

4. Begin with a statement of the thesis which you intend to make clear or the problem which you intend to discuss.

The growing feeling, extending to all classes of the community, that life is purposeless is perhaps the most significant feature of our time.

> —J. W. N. Sullivan, "What and Where Are We?" *Harper's Magazine*, vol. 175, p. 1 (June, 1937). Reprinted by permission.

The time has come for the establishing of a new branch of public education in America. It is no longer enough that we teach children. . . . In a word, we must have a comprehensive scheme of adult education.

> —Alexander Meiklejohn, "Adult Education: a Fresh Start," *The New Republic*, vol. 80, No. 1028, p. 14 (August 15, 1934). Reprinted by permission.

5. Begin by stating your purpose in writing.

I write this memoir to recapture a past.

> —Angelo P. Bertocci, "Memoir of My Mother," *Harper's Magazine*, vol. 175, p. 8 (June, 1937). Reprinted by permission.

6. Begin by setting up something to knock down (the "straw man" beginning), such as a current notion, a tradition, a theory.

There is a thesis abroad in the land today, a thesis which, by dint of much repetition, is in a fair way to become an Accepted Fact. It is this: That militant Fascism as embodied by the states of the Rome-Berlin axis is about to overwhelm the "decadent" democracies of Europe, dismember the British and French colonial empires, and divide the spoils; whereafter democracy in the Western Hemisphere may well look to itself.

> —George Fielding Eliot, "Italy's Over-Estimated Power," *Harper's Magazine*, vol. 176, p. 511 (April, 1938). Reprinted by permission.

SUBSTANCE: USE OF DETAILS

You need not be told again that to reach the mind of your reader, to make him understand and to persuade him to accept emotionally, you must be specific and concrete. Generalities will not touch him. Your outline—a very important series of generalities, it is true—is the skeleton of your theme, with the emotional appeal, the personality, and the warmth of a skeleton. You must cover the skeleton with the living flesh. Explanations, specific details, instances, illustrations, concrete examples—out of these you build your theme.

The substance of themes of definition or process is obvious enough. Themes of fact are simple, too—if you know enough facts. If not, you will get the facts you need, or take another subject. But even facts need to be interpreted, clarified, or made to appear as significant as they have a right to be. Your real problem is to be found in writing themes of ideas and opinion. Here your best procedure is to muster for your reader the evidence out of which your general idea or opinion came into existence. Take, for instance, a general subject like "College grades." You, to the surprise of your instructor, undertake to defend the system of grades, by showing that it is not an artificial system found nowhere but in schools but a valuable preparation for the realities of the workaday world. One of your general ideas is that it resembles, in a milder form, the grading that every student receives from his fellow students. "Just

—23—

what do you mean by that?" asks your reader. "What gave you that idea?" That is it. What gave you the idea? "Well," you reply, "I've noticed. . . . The men at my fraternity house discussing Ted Jones, the new freshman from my town . . . brilliant, but. . . . Blackballed him. Look at the way they ripped into the theme Miss Short read today. A trifle flowery, but honest enough. Some of the comments on it were almost sadistic. Or the way the girls talk about each other's gowns after a dance. Or the way they label a fellow . . . you're a playboy or a grind or a greasy pud." Put material like this into your theme, and your reader will react as you did. Your next general idea is that grading in college will prepare the graduate for the inevitable grading he will get from his employer. "From the very first day," you will explain, "the employer grades his man. That man is an 'A' worker, he will think. He'll bear watching; we need 'A' men. That man is doing 'C' work; he's competent enough, but uninspired, without enthusiasm. That man is an 'F.' And the grades are recorded, not, as in college, at the end of the term or the end of the year, but with the weekly pay envelope. An 'A' means a promotion; an 'F' means dismissal." Put this into your theme. That is what we mean by substance.

UNITY

Enough has been said thus far about unity in exposition so that a summary of the important principles is all that is necessary here:

1. Have an aim or objective in writing; that is, have something to say which you feel your reader wants to know.
2. Choose a subject which is neither too large nor too small for the size of the essay which you intend to write.

3. Use details which will make your essay clear, impressive, and interesting.
4. Exclude all material which might take your reader's attention from the main idea.
5. Have a plan by which you intend to make the theme idea clear to the reader.

ORDER

The order in which you present your material to your reader will depend partly on what you have to say and partly on the sort of reader you are addressing.

If you are telling how something is made, how a game is played, how a system grew or developed in the course of time, you will naturally use the order of happening, called the chronological order. In themes like the following the chronological order is inherent in the material: how to build a cold frame, how to clean a rifle, the history of tennis, the development of Fascism, learning how to tap-dance, how to prepare for a final examination. When a subject does not logically call for this order, you can often achieve a clearer presentation by changing your approach so that you can use the order of time. You can explain a social or political system, for instance, by telling how it developed.

If for any reason you think it wise to keep from the reader the central thought of your discussion until you have reached the end, you may use the inductive order. This order is adapted to compositions in which a number of instances, facts, or observations all lead to a single generalization. It is useful where it is necessary to prepare the reader's mind for a new idea by the massing of evidence. For instance, if you are advocating the paying of wages to college athletes for playing football, you may get a more favorable reaction from your readers if you convince them first that the present system of indirect and secret subsidizing is vicious.

If you can divide your subject into several parts of equal importance, you may indicate the division in your opening paragraph and then discuss the parts one by one in the selected order. For convenience, we shall label this order the order of enumeration. "Communism differs from socialism in four important aspects," you begin. "Before the Diesel engine can be used in light motor cars, automotive engineers must solve the following three problems." "The duties of a county agent may be grouped under five different heads." "Six new types of barley have been grown experimentally in the Ohio valley." You can see from these examples how a large number of subjects will naturally require the order of enumeration. In writing you will, of course, let your reader know when you have finished one part and are beginning the next one.

If your subject is a complex organization, or a complicated piece of machinery, or an idea hard to grasp, you may start with the simple elements of your subject and gradually proceed to those more difficult to understand. You may call this order "from easy to hard," if you wish, or "from known to unknown," or "from near to far." Excellent examples of this order may be found in Huxley's essays and lectures on science.

If you are dealing with a subject in which the topics may be arranged in the order of increasing importance, it may be effective to use the order of climax.

PROPORTION

The amount of space that you give to each of the topics of your theme will depend on what you have to say and on your purpose in writing. Your purpose is often determined by your selection of a reading public.

Keeping in mind the old rule of "an interesting beginning and a strong ending," you will usually give relatively more space to the important topic which you have saved for the end of your theme. You put it at the end because you feel it is more important. You want to leave the reader with that topic or idea in his mind. How can you make your reader see your intention? Yes, of course, you may introduce the topic by some such phrase as, "And, finally, the most important—," but telling your reader that an idea is important is not always the same thing as making him think so. You need evidence. You need convincing details. And you need a certain amount of time for the idea to sink into his mind.

What is unimportant? Long, rambling introductions, formal conclusions, digressions from the central idea of the theme— you know all that.

Give space to that which is important; do not waste space on what is unimportant. That is an obvious principle of proportion. The real question, however, remains: what is important? In many themes one topic is no more important than another. In discussing a subject like the work of Camp Fire Girls, it makes little difference whether you discuss citizenship, nature study, reading, or woodcraft first or last. In writing a paper on "Agriculture in the Soviet Union," what difference is there between topics like "the use of tractors," "collectives," "scientific rotation of crops," and "control of drouth"? You may arrange the topics in any order you wish and give each one approximately the same space. In some themes your purpose determines the proportion you use. In an essay on the popularity of automobile trailers, for example, you may stress mechanical improvements or problems of sanitation in trailer camps or problems of highway engineering involved, depending on whether you are addressing prospective buyers or sociologists or engineers. If you are telling how to bud a rose, you may stress the use of different root stocks if you are writing for a florists' magazine, or the actual process of budding if you are writing for amateur gardeners.

THE ENDING

In a short theme, after the writer has discussed the last phase of his topic adequately, no literary device surpasses the finality of lifting the pen from the paper. The short theme has no room for summaries or formal conclusions.

In an article of several thousand words, a quick restatement of the theme idea is effective. If a summing up of the central idea is inconvenient, the reader's mind should be directed to some important thought related to the subject, not to a subordinate detail. A study of the essays published in any of our magazines, like *Harper's Magazine*, *The Atlantic Monthly*, *Scribner's Magazine*, or *The Yale Review*, will reveal methods used by professional writers.

EXERCISES

Exercise 1, Theme subjects. In your notebook start a list of topics you can discuss, suggested by and arranged under the fifteen general topics which you find on page 5. Give a half page to each of the general topics. Add to the lists from day to day as new suggestions come to your mind. Under each heading add facts and opinions as they occur to you. You will thus have a constantly growing author's notebook.

Exercise 2, Limiting the subject. Practice cutting down a general subject to a phase of it suitable for a theme of eight hundred or a thousand words. After each general subject write a statement of the narrowed subject as in the examples given below.

General subject	*Limited subject*
World peace	What is a pacifist?
A liberal education	Is my English teacher a liberal?
Athletics	How to throw the javelin
Life on a farm	Feeding the threshing crew
College traditions	The fraternity initiation

Reading for recreation
Horses
Life in a big city
This modern generation
The summer tourist
The New Deal
Careers for women
Nature
People
Modern music

Exercise 3, Stating the objective. It will be useful to you to form the habit of stating the purpose, objective, or intention of your theme in a single declarative sentence. Your objective may be to present an opinion, to expound an idea, or to present a fact or a series of facts. The form which your statement will take will depend on the kind of theme you have planned. Study the examples and then write sentences stating the objective for each of the subjects given.

Subject:　A challenge to liberal culture
Objective:　Students may appear indifferent to cultural subjects, but so long as college teachers who teach liberal subjects

are themselves neither cultured nor liberal, students are justified in their skeptical attitude.

Subject: A good teacher
Objective: A good teacher is one who knows that his students are more important than his courses.

Subject: Trout flies
Objective: My purpose is to give clear directions for tying four or five of the most important flies used by trout fishermen in my locality.

Subject: "Don'ts" for the popular girl
Objective: My purpose is to warn the popular college girl against the danger of assuming that popularity need not be deserved or worked for.

Subjects for analysis:

> Respect for the law
> Neglected courtesies
> The perfect secretary
> How to entertain a chaperone
> To live dangerously
> Be yourself
> The intelligence of a dog
> Playing baseball for fun
> Education for leisure
> A charming girl
> Marriage for love or security
> The revolt of modern youth

Exercise 4, The plan. The statement of each of the following subjects indicates the major divisions of a theme on that subject. Construct topical outlines for each of the subjects, giving the suggested main topics and several subtopics under each main division. You are planning a theme of about a thousand words. Do not make the outlines too elaborate.

Four college traditions I could do without
Three reasons for studying a science
Four characters of fiction I should like to meet
Three ways of being unpopular
Four arguments in favor of student self-government

Exercise 5, The plan. Select a subject for a theme of facts. Begin planning a fairly extensive treatment of the subject by phrasing six questions which an average reader would ask about your subject. Use the following example for your model:

Subject: Commercialism in college football

Questions:
1. How extensive is the practice of enticing high-school stars to out-of-state colleges by offers of high salaries and easy jobs?
2. What is the effect upon education of paying coaches more than is paid to regular members of the faculty?
3. Which are the worse offenders—the state universities or the endowed colleges?
4. What effect does the system have upon the characters of the players themselves?
5. Does the system bring many boys to college who otherwise could not get a college education?
6. Is the financial investment in buildings and football fields the cause or the result of the rivalry for good football talent?

Study these questions. Now construct a topical outline on the basis of the questions.

1. The extent of proselyting
2. High salaries paid coaches
3. The worst offenders
4. Evil effects upon athletes
5. Good results of system
6. Financial investment and proselyting

You may analyze these topics to determine which one you wish to discuss first and which one is so important that it must be discussed last. The following arrangement is a possible result of your analysis:

1. The extent of proselyting
2. The worst offenders
3. Financial investment—cause or result?
4. High-salaried coaches and education
5. Evil effects upon athletes
6. The good results of the system

Any subject may be analyzed in this manner. If the example used above does not make the method clear, study the following:

Subject: College women and marriage

Questions:
1. What percentage of college women marry as compared with non-college women?
2. Do college women make better wives than non-college women?
3. What do college women who have married say about the value of the courses they took in college?
4. What do the men they married say about the value of the college courses which their wives took?
5. Does the ability to earn a living influence the willingness of college women to marry?
6. Do college graduates make their marriages more permanent or happier than the average?

Subject: National parks

Questions:
1. How did the idea of having national parks start and grow?
2. Where are the parks located, and how can I reach them?
3. What recreational facilities do they offer?
4. What will it cost me to visit one?

5. What educational benefits will I get from visiting one?
6. What plans for their future development does the government have?

Exercise 6, The beginning. Select a subject that you want to use for a theme. Write four beginnings for it:

1. Begin by using an imagined incident which illustrates the point of your theme or out of which a discussion of your subject may seem to arise.
2. Begin by stating your purpose in writing.
3. Begin by stating the thesis, or central idea, that you intend to discuss.
4. Begin with a question or a series of questions.

With the advice of your instructor pick out the most successful beginning and use it in writing your theme.

Exercise 7, Order. Select a subject which can be developed by using the chronological order. Construct an outline for your theme. The following are subjects which may be used. Others will readily suggest themselves to you.

1. An issue of the college newspaper
2. How to bind a book
3. Learning to skate
4. Make your own Christmas cards
5. How to train a dog
6. Delivering your morning paper
7. The hostess at an informal dinner
8. How to entertain a chaperone
9. An issue of the literary magazine
10. How to explore the city

Exercise 8, Order. Make a list of five subjects which can be best presented by using the inductive order. Use two reasons for selecting subjects: you want to prepare your reader for an idea to which he is naturally antagonistic; you want to use a number of concrete instances so as to prepare his mind for a generalization.

Exercise 9, Proportion. Select an article that you like from the current issue of one of the better magazines. Let it be one of the shorter articles. Indicate the main divisions of the outline upon which it is based. Count the number of lines of print given to each main topic. Bring this analysis to class with you. A single essay may show you nothing of importance, but surely you will learn something valuable if all the members of the class pool their findings. What generalization can you make about proportion as a result of the study made by your class?

Exercise 10, The ending. Bring to class the concluding paragraphs or sections of three good magazine essays or articles. What does the author do in each case? Does he summarize? Does he stress an idea that he has already used? Does he introduce a new idea? Does he end with a minor detail?

THE SENTENCE

Grammar: The Tool of Effective Writing

A school superintendent once solemnly admonished a group of English teachers: "We need more useful grammar. We need less useless grammar." What part of grammar is useful? What part is useless? No one can say with absolute certainty. Much of the grammar that you will learn will be useless to you if you make it so. All of it will be useful to you if you study it not for itself but for what it will eventually give you—a greater ease, effectiveness, and interest in your writing. In your study of grammar keep the purpose always in view. The ability to pick out subjects and verbs and modifiers is not a virtue in itself. If you think that you can write well because you can tell the difference between a cognate accusative and an objective predicate, you are like a carpenter who thinks he can build a house because he can distinguish between a plane and a spirit level. Grammar is a tool of expression—rather, a chest of tools. You must learn how to use your tools, but before you can use them you must know what they are.

THE PARTS OF SPEECH

The following definitions are condensed and simplified, and therefore open to academic quibbling, but they will serve their purpose. You will probably learn more from the examples than from the definitions.

Words are classified according to their function or use in the sentence into classes called the parts of speech. Notice that the use in a sentence always determines the part of speech to which a word belongs.

1. A **noun** is a word that names something. It may name an object, a person, a place, or a quality.

The perfect *historian* is he in whose *work* the *character* and *spirit* of an *age* is exhibited in *miniature*.—Macaulay.

Space, time, society, labor, climate, food, locomotion, the *animals*, the mechanical *forces*, give us sincerest *lessons* . . . whose *meaning* is unlimited.—Emerson.

2. A **verb** is a word that asserts action, being, or state of being.

Birds *sing*. Why *are* you *crying?* I *did* not *think* about you. They *have brought* their relatives. I *am being spoiled* by too much attention.

3. A **pronoun** is a word that takes the place of a noun. Pronouns are classified as personal, demonstrative, relative, interrogative, and indefinite.

Personal: *I, you, he, she, it, they, we, them, thee, thou.*
Demonstrative: *this, that, these, those.*
Relative: *who, which, what, that, whoever, whatever, whichever.*
Interrogative: *who, which, what.*
Indefinite: *one, none, some, any, anyone, anybody, some one, somebody, no one, nobody, each, everyone, everybody, either, neither, both.*

4. An **adjective** is a word that modifies (describes or limits) a noun or pronoun. The articles *a, an, the,* and the possessive forms of nouns and pronouns, when used to modify nouns, are classed as adjectives.

The place through which he made *his* way at leisure was one of *those* receptacles for *old* and *curious* things which seem to crouch in *odd* corners of *this* town, and to hide *their musty* treasures from the *public* eye in jealousy and distrust.—Dickens.

A *high, clear* flame, *an immense* and *lonely* flame, ascended from *the* ocean, and from *its* summit *the black* smoke poured continuously at *the* sky.—Joseph Conrad.

5. An **adverb** is a word that modifies a verb, an adjective, or another adverb. Occasionally an adverb will modify a phrase, a clause, or a whole sentence.

He took his defeat *cheerfully*. Do *not* drive *so fast* around the corners. I *seldom* drive *fast*. The sermon was *rather* dull. He did *not* look *up*. *Yes*, he is *here*. *No*, we left *immediately* after the game. *Certainly*, I will return your book *soon*.

6. A **preposition** is a word used to show the relation between a noun or pronoun, called its object, and some other word in the sentence.

He wandered *about* the town. He looked *at* the blue sky *above* his head. The girl swam *across* the river. *Behind* the barn, *near* the apple tree, grew a lilac bush. It was now *in* full bloom.

The wind swept past *in* hissing floods, grinding the snow *into* meal and sweeping down *into* the hollows *in* enormous drifts all the heavier particles, while the finer dust was sifted *through* the sky, increasing the icy gloom.—John Muir.

7. A **conjunction** is a word which connects words, phrases, or clauses. Conjunctions are co-ordinating and subordinating. Conjunctions used in pairs are called correlatives. Adverbs used as connectives, either co-ordinating or subordinating, are called conjunctive adverbs.

The chief co-ordinating conjunctions are: *and, for, but, or, nor, yet, both . . . and, not only . . . but also, either . . . or, neither . . . nor.*

The following are some of the subordinating conjunctions: *if, although, though, that, because, since, so that, in order that, as, unless, before, than, where, when.*

Correlative conjunctions are: *both . . . and, not only . . . but also, either . . . or, neither . . . nor.*

Some adverbs used as conjunctions are: *how, why, where, while, before, after.* Such connectives as *however, therefore, nevertheless, hence, accordingly,* are often classed as conjunctive adverbs. In modern prose they are commonly used as transitional expressions, although it is hard to say just how a transitional expression of this sort differs from a true conjunction or a conjunctive adverb.

8. An **interjection** is a word used as an exclamation expressing sudden or strong feeling.

Oh! Ah! Bravo! Alas! Dear me! Why!

The English language also has another class of words called verbals, which are formed from verbs and resemble verbs but which are used as other parts of speech. See section 9 in the handbook.

1. A **gerund** is a verbal used as a noun.

Try *hitting* the ball a little harder. *Working* in a factory is a valuable education. I tried to keep him from *asking* too many questions.

2. A **participle** is a verbal used as an adjective.

I put the *broken* dish on the shelf. *Tired* and hungry, he started to walk home. *Having sold* his last paper, Tom returned for a new supply.

3. An **infinitive** is a verbal which may be used as a noun, an adjective, or an adverb.

Wilbur tried *to climb* a tree. I want *to be* an engineer. Give me a horse *to ride*. I did not stop *to ask* his name.

EXERCISES

Exercise 1, Parts of speech. In the following sentences name the part of speech to which each word belongs. The sentences are purposely made elementary. You should have no difficulty with this exercise. It is just a preliminary workout.

1. Theodore sold his car for twenty dollars.
2. On his head he wore a ridiculous green cap.
3. Stealthily the beast crept upon its prey.
4. Sincere praise is welcomed by every student.
5. Lift up your eyes to the hills.
6. Thunder roared and lightning flashed, although no **rain fell.**
7. What! Are you here again?
8. His life was a battle against disease and misfortune.
9. Our football team is playing a game in Texas.
10. Oswald does not care for books or music.

Exercise 2, Verbals. Identify the verbals in the following sentences. The verbals are gerunds, participles, and infinitives.

1. Gordon was trying to write a theme.
2. Look at that quarterback trying to sneak through the line.
3. The grey uniform, faded and mended, hung on his emaciated frame.
4. Having won the match, Nagurski claimed the heavyweight championship.
5. I seem to recall his saying that he was going to write to me.
6. The weeping child seemed unable to control itself.
7. Many of the spectators, having decided that the game was **won,** were leaving the stands.

8. A barking dog never bites, but no one knows when he will stop barking.
9. The old shed, having weathered many storms, was in need of repair.
10. All doors having been locked, we were forced to spend the night at a neighbor's home.

THE SENTENCE

A sentence is a word or a group of words that expresses a thought or feeling. The normal sentence must have two elements—the subject and the predicate. The subject is that about which something is said. The predicate is that which asserts or states something about the subject.

Subjects: Birds sing. *Hercule* solved the mystery. *Loyalty* is a virtue. *Fishing* is his recreation. *To work* is to pray. *What he did there* was never known.

Predicates: He *should have left sooner.* The ships *were sailing into the harbor.* He *is going home. Will* you *go now?*

With certain types of verbs a third element is essential to the formation of a complete thought—a complement. There are three main kinds of complements—direct objects, indirect objects, and subjective complements. Less common are the objective complement and the retained object.

1. The **direct object** of a verb denotes that which is immediately acted upon.

Harold took my *cap.* I saw *him* at the game. Little Audrey recited a *poem.* We learned our *lesson.*

2. The **indirect object** names, without the use of the preposition, the one to whom or for whom the action is done.

Tell *her* a bedtime story. We gave the *man* our tickets. The agent made *me* an offer. We sent *Mary* some flowers.

3. The **subjective complement** refers to the subject and describes or limits it. It may be a noun, a pronoun, or an adjective. It is often called the *predicate substantive* and the *predicate adjective.*

It must be *they*. The tackles are *veterans* from last season. The book became *popular* over night. The quarterback is too *heavy* and *slow*. Our old tent proved very *convenient*. The roses smell *sweet*.

4. The **objective complement,** used with verbs like *elect, choose, call, appoint,* or the like, refers to the direct object.

The committee made Ashley their *chairman*. They call their dog *Goofy*. The jury found him *guilty*. Army life has made him *stern*.

5. The **retained object** is used with a verb in the passive voice.

The children were given some *candy*. The students were granted an additional *holiday*. The visitors were shown every possible *courtesy.*

KINDS OF SENTENCES

A group of words having a subject and a predicate, if the group stands as an independent unit, is a sentence. There are, however, dependent groups of this nature, groups which act as parts of speech. We must therefore have a common name for both types; we call them clauses, or predications, or propositions. If a clause expresses a complete thought, it is called independent or principal. If it does not express a complete thought, it is called subordinate or dependent.

Sentences are divided according to their structure into four classes: simple, complex, compound, and compound-complex.

1. The **simple sentence** is one which contains a single independent clause. A simple sentence may have as subject

more than one noun or pronoun and as predicate more than one verb.

He gave his money to the poor. Howard and his brother now own the mill. Professor Jones and his students laughed and shouted at the sight of his confusion. She powdered her nose and put on her hat.

2. The **complex sentence** is one which contains one independent clause and at least one dependent clause. In the following sentences the dependent clauses are in italics.

Jones made a remark *which I did not like*. *Although he appeared prosperous*, I knew *that he was badly in debt*.

3. The **compound sentence** is one which contains two or more independent clauses.

Mrs. Heath is an excellent cook, but her daughter cannot boil water without burning it. Tom and Val just smiled; they had heard the story before.

4. The **compound-complex sentence** is one which contains two or more independent clauses and at least one dependent clause. In the following sentences the dependent clauses are in italics.

The senator spoke eloquently in favor of a large navy, but he did not mention the fact *that all of his money was invested in the steel industry*.

The chessboard is the world, the pieces are the phenomena of the universe, the rules of the game are *what we call the laws of nature*.

EXERCISES

Exercise 1, Subject, verb, complement. In each of the following sentences pick out the subject, the verb, and the complement.

1. At three o'clock in the morning he arose and saddled his horse.
2. Each of the players picked up his cards.
3. Without a word of warning, Desmond stood up and left the room.
4. Jumping up in confusion, Stella tossed the letter into the fire.
5. Which story have you read?
6. Come here quickly and move the table for me.
7. The sight of the injured man terrified the little girl.
8. Two of the prisoners, however, had eluded the guard and escaped.
9. How can you laugh on a day like this?
10. Apparently gratitude was not one of his virtues.

Exercise 2, Kinds of sentences. Pick out the independent and dependent clauses in the following sentences. Classify the sentences (simple, complex, compound, compound-complex).

1. Those slight labors which afford me a livelihood, and by which it is allowed that I am to some extent serviceable to my contemporaries, are as yet commonly a pleasure to me, and I am not often reminded that they are a necessity.—Thoreau.

2. He had a directness of action never before combined with so much comprehension.—Emerson.

3. The rapidity with which ideas grow old in our memories is in direct ratio to the squares of their importance.—Holmes.

4. Men whose minds are possessed with some one object take exaggerated views of its importance, are feverish in the pursuit of it, make it the measure of things which are utterly foreign to it, and are startled and despond if it happens to fail them.
—Newman.

5. Style should for this very reason never be subjective, but objective; and it will not be objective unless the words are so set down that they directly force the reader to think precisely the same thing as the author thought when he wrote them.

—Schopenhauer.

PHRASES

In the general sense, a phrase is any group of words less than a sentence. The word in its general sense has its place. In the study of grammar, however, the word "phrase" refers to one of two kinds: prepositional phrases and verbal phrases. A **prepositional phrase** consists of a preposition, its object, and modifiers of the phrase or any of its parts. **Verbal phrases** are made up with the verbals: gerunds, participles, and infinitives.

1. A prepositional phrase may be used as an adjective.

The amount *of work* he could do was incredible. The boy *with the books under his arm* is my brother. The explanation *in our book* is confusing. She married a man *of great wealth*. As entertainment it is *without its equal*. His comment is *of no importance*.

2. A prepositional phrase may be used as an adverb.

Mary seemed to be inquisitive *about my affairs*. He plunged *into the pool*. *For an hour* he played *in the water*. Try to be careful *with that vase*. Francis was true *to his word*.

3. A prepositional phrase may be used as a noun.

The best time for study is *in the morning*. He crawled from *under the debris*. *On the mantel* would be a good place for it.

A **participial phrase** consists of a participle, its complement, if it has one, and any modifiers of the phrase or any of its parts. It is used as an adjective.

PHRASES

The boy *now playing center* is a substitute. She entered a field *overgrown with weeds and briars*. *Talking with him*, I realized how lonely he had been. *Frightened by the sudden noise*, the deer plunged into the brush. His face, *freshly scrubbed*, shone in the morning light.

A special kind of participial phrase, called the **absolute phrase,** is made up of a substantive followed by a participle. It differs from the usual participial phrase in that it does not modify any single word in the sentence; grammatically it is an independent element.

We hunted toward the north, *each taking one side of the ridge*. *Their morale shattered*, the strikers fled in disorder. *The game being over*, we returned to our rooms.

A **gerund phrase** consists of a gerund, its complement, if it has one, and any modifiers of the phrase or any of its parts. The gerund phrase is used as a noun.

Repeating an explanation for the benefit of the deaf girl irritated him. *Staying out late at night* will not help your reputation. *Listening to his lecture* is as interesting as *watching a play*. Oswald enjoyed *mowing the lawn*. I should call that *violating the spirit of our agreement*. You can get the address by *stopping at our house*.

An **infinitive phrase,** like other verbal phrases, may have a complement and modifiers. In addition it may have what is called the assumed subject of the infinitive. The assumed subject of the infinitive is in the objective case. An infinitive phrase may be used as an adverb, an adjective, or a noun.

Tommy did not stop *to pick up his toys*. He is sure *to be there on time*. She stooped low *to pass under the rail*. Their attempts *to cut the line* were futile. *Whether to believe him or to call mother* was a real problem for me. We knew *him to be the most hardened gambler of the regiment*. It is our duty *to help our less fortunate neighbors*.

DEPENDENT CLAUSES

A dependent clause is distinguished from a sentence in that it does not make complete sense by itself; it depends upon something else in the sentence for its full meaning. Like phrases, dependent clauses are used as single parts of speech.

1. A dependent clause may be used as a noun.

As subject of a verb: *What he did at the dance* shocked me greatly.
As object of a verb: Harry thought *that he would not be recognized*.
As subjective complement: This is *where I caught the largest salmon*.
As object of a verbal: Be sure to accept *whatever she offers you*.
As object of a preposition: It depends upon *how many will pay their dues*.

2. A dependent clause may be used as an adjective. Adjective clauses are either restrictive or nonrestrictive. An important thing to remember in this connection is that restrictive clauses are *not* set off by commas.

Restrictive: I like a roommate *who is thoughtful and generous*.
A teacher *who speaks poor English* is badly handicapped.
We visited the ship *on which he returned from France*.
A girl *who knows shorthand and typing* can easily get work.
He *who is willing to learn* will advance rapidly.

Nonrestrictive: Our janitor, *who used to be a sailor*, strapped and tied our boxes.
My mother, *who is usually as light-hearted as a girl*, seemed strangely depressed.
The Minnesota team, *which has not lost a game in three years*, will play at Evanston tomorrow.

DEPENDENT CLAUSES

3. A dependent clause may be used as an adverb to show time, place, cause, purpose, result, condition, concession, manner, or comparison.

Time: You may leave *when the whistle blows.*
Before you leave the room, close the windows and pull down the shades.
We played cards *until our father returned.*
After you finish your test, hand in your papers.
While Mother entertained her guests, we children played in the orchard.

Place: These men will go *wherever they can find work.*

Cause: I came late *because I was delayed by a wreck.*
As I could not understand the painting, I kept silent.
Since no one volunteered, James finished the work himself.

Purpose: They came to America *in order that they might find religious freedom.*

Result: Every door was locked, *so that it was impossible to leave the building.* The night was so dark *that we could travel no farther.* Every door was so well barred *that it was impossible to leave the building.*

Condition: *If you want to go home,* I shall call a cab.
Should you find yourself on the wrong trail, return to the starting point.
Children will not be admitted *unless they are accompanied by their parents.*

Concession: *Although I did not understand his question,* I attempted a reply.
No matter what he says, I shall not be angry.

Manner: Let us sing *as the birds sing.*
Marion Jean looks *as if she were ready for bed.*

Comparison: They are as free *as we are.*
They are not so free *as we are.*
Ralph is older *than I am.*

EXERCISES

Exercise 1, Phrases. In the following sentences pick out each phrase and tell whether it is prepositional, participial, gerund, or infinitive.

1. Father advised me not to bet on the game.
2. Against his advice I bet Harold that we would win by three touchdowns.
3. This is a doctrine dangerous to liberty of opinion.
4. As he was horribly afraid of snakes, he did not try to sleep in the tent.
5. Roger stopped pulling the weeds out of his garden and turned to greet us.
6. We always considered her to be the most brilliant girl in our class.
7. His face, blackened with grime and sweat, was covered with a week's growth of hair.
8. He will try to find relief in his music.
9. The pounding waves and the whistling winds kept him from sleeping at night.
10. To be a radio announcer is my greatest ambition.

Exercise 2, Noun clauses. In the following sentences pick out each noun clause and tell whether it is used as the subject of a verb, as the complement of a verb, or as the object of a preposition.

1. What he saw in that room must have frightened him terribly.
2. Cover the plants with whatever is convenient.
3. What these people have left behind is full of meaning.
4. This is where I live.
5. Brother Jackson announced solemnly that he did not like modern music.
6. I learned how the tarantula hawk kills its victim and drags it to its tomb.

7. How he disappeared so completely is a mystery to me.
8. Give the message to whoever opens the door.
9. It is not known who the author of this play was.
10. I do not know why I came to college.

Exercise 3, Adjective clauses. Pick out the adjective clauses in the following sentences. Tell what word each clause modifies.

1. This is the book I referred to last night.
2. My brother, who is an ardent philatelist, received a set of coronation stamps.
3. All that I am I owe to my mother.
4. This is the place where the first battle of the war was fought.
5. We met on the day when I entered the academy.
6. The rock from which he leaped is called Suicide Peak.
7. We reached the cabin the minute before the storm broke.
8. That was a side of her character I had not known before.
9. Diamond Lake is the place where we expect to fish.
10. I like to be with Mary, who is a sweet and agreeable child.

VARIETY IN SENTENCE PATTERNS

"Style is the man himself," said Buffon, a French naturalist, in his inaugural address before the French Academy. It may be well for you to take this widely quoted definition of style with a bit of prudent distrust. Like many attempts at epigrams, this one is but a half-truth, and you must remember that the other half of a half-truth is a lie. If a man writes as he is, as he has lived, then he who writes in a dull, flat manner has lived a dull, flat life. Conversely, he who has lived a rich, exciting life will write in a rich, exciting manner. Neither statement, as you well know, is true. The man who has served in the Foreign Legion, the man who has designed bridges of breath-taking beauty, the man who has explored African jungles, needs, like as not, the aid of a ghost writer to put his experiences into words. And the author of thrilling yarns of adventure in the South Seas may be an inhibited teacher of English in a small Iowa town. Whatever style is, it is not an unchangeable attribute of personality.

Without troubling yourself too much about the subtle interrelations between style and personality, you can improve your manner of writing by attention to those things which are learnable. For writing, like any other craft, may be learned. Some of the qualities of good writing are stressed so often in this book that they need but to be recalled to your attention here. You know that it is important to choose exact words. Not only that, the words you choose must be sound and fresh, not jaded by too much labor. You know about picture-making words, about comparisons and figures of speech. You know that a fresh point of view will give flavor to your style, that humor will lighten it. In this section, however, we are dealing not with the choice but with the grouping of words. Now that we are familiar with grammatical patterns—parts of speech, verbals, phrases, clauses—we shall see how grammar may be used as a means toward a more flexible and pleasing style.

VARIETY IN STRUCTURE

The normal order of an English sentence, subject-verb-complement, is so natural, so instinctive, that the untrained writer tends to cast all his thoughts in this one mold. "Father is an exceptionally calm person," he writes. "He takes everything as a matter of fact. He is slow and easy-going. It doesn't make any difference what happens, he retains his calmness. He is considerate of other people's feelings. He doesn't try to keep us from making too much noise when he is reading. But this reminds me when he speaks he means business." Now, quite obviously, no matter how important father is, it is neither accurate nor pleasing to give every detail about him the importance and dignity of a separate sentence. When the writer does recognize a causal relationship between two statements, he indicates the fact by running the two statements together in the same sentence. The result is sameness, a tedious monotony. Nor is the monotony relieved when a writer, in a helpless gesture toward smoothness and continuity, strings his clauses out with a series of *and's, but's,* and *so's.*

If you do not like to be the owner of a monotonous style (and who does?), you have several means of reclaiming it. Let us see, first, what can be done with the sentences about father: "Father, a calm, slow, easy-going, matter-of-fact person, does not lose his temper no matter what the provocation." One sentence takes care of five, more effectively, too, than the five did, for the grouping of adjectives in the appositive position is emphatic. Scattered through five sentences, they are lost.

The revised sentences below contain further illustrations of the use of the appositive:

Awkward: Father is a congenial sort of person, and he hasn't made an enemy in his life.
Improved: Father, a congenial sort of person, has not made an enemy in his life.

Awkward: Many owners of house trailers pay their traveling expenses by engaging in some trade or occupation. They do carpenter work or repair automobiles or sell insurance.
Improved: Many owners of house trailers pay their traveling expenses by engaging in some trade or occupation, such as carpentering, repairing automobiles, or selling insurance.

Awkward: Industry and determination are the traits of the beaver. These traits represent the attitude of some students at Oregon State College.

Improved: Industry and determination, the traits of the beaver, characterize the attitude of some students at Oregon State College.

You see how a change from a clause to an appositive can make a sentence smoother, more compact, more emphatic. A word of caution, however: do not think that an appositive is always better than a clause. Look upon it merely as a resource at your command, to be used for greater exactness in expression as well as for a welcome variety.

Occasionally the thought in a compound sentence is better expressed in a simple sentence with a compound verb:

Awkward: The wise student budgets his time for study, and he prepares his lessons according to a schedule.

Improved: The wise student budgets his time for study and prepares his lessons according to a schedule.

A co-ordinate clause may often be better expressed in a participial phrase:

Awkward: My decision to enter college came suddenly, and I encountered several obstacles.

Improved: Having made a sudden decision to enter college, I was unprepared for the difficulties which I encountered.

Awkward: The inexperienced camper usually sleeps on the ground for several nights, and so he decides that a bed of fir boughs is worth his effort.

Improved: Having endured sleeping on the ground for several nights, the inexperienced camper usually decides that a bed of fir boughs is worth his effort.

Awkward: He looks at his teacher. His mind is in a whirl, his mouth is dry, so he makes some worthless answer.

Improved: The confused student stares at his teacher—his brain in a whirl, his dry mouth stuttering some incoherent response.

A similar effect may be produced with gerund or infinitive phrases:

Awkward: Their working hours were shortened. This resulted in more spare time for recreation and enjoyment.

Improved: Shortening their hours of work resulted in more time available for recreation and enjoyment.

Awkward: The wife has children which she must clothe. She must take care of them and worry about them. The business woman does not have anybody except herself to whom she is obliged to pay any attention.

Improved: The wife has children to clothe, to care for, to worry about; the business woman has no one but herself to think of.

Awkward: The necessary preparation is simple. You get dressed and pull your old shotgun out of the corner. Then you are ready to start for the duck ponds.

Improved: Having dressed and pulled the old shotgun out of the corner—all the preparation really necessary—the hunter is ready to start for the duck ponds.

Clauses—noun, adjective, and adverb—are a means of relieving the monotony of too much co-ordination:

Awkward: The reason for his failure was plain. In college he had depended upon his fraternity brothers to help him and to keep him at work.

Improved: The plain cause of his failure was that in college he had depended upon his fraternity brothers for help and incentive.

Awkward: My roommate stared at me in unconcealed dismay. She is the chairman of the house scholarship committee.

Improved: My roommate, who is the chairman of the house scholarship committee, stared at me in unconcealed dismay.

Awkward: The high-school principal had forgotten to mail my credits to the registrar, so I had to make a special trip to get them.

Improved: As the high-school principal had forgotten to mail my credentials to the registrar, I had to make a special trip to get them.

Awkward: Do not be in too much of a hurry to join an organization. Study the membership before you join.

Improved: Before you join an organization, investigate its membership.

Awkward: I had heard stories of the way freshmen were treated, but I have seen no bitter rivalry between the classes thus far.

Improved: Although I had heard stories of ill-treatment of freshmen, thus far I have observed no bitter rivalry between the classes.

VARIETY IN ORDER

You may also relieve a monotonous style by occasionally varying the order of the sentence elements. Here, again, you should keep in mind the fact that variety is a departure from the normal or natural. The normal order in the English sentence—subject, verb, complement—still remains the pattern into which most of your sentences will fall without much effort on your part. In the following examples of various sentence patterns notice the difference in effect. One pattern is not necessarily better than another; it is merely different.

In a home there is love.
There is love in a home.

To be a home, a house must be occupied by a congenial group of people.
A house, to be a home, must be occupied by a congenial group of people.

The work of the night shift was the same, although it seemed much harder to me.

Although it seemed much harder to me, the work of the night shift was the same.

It is very seldom that one is privileged to see such a story-book ending as this game had.

Seldom is one privileged to see such a story-book ending as this game had.

My delicate and fragile dream faded at the sight of her stupid face.

My dream, so delicate and fragile, faded at the sight of her stupid face.

A corsage was delivered at my door just after dinner. It was a huge affair of violets.

Just after dinner, a corsage, a huge affair of violets, was delivered at my door.

Expressed in terms of grammar, the various devices for securing variety in sentence order may be summarized as follows:

1. You may reverse the normal order of subject and verb in a sentence. This device must be used with caution lest it become a mannerism. But an occasional inversion like one of the following may be used effectively.

Said he. Into their midst stormed the principal. Straight across his garden raced the terrified dogs. Over the rail fence and into the brush stampeded the herd of longhorns. Like a ship under full sail came Aunt Sophronia.

2. You may begin with an adverb or an adverbial phrase.

Seldom do they come back for more. During the heat of the day he must not leave his post. Suddenly the crew swing into action. Narrowly he missed the concrete post.

3. You may put adjectives and participles after the words they modify.

Her voice, low and pleasant, banished my fear. Her roommate, angry and impatient, threw her hat upon the bed. The children, sullen and rebellious, refused to answer her questions.

4. You may begin with a clause.

That he lacked physical courage was only too evident. If I were the coach, I would send McCorkle into the game. When it does not rain it snows.

5. You may change a clause to an appositive.

The author of the book, a former member of a notorious Chicago gang, lets his readers infer his social philosophy. The next morning he decided to tell the truth, a course which should have occurred to him the day before. She arose at seven, an unpleasantly early hour for her. He found himself engaged to three girls at once, a situation fraught with more danger than glamor.

PARALLEL CONSTRUCTION

You have just been warned not to use the same sentence structure repeatedly; now you are to be told to express similar ideas in similar sentence patterns. This looks like a contradiction, yet each principle is sound, as a little thought on your part will show you. All sentences must, after all, be built to fit the thoughts they express. If several ideas are of equal importance, they properly belong in a series of co-ordinate clauses. If some of the ideas are less important than others, they should be given a subordinate position in sentences. The warning against excessive co-ordination was directed as much against inaccuracy of expression as against monotony of effect. Parallel structure, likewise, becomes monotonous when it is carried too far. If it is used naturally, to fit the thought, it will seldom be overused. You will not have frequent occasions to say, "To err is human, to forgive divine," or "You can take a boy out of the country, but you cannot take the country out of the boy." Even Francis Bacon, writing in an age when rhetorical mannerisms were fashionable, did not often find it possible to balance phrases as he did in his essay about studies: "Reading maketh a full man; conference a ready man; and writing an exact man. And therefore, if a man write little, he had need have a great memory; if he confer little, he had need have a present wit; and if he read little, he had need have much cunning, to seem to know what he doth not."

A fine example of skillful use of parallel structure is Abraham Lincoln's famous letter to Horace Greeley:

Dear Sir:

I have just read yours of the 19th instant, addressed to myself through the New York *Tribune.* If there be in it any statements or assumptions of fact which I may know to be erroneous, I do not now and here controvert them. If there be in it any inferences which I may believe to be falsely drawn, I do not now and here argue against them. If there be perceptible in it an impatient and dictatorial tone, I waive it in deference to an old friend whose heart I have always supposed to be right.

As to the policy I "seem to be pursuing," as you say, I have not meant to leave anyone in doubt.

I would save the Union. I would save it by the shortest way under the Constitution. The sooner the national authority can be restored, the nearer the Union will be "the Union as it was." If there be those who would not save the Union unless they could at the same time save slavery, I do not agree with them. If there be those who would not save the Union unless they could at the same time destroy slavery, I do not agree with them. My paramount object in this struggle is to save the Union, and not either to save or to destroy slavery. If I could save the Union without freeing any slave, I would do it; if I could save it by freeing all the slaves, I would do it; and if I could save it by freeing some and leaving others alone, I would also do that. What I do about slavery and the colored race, I do because I believe it helps to save the Union; and what I forbear, I forbear because I do not believe it would help to save the Union. I shall do less whenever I shall believe that what I am doing hurts the cause; and I shall do more whenever I shall believe doing more will help the cause. I shall try to correct errors when shown to be errors, and I shall adopt new views as fast as they shall appear to be true views.

I have here stated my purpose according to my views of official duty, and I intend no modification of my oft expressed personal wish that all men everywhere could be free.

Yours,

A. LINCOLN.

As an approach to the improvement of style through the use of parallel structure, we may again express rhetorical principles in terms of grammar. Logically, a noun is made parallel with another noun, a gerund with another gerund, a phrase with another phrase, a clause with another clause. Lincoln's letter is the work of a true craftsmaster; it cannot be duplicated by every apprentice. Even the inexperienced writer, however, can achieve a symmetry in his sentences where the thought logically calls for symmetry.

Awkward: All freshmen assembled in the men's gymnasium for general talks and to give us an idea of the procedure of registration.

Improved: All freshmen assembled in the men's gymnasium to listen to general talks and to learn the registration procedure.

Awkward: Since he spends most of his time before the public, he must be popular, energetic, and have a winning personality.

Improved: Since he spends most of his time before the public, he must have popularity, energy, and a winning personality.

Awkward: I have learned better manners and how to make myself look better to others.

Improved: I have acquired better manners and the ability to make myself attractive.

EUPHONY AND RHYTHM

In your study of writing you finally reach a point beyond which grammar will not help you. You must depend upon your feeling for rhythm. Good prose should have a pleasant sound when it is read aloud. It should form patterns of sound —patterns which the reader somehow feels to be an appropriate and harmonious accompaniment of the thought expressed. But no one can give you a sense of rhythm. If you do not have it, you must be satisfied to begin with a few elementary cautions, purely negative in character. As a rule, recast every phrase that is difficult to read aloud. Avoid the chime of unintentional rhyme. Avoid accidental alliteration. Shun a succession of hissing sibilants!

Here are a few examples of what you must NOT do, either by intention or by accident:

We could use the cart and carry Mary and supplies for the expedition.

What equipment does an author need in order to succeed?

Can't you plant alfalfa for forage?

When submission is inevitable, it is vain to complain.

Bring around to the house about an hour from now a half pound of ground round steak.

Weber's unusual musical career extended to the year 1836.

You and I were born to be, but why?

Lack of water caused my eight young larch trees to parch to death.

He stuck a stick through the steak.

But if you pride yourself on being sensitive to music, you can do much to cultivate your feeling for good prose rhythm. The subject is really beyond the scope of this book. All that we can do here is to recommend extensive reading and a thoughtful attention to the sound patterns of well-built sentences. Read the following selections aloud and make your own comments:

A man may read a sermon, the best and most passionate that ever man preached, if he shall but enter into the sepulchres of kings. In the same Escurial where the Spanish princes live in greatness and power, and decree war or peace, they have wisely placed a cemetery, where their ashes and their glory shall sleep till time shall be no more; and where our kings have been crowned, their ancestors lie interred, and they must walk over their grandsire's head to take his crown. There is an acre sown with royal seed, the copy of the greatest change, from rich to naked, from ceiled roofs to arched coffins, from living like gods to die like men. There is enough to cool the flames of lust, to abate the heights of pride, to appease the itch of covetous desires, to sully and dash out the dissembling colors of a lustful, artificial, and imaginary beauty. There the warlike and the peaceful, the fortunate and the miserable, the beloved and the despised princes mingle their dust, and pay down their symbol of mortality, and tell all the world that when we die our ashes shall be equal to kings', and our accounts easier, and our pains and our crowns shall be less.—Jeremy Taylor.

Every heart that has beat strong and cheerfully has left a hopeful impulse behind it in the world, and bettered the tradition of mankind. And even if death catch people, like an open pitfall, and in mid-career, laying out vast projects, and planning monstrous foundations, flushed with hope, and their mouths full of boastful language, they should be at once tripped up and silenced: is there not something brave and spirited in such a termination? and does not life go down with a better grace, foaming in full body over a precipice, than miserably straggling to an end in sandy deltas?
—Robert Louis Stevenson.

Neither party expected for the war the magnitude or the duration which it has already attained. Neither anticipated that the cause of the conflict might cease with, or even before, the conflict itself should cease. Each looked for an easier triumph, and a result less fundamental and astounding. Both read the same Bible, and pray to the same God; and each invokes His aid against the other.

It may seem strange that any men should dare to ask a just God's assistance in wringing their bread from the sweat of other men's faces; but let us judge not, that we be not judged. The prayers of both could not be answered—that of neither has been answered fully.

The Almighty has His own purposes. "Woe unto the world because of offenses! for it must needs be that offenses come; but woe to that man by whom the offense cometh." If we shall suppose that American slavery is one of those offenses which, in the providence of God, must needs come, but which, having continued through His appointed time, He now wills to remove, and that He gives to both North and South this terrible war, as the woe due to those by whom the offense came, shall we discern therein any departure from those divine attributes which the believers in a living God always ascribe to Him? Fondly do we hope—fervently do we pray—that this mighty scourge of war may speedily pass away. Yet, if God wills that it continue until all the wealth piled by the bondman's two hundred and fifty years of unrequited toil shall be sunk, and until every drop of blood drawn with the lash shall be paid by another drawn with the sword, as was said three thousand years ago, so still it must be said, "The judgments of the Lord are true and righteous altogether."—Abraham Lincoln.

THE PARAGRAPH

WHAT IS A PARAGRAPH?

A paragraph of exposition or argument is usually defined as a sentence or a group of sentences developing a single, complete idea. A definition of a paragraph is valuable to you only as it helps you to write good paragraphs or to read them with greater ease or understanding. Let us therefore make our definition less arbitrary by adding to it several comments.

Just what is meant by "develop an idea"? Various degrees of development are possible. The same idea may be the subject of a sentence, a paragraph, a group of paragraphs, a chapter, or a book. It is quite possible that an idea may be *developed* by a single sentence; on the other hand, it is also possible that another idea may take several paragraphs for an adequate *statement*. There are further possibilities. One idea may be developed by several paragraphs. One idea may be stated in a paragraph of a single sentence, and the various units composing it may be developed in a series of paragraphs following, each unit in a separate paragraph. An idea composed of several subordinate ideas may be stated in the first sentence of a paragraph, the first subtopic developed in the same paragraph, and the other subtopics developed in succeeding paragraphs.

We may therefore revise our first definition by saying that a paragraph is a unit of thought—or, more exactly, a unit of the expression and communication of thought—larger than the sentence and smaller than the section or the chapter. Modern writers and publishers have recognized the need of units of writing larger than the paragraph and smaller than the chapter. These divisions, or sections, are usually composed of the paragraphs discussing one of the main divisions of the theme idea.

LENGTH OF PARAGRAPHS

The length of a paragraph depends on several considerations: the thoroughness or completeness with which the writer wishes to develop the topic or idea he is trying to make clear; the class of readers for whom he is writing; and present-day conventions governing paragraph length. Essays written for serious or leisurely study may use more complete development of topics and therefore longer paragraphs. Essays written for hasty reading or for immature minds should use smaller units and therefore shorter paragraphs.

The following analysis, showing the number of words used in a series of paragraphs, will tell you more than an arbitrary rule governing paragraph length. The selections analyzed are fairly representative of contemporary writing of the serious type. One is a popular treatment of science; another is a mixture of autobiography and essay; the third is a magazine article. Compute the average length of these paragraphs, if you wish, but remember that averages will not reveal to you the range and variety of paragraph sizes as accurately as will this analysis.

Number of Words

Sir James Jeans, *The Mysterious Universe*, The Macmillan Company, New York, 1934, chap. 1:

99 – 106 – 181 – 149 – 141 – 246 –
55 – 100 – 113 – 71 – 289 – 31 –
261 – 168 – 94 – 171 – 199 – 169 –
57 – 64 – 57 – 251 – 100 – 93 –
110.

Henry S. Canby, *Alma Mater*, Farrar & Rinehart, New York, 1936, chap. 3:

140 – 80 – 80 – 109 – 99 – 61 – 275 – 278 – 219 – 279 – 221 – 117 – 151 – 164 – 77 – 77 – 111 – 338 – 283 – 175 – 266 – 176 – 225 – 177 – 561.

Nathaniel Peffer, "Is Capitalism to Blame?" *Harper's Magazine*, vol. 170, pp. 549–556 (April, 1935):

141 – 188 – 175 – 324 – 188 – 201 – 213 – 154 – 219 – 150 – 146 – 160 – 224 – 354 – 215 – 215 – 358 – 122 – 378 – 110.

These figures may be analyzed in another way that should prove helpful to you:

Number of paragraphs below 100 words...... 15
Number between 100 and 200 words......... 31
Number between 200 and 300 words......... 18
Number between 300 and 400 words......... 5
Number above 400 words................. 1

THE TOPIC SENTENCE

A sentence which expresses the central idea of an expository paragraph is called a topic sentence.

A topic sentence may or may not be actually present in a written paragraph. It may be implied or understood. While you are learning to write, however, it is good practice for you to state the central idea of every paragraph in the form of a topic sentence. The practice is an aid to clearer thinking. It is a safeguard against spineless paragraphs. It is good mental discipline. If you write a paragraph without an expressed topic sentence, you must be sure that your paragraph does have a central idea and that your reader will have no difficulty in finding it.

The position of the topic sentence in a paragraph depends on the effect desired. It usually comes first. It may include a transitional phrase, or it may follow the necessary transitional sentence. Placing the topic sentence first has the merit of setting before the reader a guide to the contents of the paragraph. It leads to clearness and directness in writing. The topic sentence may come last in the paragraph. This method may be used when the writer wishes to prepare his reader for the central idea, or to produce an effect of climax. The topic sentence may come both first and last. The entire idea may be repeated by the last sentence, or a part may be stated by the first sentence and a part by the last. And, finally, in some paragraphs the topic sentence appears within the paragraph, whenever the writer is ready for it, usually after a preparation for it by means of examples or details.

UNITY IN A PARAGRAPH

Knowing the essential function of paragraphing, you can now formulate for yourself the principles governing paragraph unity. Since a paragraph is a unit of structure, dealing with one topic or subtopic, it is obvious that if you include in the paragraph any material not related to the central idea you are violating unity and weakening the effect you wish to produce.

HOW TO WRITE A PARAGRAPH

In general, whatever you have learned about the writing of an effective theme applies to the writing of an effective paragraph. Conversely, whatever you learn here about paragraphs will help you to write a good theme.

Since a topic sentence (expressed or implied) is the core of an expository paragraph, it follows that the writing of a paragraph is simply a development of this topic idea to the extent that the writer deems necessary. At the outset, you may be mystified by the term "development." What does it mean? To you, it should mean, in most cases, "make clear." It may also mean "make impressive" or "make convincing." How an idea may be made clear or impressive or convincing may be learned from an analysis of paragraphs written by professional writers. If you analyze paragraphs in a group of essays, you will quickly discover that all types of paragraph development depend ultimately on the use of specific and concrete details. Let this principle be your key to good paragraphs—or, for that matter, to good themes. To make a general idea clear to the mind of your reader, arrange and present the evidence which made the idea clear to you.

It may be necessary at this point in your study to rid your mind of some hazy doubt, or even outright skepticism, about the methods actually used by professional writers. Does the experienced writer hesitate before each paragraph and ask, "Now what method shall I use?" Does a champion golfer stop to worry about grip and stance or follow-through in a match game? But think of the years of worrying before he became a champion. Does Paderewski worry about the position of his hands when he plays a Chopin *étude*? And even Paderewski practices several hours each day during a concert tour. You are not yet a skilled writer. As a learner you must patiently master the tools of your trade, always comforted by the knowledge that a time will come when you will reach for the right tools almost instinctively.

If you are really interested in the craft of writing, you can discover for yourself the following methods used by professional writers in developing paragraphs:

1. **Development by particulars and details,** the method used in nine out of every ten expository paragraphs written, follows one of the most common processes of thought. We observe a number of details; our minds formulate thoughts which relate these details to one another, which give them a connection, a unity, a meaning. If we write a paragraph in this way, we have a paragraph developed by particulars and details with a topic sentence at the end. We may, however, wish to reverse the process and begin with a general statement. The procedure is not always as simple as this explanation of it, yet the explanation will serve our purpose. The paragraphs quoted below will help to explain the method. The topic sentences are italicized.

There are other conventions concerning safe driving at intersections that cannot be omitted from a discussion of this kind. You should never pass another vehicle, particularly a large truck, at an intersection. As you pass, your view to the right is cut off, and the truck driver may be waving a motorist to pass in front of him and into your path. Show consideration for pedestrians by stopping for a traffic signal behind the crosswalk, so that people on foot do not have to walk out around your machine. A dangerous practice is to approach a corner at high speed, depending on your brakes to bring you safely to a sudden stop. To do so frightens pedestrians who do not know that you can stop and are not sure that you intend to. In addition, the driver coming up from the rear may not have brakes as efficient as yours, and he may crash into you.

> —Curtis Billings, "Rules of the Road," *The Atlantic Monthly*, vol. 154, p. 341 (September, 1934). Reprinted by permission.

What, if anything, does literature show to be the prevailing time-current of the thirties? *I believe it to be fear, although fear is too strong a word for its quiet margins, and panic would better describe some of its hurrying tides.* This fear is sometimes conscious, sometimes subconscious. It ranges from a skeptical inquiry into the possible disintegration of culture as we have known it, to the deep pessimism of convinced alarm. Sometimes the writer is inspired by what he may call the decline of capitalism. Sometimes the underlying fear is of war. Sometimes, and very commonly, the writer is concerned with the revival of the brutality of more desperate ages. Sometimes the unrest which spreads through a book is a reflection of the author's belief that democracy is bankrupt; sometimes jubilantly or fearfully he hails the rise of the proletariat, or the reappearance of the strong arm and submission to the state. More subtle is what has been recently called the flight from reason toward pure emotionalism, where men are encouraged to exchange their liberties for the joys of being the most powerful of animals. Again, this fear is only the weariness of a trading civilization, such a weariness as may have overcome the initiative of the Byzantines. Any of these fears, skepticisms, distrusts may be justified or unjustified. The fear remains.

> —Henry Seidel Canby, "The Threatening Thirties," *The Saturday Review of Literature*, vol. 16, No. 4, p. 3 (May 22, 1937). Reprinted by permission.

2. **Development by examples or typical instances** does not, like development by particulars and details, take the idea apart to see what it means. It uses examples of the working of the general idea stated in the topic sentence. "To be great is to be misunderstood," wrote Emerson. "Is that so?" you wonder. "Kindly explain what you mean by that statement." But, instead, Emerson continues: "Pythagoras was misunderstood, and Socrates, and Jesus, and Luther, and Copernicus, and Galileo, and Newton, and every pure and wise spirit that ever took flesh." And because these examples are familiar to us, Emerson does not need to explain why these men were great or how they were misunderstood. A familiar example carries with it its own explanation. An unfamiliar one must be interpreted.

Literature, when supplemented by intelligent observation, can teach us much about human nature. The number of interesting people whom most of us know is quite limited. Literature offers us a means of extending our experiences almost indefinitely. Biography and history can bring back the great men of the past—Johnson, Napoleon, Lincoln, Franklin. Individuals whom in actual life we should avoid may become extraordinarily interesting in the pages of a novel or upon the stage. In real life few of us have known such men and women as Huckleberry Finn, Uncle Remus, Falstaff, Hamlet, Becky Sharp, Jeanie Deans, Sam Weller, Eustacia Vye, Tartuffe, Jean Valjean, or Silas Lapham.

Literature is not a substitute for living; it is a way of living—a means of widening and intensifying one's life. When we have read a play by Shakespeare or a novel by Thackeray, we ought for days afterwards to be able to see the world and its people through the far-seeing eyes of the poet or the novelist. After reading the poems of Burns or Wordsworth, one ought to be able to find unsuspected beauty in a Texas prairie, a Carolina cotton field, or a back street in any town or city. If one knows how to read, the accomplishment places the reader temporarily on a footing of something like equality with the masters. "We are all poets," said Carlyle, "when we *read* a poem well."

—Jay Broadus Hubbell, *The Enjoyment of Literature.* By permission of The Macmillan Company, publishers.

3. **Development by definition** again makes use principally of details and examples. A definition is written in answer to an implied question: What do you mean by this? In what sense are you using this or that word? What—to use an example— is a good sport? You explain by analyzing the qualities of sportsmanship—particulars and details—or you say that John Smith is a good sport—an example. What do you mean by "courage"? You may say that courage is a quality that differs from daring, valor, or heroism in that it is more rational, quiet, and considered, or you may say that Private Blank, who volunteered as a human guinea pig in the fight against yellow fever, showed more true courage than Private Brown, who received a medal for gallant conduct at Château-Thierry.

Truth,—which is a concept conforming to reason, experience, and knowledge,—is the breath of the poet, the vision of the artist and prophet, the quarry of the scientist, the haunted house of the fundamentalist, the bone of contention between bone-headed contenders, the toy of the careless, the *bête noire* of the politician, the elixir of life to the sage, and the embalming fluid for fools. It is the weapon of offense against ignorance, and the offensive weapon of the prejudiced. Truth is the voice of God speaking to the inner ear of man.

> —Reverend Myron Lewis Morley, "What Is Truth?" *The Forum*, vol. 78, p. 614 (October, 1927). Reprinted by permission.

A Good Sport is a combination of a hero, a martyr, and a humorist, with a deep sense of justice in acknowledging the rights of others at the cost of his own disadvantage and discomfort, relieving the harsh realities in life's drama with the brighter and warmer color of good fellowship and generosity without spoiling the comedy through self-love and false susceptibility. He can smile when it rains on a picnic day, laugh at a joke about himself, shake hands with a man who inadvertently knocks him down with his car, forgive the friend who marries the girl he loves, and die on the battlefield for his country with a smile on his lips.

> —O. F. Page, "What Is a Good Sport?" *The Forum*, vol. 77, p. 243 (February, 1927). Reprinted by permission.

4. **Development by comparison or contrast** likewise involves the use of particulars, details, and even examples. Comparison is telling what a thing is like. Usually the more familiar thing or idea is used to explain the less familiar one. If you were to explain the game of badminton, for instance, you could show how it was similar to tennis, the more familiar game. Or in attempting to get students to understand the times in which Chaucer lived you could compare his century with our century. Professor Kittredge used this device brilliantly in one of his books. Contrast is telling what a thing is not like. How does

college football differ from professional football? How does the American way of living differ from the Oriental way? How does democracy differ from communism? These are typical subjects which invite treatment by contrast, not in paragraphs alone but also in entire essays and even books.

Tolerance is that state of mind which regards truth as being always relative and never absolute. It arrives at opinions, but never reaches conclusions; it entertains persuasions, but avoids convictions; it ignores verdicts, but courts facts. Tolerance indicates an intellect hitting on all six; it mirrors a mind mellow with good humor. It loves light and laughter, and hates nothing, save intolerance. It is the Nirvana of the dreamer, but Pandemonium to the doer. Tolerance first visions the plan. But in the end Intolerance does the job.

> —Dwight T. Scott, "What Is Tolerance?" *The Forum*, vol. 77, pp. 749–750 (May, 1927). Reprinted by permission.

The chief difference between the fourteenth century and our own, in intellectual matters, lies, I think, in a different attitude toward specialization. Our tendency is to exhaust one subject, if we can, and ignore the rest; theirs was to aspire to an encyclopaedic grasp of the universe. Other points of contrast are usually emphasized. We hear, for instance, that our times are blessed with a critical or questioning spirit, whereas our mediaeval ancestors believed what they were told, with blind faith. This, however, is at best a very crude antithesis and it has no merit whatever when applied to Chaucer's lifetime. Then, if ever, the spirit of radicalism was abroad in the land. To describe as an era of dumb submissiveness the age of Wyclif, and John Huss, and the Great Schism, of the Jacquerie in France and Tyler and Ball in England, is to read both literature and history with one's eyes shut. Equally fallacious is the alleged contrast as to what is called the scientific temper, with its appendage the inductive method. We have shifted our ground, perhaps, in some particulars, but we have not much changed our mental habits. We are still led by generalities, quite as much as by experience, though we may apply them rather to politics and the social system than to the natural sciences. And even there, one must not be too confident of an actualized millennium now, or too incredulous of enlightenment then. Empiricism was the sole guide, in practice, of the alchemical brethren to whom the Canon's Yeoman had attached himself. It was not the calm precepts of placid deduction that scattered their gold, and blew up their laboratories, and poisoned them with the fumes of sulphur and antimony.

> —George Lyman Kittredge, *Chaucer and His Poetry*,
> Harvard University Press, Cambridge, 1924, pp. 7–8.
> By permission of the President and Fellows of Harvard
> College.

5. **Development by repetition** implies more than mere restatement. It implies a change, a modification of the idea to make it more exact or more specific. The process of restatement usually requires the use of supporting details.

6. **Development by analogy** is used by a writer when he wishes to make something clear by comparing it with something from a different, and to the reader a more familiar, field of experience. Literature as well as popular speech is full of analogies. Life, wrote Shakespeare, is "a tale told by an idiot"; it is a "bowl of cherries," says the popular-song writer. Life is "a narrow vale between the mountain peaks of two eternities." It is "an empty dream," a "fleeting breath," a "short summer." All these, when expanded by the use of supporting details, are analogies.

Similar to the analogy is the illustration or the anecdote or even the figure of speech. James Russell Lowell, speaking of Wordsworth, said: "Even where his genius is wrapped in clouds, the unconquerable lightning of imagination struggles through, flashing out unexpected vistas, and illuminating the humdrum pathway of our daily thought with a radiance of momentary consciousness that seems like a revelation." In his essay on "Rousseau and the Sentimentalists" he used this anecdote:

There is an old story in the *Gesta Romanorum* of a priest who was found fault with by one of his parishioners because his life was in painful discordance with his teaching. So one day he takes his critic out to a stream, and, giving him to drink of it, asks him if he does not find it sweet and pure water. The parishioner, having answered that it was, is taken to the source, and finds that what had so refreshed him flowed from between the jaws of a dead dog. "Let this teach thee," said the priest, "that the very best doctrine may take its rise in a very impure and disgustful spring, and that excellent morals may be taught by a man who has no morals at all." It is easy enough to see the fallacy here. Had the man known beforehand from what a carrion fountain-head the stream issued, he could not have drunk of it without loathing. Had the priest merely bidden him to *look* at the stream and see how beautiful it was, instead of tasting it, it would have been quite another matter. And this is precisely the difference between what appeals to our aesthetic or to our moral sense, between what is judged of by the taste or by the conscience.

7. **Development by giving causes or effects** is another variation of development by particulars and details.

In analyzing paragraphs to learn the methods used by professional writers, you must not be confused by a possible complexity of paragraph structure. A writer may use these methods singly or in various combinations, and the combinations may be intricate. It is not always possible to pick out a sentence and say, "This is example; this is definition." Frequently you will find several methods used in the same sentence. At times you may even find that example, analogy, or definition is used to make clear, not the topic idea, but a subordinate idea. Remember also that some of the words or even sentences in a paragraph must do other things than develop the topic idea.

THE PARAGRAPH

Notice the transitions and connecting links in the following paragraph:

Literature, although it stands apart by reason of the great destiny and general use of its medium in the affairs of men, is yet an art like other arts. Of these we may distinguish two great classes: those arts, like sculpture, painting, acting, which are representative, or, as used to be said very clumsily, imitative; and those, like architecture, music, and the dance, which are self-sufficient, and merely presentative. Each class, in right of this distinction, obeys principles apart; yet both may claim a common ground of existence, and it may be said with sufficient justice that the motive and end of any art whatever is to make a pattern; a pattern, it may be, of colors, of sounds, of changing attitudes, geometrical figures, or imitative lines; but still a pattern. That is the plane on which these sisters meet; it is by this that they are arts; and if it be well they should at times forget their childish origin, addressing their intelligence to virile tasks, and performing unconsciously that necessary function of their life, to make a pattern, it is still imperative that the pattern shall be made.

—Robert Louis Stevenson, *On Some Technical Elements of Style in Literature.* Reprinted by permission of Charles Scribner's Sons, publishers.

HOW TO WRITE A PARAGRAPH

In the following selection draw lines connecting the under-lined words and phrases which Abraham Lincoln used to tie together the thoughts of his famous address.

Fourscore and seven years ago our fathers brought forth on this continent a new nation, conceived in Liberty, and dedicated to the proposition that all men are created equal.

Now we are engaged in a great civil war, testing whether that nation, or any nation so conceived and so dedicated, can long endure. We are met on a great battlefield of that war. We have come to dedicate a portion of that field as a final resting-place for those who here gave their lives that that nation might live. It is altogether fitting and proper that we should do this.

But, in a larger sense, we cannot dedicate—we cannot consecrate —we cannot hallow this ground. The brave men, living and dead, who struggled here, have consecrated it, far above our poor power to add or detract. The world will little note nor long remember what we say here, but it can never forget what they did here. It is for us, the living, rather, to be dedicated here to the unfinished work which they who fought here have thus far so nobly advanced. It is rather for us to be here dedicated to the great task remaining before us—that from these honored dead we take increased devotion to that cause for which they gave the last full measure of devotion; that we here highly resolve that these dead shall not have died in vain; that this nation, under God, shall have a new birth of freedom; and that government of the people, by the people, for the people, shall not perish from the earth.

They may be used to relate the topic idea to ideas that came before it or that may come after it, or to establish connections between the subordinate ideas in the paragraph.

ORDER AND TRANSITIONS

The ideal paragraph has often been defined as one in which each sentence grows so naturally out of the one before it that the reader *feels* the natural, logical growth of the paragraph idea. It is pointless to quibble over the question whether such a paragraph is any closer to the ideal than one which is liberally sprinkled with connective words. Good paragraphs may be written either with or without connecting links or transitions. When two ideas are set side by side, the mind naturally assumes that the ideas are related. Not all paragraphs, however, are so simple that the ideas in them may be stacked like bricks in a pile. If a writer is building a wall, instead of piling bricks, he may need to work out a complex pattern, and—to extend the analogy—he may find it necessary to use mortar.

The mortar which holds the bricks of thought together in a paragraph may be one of three different kinds. Assuming that the thoughts have been properly arranged, they may be further tied to each other by linking, transitional, or directive words or expressions, by pronouns, and by echo-words. In the first class are such words as *moreover, therefore, consequently, for example, for instance, as a result, nevertheless, on the other hand, similarly, first, second, third, in conclusion, that is, that is to say, on the contrary, conversely.* This list is by no means complete. Pronouns, as you can readily see, carry the reader's mind back to their antecedents. Echo-words have the same function. By repeating a word, a phrase, or a part of a phrase, the writer *echoes* what has been said earlier in the paragraph.

But, again, your best method of learning how to use connectives is to analyze paragraphs written by skilled writers.

HOW MODERN WRITERS BUILD PARAGRAPHS

In the two paragraphs quoted below, Hilaire Belloc is defining a term, "the love of England"; you may consequently take these to be paragraphs of definition. But the term is defined by means of numerous particulars and details, and in the middle of the first paragraph you will find an analogy being used. Puzzle over these two paragraphs as long as you will, you will hesitate to put your finger on any one sentence that even remotely resembles a topic sentence. Then, too, you may ask why there are two paragraphs instead of one. Combine them into one and you have a paragraph that is unified, coherent, and logical. The author chose to group his details into two paragraphs, indicating the break between the two by repeating the phrase with which he began the first one.

The love of England has in it the love of landscape, as has the love of no other country: it has in it as has the love of no other country, the love of friends. Less than the love of other countries has it in it the love of what may be fixed in a phrase or well set down in words. It lacks, alas, the love of some interminable past nor does it draw its liveliness from any great succession of centuries. Say that ten centuries made a soil, and that in that soil four centuries more produced a tree, and that the tree was England, then you will know to what the love of England is in most men directed. For most who love England know so little of her first thousand years that when they hear the echoes of them or see visions of them, they think they are dealing with a foreign thing. All English men are clean cut off from their long past which ended when the last Mass was sung at Westminster.

—77—

The love of England has in it no true plains but fens, low hills, and distant mountains. No very ancient towns, but comfortable, small and ordered ones, which love to dress themselves with age The love of England concerns itself with trees. Accident has given to the lovers of England no long pageantry of battle. Nature has given Englishmen an appetite for battle, and between the two, men who love England make a legend for themselves of wars unfought, and of arms permanently successful; though arms were they thus always successful would not be arms at all.

—Hilaire Belloc, *This and That and the Other*, Dodd, Mead & Company, New York, 1912, pp. 219–220. Reprinted by permission.

The following paragraph begins with a topic sentence. The first half of the paragraph makes use of an example. Then after a comment on the example, the author repeats his topic idea, briefly suggests other examples, and finally concludes with an instance of the recognition of the truth of his topic idea. The last sentence should reveal to you the fact that examples often need to have their pertinence or application interpreted if they are to be effective.

The [honor] system works, of course, only in those colleges which have sufficient social solidarity to ensure that any offender will promptly be 'sent to Coventry' by undergraduate sentiment. One of the two violations of the code which occurred during my years at Princeton was in an examination in one of my own courses. I had left the room as soon as the papers were distributed, and there were no longer any 'proctors.' But a boy was seen to cheat, was reported by his classmates to the undergraduate 'honor committee,' and told to leave Princeton forever that afternoon. I knew nothing about it until Dean Murray announced at the next faculty meeting that Mr. X, on recommendation of the student committee, had severed his connection with the college. Only those professors who have taught under the humiliating police system and then under the honor system can understand the happy difference made in relations between professors and students. Yet without the requisite social solidarity the system is doomed to failure. It worked admirably at Williams, for example, and at many other of the smaller institutions. Some of us made a futile effort, many years ago, to persuade the Harvard authorities to try it, but even Dean Briggs, generous and idealistic as he was, was not to be convinced that the scheme was workable at Cambridge. There are, alas, too many 'Untouchables' in every great university, as Briggs knew sadly well, and you cannot send a boy to Coventry if he lives in Coventry already.

—Bliss Perry, *And Gladly Teach*, Houghton Mifflin Company, New York, 1935, p. 131. Reprinted by permission.

Effective use of concrete examples gives the following paragraph its cumulative force. The first two sentences are transitional. Yet if you still have a notion lingering in your mind that transitional sentences are minor details that may be added after a paragraph has been written, read the part of the essay that precedes this selection. "I am not referring to direct physical contact" is Mr. Gunther's beginning of one paragraph. "Nor do I mean to discuss the psychological effects of Chicago crime," starts the next paragraph on its way. The third paragraph brings us closer to his announcement of the subject: "Nor do I mean to elaborate on the larger political issues." What we have called a transition, then, is really a statement of the subject of the entire essay. The topic sentence follows, repeated with more specific application, and then made clear and convincing by a piling up of example after example.

What I am after is something newer, more intimate, and more definite. I mean racketeering. Crime is affecting the Chicago citizen in a new fashion. A system of criminal exploitation, based on extortion, controlled by hoodlums, and decorated with icy-cold murder, has arisen in the past five or six years, to seize the ordinary Chicagoan, you and me and the man across the street, by the pocket-book if not the throat. Crime is costing me money. It is costing money to the taxi-driver who took me to the office this morning, the elevator boy who lifted me ten stories through the steel stratifications of a great skyscraper, the waiter who served me my luncheon, the suburban business man who sat at the next table. Very few persons, in Chicago or out of it, realize that the ordinary citizen is paying literal tribute to racketeers. This tribute is levied in many ways. The ordinary citizen pays it, like as not, whenever he has a suit pressed and every time he gets a haircut; he may pay it in the plumbing in his house and the garaging of his car; the very garbage behind his back door may perhaps mean spoils for someone.

 —John Gunther, "The High Cost of Hoodlums," *Harper's Magazine*, vol. 159, p. 530 (October, 1929). Reprinted by permission.

The following is an excellent example of a paragraph of definition. Notice how carefully and how exactly the authors specify the sense in which they will use the term "virtues," and then, because in defining virtues they had to use two other disputable terms, how most of the paragraph becomes an attempt to clarify these two terms.

I shall define as virtues those mental and physical habits which tend to produce a good community, and as vices those that tend to produce a bad one. Different people have different conceptions of what makes a community good or bad, and it is difficult to find arguments by which to establish the preferability of one's own conception. I cannot hope, therefore, to appeal to those whose tastes are very different from my own, but I hope and believe that there is nothing very singular in my own tastes. For my part, I should judge a community to be in a good state if I found a great deal of instinctive happiness, a prevalence of feelings of friendship and affection rather than hatred and envy, a capacity for creating and enjoying beauty, and the intellectual curiosity which leads to the advancement and diffusion of knowledge. I should judge a community to be in a bad state if I found much unhappiness from thwarted instinct, much hatred and envy, little sense of beauty, and little intellectual curiosity. As between these different elements of excellence or the reverse, I do not pretend to judge. Suppose, for the sake of argument, that intellectual curiosity and artistic capacity were found to be in some degree incompatible, I should find it difficult to say which ought to be preferred. But I should certainly think better of a community which contained something of both than of one which contained more of the one and none of the other. I do not, however, believe that there is any incompatibility among the four ingredients I have mentioned as constituting a good community; namely, happiness, friendship, enjoyment of beauty, and love of knowledge.

> —Bertrand and Dora Russell, *Prospects of Industrial Civilization*, "Moral Standards and Social Well-Being," D. Appleton-Century Company, New York, 1923, pp. 161–162. Reprinted by permission.

Concrete details, a number of examples, and an interesting analogy form the substance of the following paragraph. The first sentence is the topic sentence.

I suppose the truth is that Americans are really more kindly and more sensitive and more vulnerable than English people, with the result that their manners are more unreliable. Social life in America is not smooth. It is jerky, turbulent, changeable. The social climate is an April climate. Clouds rush up, storms break, the skies clear again, all in the course of an evening party. As I have said elsewhere, one is reminded of children. Observe a children's party. The youngsters to begin with are on their best behavior, but presently they grow excited, boisterous, rows begin, tears are shed, and so on. Self-control, an iron self-discipline, an invincible quiet under provocation are not striking characteristics of the American. If he is annoyed he loses his temper. If he is amused he shouts with laughter. If she is jealous she shows it. Indeed, Americans almost always show their feelings too much for perfect manners. Good manners demand that one should ignore one's personal feelings and, if they are disagreeable, that one should hide them.

> —Mary Borden, "Manners," *Harper's Magazine*, vol. 160, p. 81 (December, 1929). Reprinted by permission.

Three paragraphs where one would produce the same effect —that may be your comment on the following selection. You are quite right, and yet when Galsworthy chose to make the subtopic the unit of paragraph structure he was doing what modern writers do frequently. Notice that the topic sentence not only expresses the general idea but also forecasts the structure.

Now, in writing plays, there are, in this matter of the moral, three courses open to the serious dramatist. The first is: To definitely set before the public that which it wishes to have set before it, the views and codes of life by which the public lives and in which it believes. This way is the most common, successful, and popular. It makes the dramatist's position sure, and not too obviously authoritative.

The second course is: To definitely set before the public those views and codes of life by which the dramatist himself lives, those theories in which he himself believes, the more effectively if they are the opposite of what the public wishes to have placed before it, presenting them so that the audience may swallow them like powder in a spoonful of jam.

There is a third course: To set before the public no cut-and-dried codes, but the phenomena of life and character, selected and combined, but not distorted, by the dramatist's outlook, set down without fear, favour, or prejudice, leaving the public to draw such poor moral as nature may afford. This third method requires a certain detachment; it requires a sympathy with, a love of, and a curiosity as to, things for their own sake; it requires a far view, together with patient industry, for no immediately practical result.

> —John Galsworthy, *Candelabra*, "Some Platitudes concerning Drama," Charles Scribner's Sons, New York, 1933, pp. 3–4. Reprinted by permission.

Development by the use of contrast, particulars and details, and citing results is illustrated in the following paragraph.

We went to science in search of light, not merely upon the nature of matter, but upon the nature of man as well, and though that which we have received may be light of a sort, it is not adapted to our eyes and is not anything by which we can see. Since thought began we have groped in the dark among shadowy shapes, doubtfully aware of landmarks looming uncertainly here and there—of moral principles, human values, aims, and ideals. We hoped for an illumination in which they would at least stand clearly and unmistakably forth, but instead they appear even less certain and less substantial than before—mere fancies and illusions generated by nerve actions that seem terribly remote from anything we can care about or based upon relativities that accident can shift. We had been assured that many troublesome shadows would flee away, that superstitious fears, irrational repugnances, and all manner of bad dreams would disappear. And so in truth very many have. But we never supposed that most of the things we cherished would prove equally unsubstantial, that all the aims we thought we vaguely perceived, all the values we pursued, and all the principles we clung to were but similar shadows, and that either the light of science is somehow deceptive or the universe, emotionally and spiritually, a vast emptiness.

> —Joseph Wood Krutch, *The Modern Temper*, Harcourt, Brace & Company, New York, 1929, pp. 68–69. Reprinted by permission.

The "Diagnosis of an Englishman," a paragraph packed full of concrete details, should challenge you to attempt a similar diagnosis of an American—or a Southerner, or an Oregonian, or a New Yorker, whichever commands your loyalty.

Diagnosis of an Englishman

The Englishman must have a thing brought under his nose before he will act; bring it there and he will go on acting after everybody else has stopped. He lives very much in the moment because he is essentially a man of facts and not a man of imagination. Want of imagination makes him, philosophically speaking, rather ludicrous; in practical affairs it handicaps him at the start; but once he has "got going"—as we say—it is of incalculable assistance to his stamina. The Englishman, partly through his lack of imagination and nervous sensibility, partly through his inbred dislike of extremes and habit of minimising the expression of everything, is a perfect example of the conservation of energy. It is, therefore, very difficult to come to the end of him. Add to this his unimaginative practicality, and tenacious moderation, his inherent spirit of competition—not to say pugnacity—a spirit of competition so extreme that it makes him, as it were, patronize Fate; add the sort of vulgarity that grows like fungus on people who despise ideas and analysis, and make a cult of unintellectuality; add a peculiar, ironic, "don't care" sort of humour; an underground humaneness, and an ashamed idealism—and you get some notion of the pudding of English character. It has a kind of terrible coolness, a rather awful level-headedness—by no means reflected in his Press. The Englishman makes constant small blunders; but few, almost no, deep mistakes. He is a slow starter, but there is no stronger finisher, because he has by temperament and training the faculty of getting through any job he gives his mind to with a minimum expenditure of vital energy; nothing is wasted in expression, style, spread-eagleism; everything is instinctively kept as near to the practical heart of the matter as possible. He is—to the eyes of an artist—distressingly matter-of-fact; a tempting mark for satire. And yet he is at bottom an idealist, though it is his nature to snub, disguise, and mock his own inherent optimism. To admit enthusiasm is "bad form" if he is a "gentleman"; and "swank," or mere waste of good heat, if he is not a "gentleman." England produces more than its proper percentage of cranks and poets; this is nature's way of redressing the balance in a country where feelings are not shown, sentiments not expressed, and extremes laughed at. Not that the Englishman is cold, as is generally supposed in foreign countries—on the contrary he is warm-hearted and feels strongly; but just as peasants, for lack of words to express their feelings, become stolid, so does the Englishman, from sheer lack of habit of self-expression. The Englishman's proverbial "hypocrisy"—that which I myself have dubbed his "island Pharisaism"—comes chiefly, I think, from his latent but fearfully strong instinct for competition which will not let him admit himself beaten, or in the wrong, even to himself; and from an ingrained sense of form that impels him always to "save his face"; but partly it comes from his powerlessness to explain his feelings. He has not the clear and fluent cynicism of expansive natures, wherewith to confess exactly how he stands. It is the habit of men of all nations to want to have things both ways; the Englishman wants it both ways, I think, more strongly than any; and he is unfortunately so unable to express himself, *even to himself*, that he has never realized this truth, much less confessed it—hence his "hypocrisy."

> —John Galsworthy, *Candelabra*, "Diagnosis of an Englishman," Charles Scribner's Sons, New York, 1933, pp. 57–59. Reprinted by permission.

The next two paragraphs, both of them developed largely by particulars and details, are good examples of scientific writing. Each begins with a topic sentence.

Looked at in its broad implications, the law of gravitation was important, not so much because it told us why an apple fell to the ground, or why the earth and planets moved around the sun, as because it suggested that the whole of Nature was governed by hard and fast laws. For instance, to the ancients comets had been fearsome portents of evil, of famines or pestilences, of wars or the death of kings; seen in the light of Newton's work, they became mere inert chunks of matter, following their predestined paths as they were dragged about in space by the gravitational pull of the sun. Clearly, their motions could have nothing to do with the deeds or misdeeds of men. In the same way, darkness spread over the earth at an eclipse of the sun, not because the gods were angry with men, but because gravitation had pulled the moon into a position in which it temporarily shut off the sun's light—a position to which it had been predestined from the beginning of time. The tyranny of superstition and magic was broken, and Nature became something to study, not something to fear. Man began to see that he was free to work out his own destiny without fear of disturbance from interfering gods, spirits, or demons.

> —Sir James Jeans, "Man and the Universe," from *Scientific Progress*, 1936, pp. 15–16. By permission of The Macmillan Company, publishers.

We of these later days, living in the narrow temperate zone surrounding our sun and peering into the far future, see an ice-age of a different kind threatening us. Just as Tantalus, standing in a lake so deep that he only just escaped drowning, was yet destined to die of thirst, so it is the tragedy of our race that it is probably destined to die of cold, while the greater part of the substance of the universe still remains too hot for life to obtain a footing. The sun, having no extraneous supply of heat, must necessarily emit ever less and less of its life-giving radiation, and, as it does so, the temperate zone of space, within which alone life can exist, must close around it. To remain a possible abode of life, our earth would need to move in ever nearer and nearer to the dying sun. Yet, science tells us that, so far from its moving inwards, inexorable dynamical laws are even now driving it ever farther away from the sun into the outer cold and darkness. And, so far as we can see, they must continue to do so until life is frozen off the earth, unless indeed some celestial collision or cataclysm intervenes to destroy life even earlier by a more speedy death. This prospective fate is not peculiar to our earth; other suns must die like our own, and any life there may be on other planets must meet the same inglorious end.

—Sir James Jeans, *The Mysterious Universe*, 1934, pp. 14–15
By permission of The Macmillan Company, publishers.

When a scientist sets out to write an interesting definition, he produces a paragraph like this one. Notice again that definition depends entirely on the use of concrete details.

Proteins are bodies of complicated composition and structure which play a fundamental part in animal life. They are essential constituents of muscle and nerve, skin and hair and wool: the values of our foods are related to protein-content, since the body's store must be continually replenished. We have long known that carbon, nitrogen, oxygen, hydrogen, sulphur, and other atoms are elements of the protein molecule, and that its molecular structure must in some ways be very variable, whence its name. Only recently we have acquired new information about the general plan, mainly from our X-ray studies, and it is extremely curious and interesting. Every protein molecule has a backbone or central framework, consisting of an atomic chain in which carbon and nitrogen atoms recur with perfect regularity, two of the former to one of the latter. The chain cannot be pulled into a straight line because the two links that join each atom to its neighbors in the chain make with each other an invariable angle. This angle, which can be measured with great exactness, as can also the distance between each pair of atoms, is rather more than a right angle. Although there is this element of rigidity the chain as a whole can be crumpled up because any part of the chain can turn around the link that connects it to the remainder, as if the link were an axle. It is the shortening of the protein chains in this way which constitutes the contraction of our muscles, or the shrinking of a textile fabric. All animal movements are produced by the contraction and extension of muscular fibre, and directed by way of nerves, in which also protein is the important constituent.

—Sir William Bragg, "The Progress of Physical Science," from *Scientific Progress*, 1936, pp. 70–72. By permission of The Macmillan Company, publishers.

Here is a paragraph developed inductively with the topic sentence at the end.

On the whole, the Fathers of the Republic believed that war was principally a wicked trade of princes and tyrants, and that the United States, by keeping out of the brawls of Europe, might steadily enjoy peace as a national blessing. If, being practical men, they took into account the possible recurrence of war and made ample provision in the Constitution for defense, they did it with reference to the chances of life, not in praise of war as a manly exercise. By and large, the creed of peace, scorned by feudal aristocracies as the craven ethics of commercial huckstering, became a kind of national tradition, although nearly every generation after the establishment of independence passed through an armed conflict. Even while condemning pacifists privately as weaklings, cowards, and near-traitors, President Roosevelt never publicly exalted war as a virtue in itself but only when waged for a "righteous" cause. President

Wilson branded it as an evil and called on the nation to help him "end war." It is not surprising, therefore, that some haziness exists in the American mind on the subject of armed combat and its uses in world economy.

> —Charles A. Beard and William Beard, *The American Leviathan*, 1931, pp. 754–755. By permission of The Macmillan Company, publishers.

This is a paragraph developed by analogy, showing you the usefulness of this method in explaining an abstruse scientific concept.

Roughly, one might say that the atoms correspond to the members of the engineer's structure and the electrons to the rivets which hold the members together. With a little greater license one might compare the energy-quanta to the exertions of the workmen who insert or remove the rivets. In these terms the construction or alteration of the engineer's design is a fairly close analogue to physical and chemical operations, such as the melting of wax or the growth of a plant in the rays of the sun. Bonds are broken and re-formed, and energy-quanta are derived from the radiant light and heat.

> —Sir William Bragg, "The Progress of Physical Science," from *Scientific Progress*, 1936, pp. 50–51. By permission of The Macmillan Company, publishers.

And here is a paragraph of summary and transition, with the topic sentence first.

Before turning to the medical advances of the present century, let us just briefly recapitulate the changes that have been mentioned above. We have seen medicine emerge from a period of magic and religion to a stage where disease came to be accepted as a phenomenon of nature. Following this there came a time when the structure of the body was investigated; this led to the further stage in which clinical signs and symptoms and anatomical structures of diseased organs were correlated. Ultimately, the present era arrived, when the experimental method was seriously applied to the study of the body, with the result that big strides were made not only in knowledge of the actions of many organs, but also of the causes of many diseases. There were still, however, at the beginning of the present century, many diseases which had been distinguished as entities but about which we knew little or nothing as to causation or treatment, and, although this is still the case, the work of the last thirty years has helped to fill in many blanks.

—Edward Mellanby, "Progress in Medical Science," from *Scientific Progress*, 1936, pp. 116–117. By permission of The Macmillan Company, publishers.

THE USE OF THE LIBRARY

The purpose of this chapter is to give you information helpful to you in getting books from your library and in getting information from books and periodicals which ordinarily cannot be taken out of a library.

The starting point for your explorations of the library is, logically, the card catalogue. This is a collection of cards listing every book, bulletin, pamphlet, or periodical which the library owns. The cards are arranged alphabetically according to authors, titles, and subjects. In other words, every book is listed on at least three separate cards. You can therefore find a book if you know the author's name, or the title, or the subject with which it deals. Magazines and bulletins are usually listed by title; that is, the card catalogue will tell you whether or not the library possesses a certain magazine or series of bulletins. For detailed information about the contents of these periodicals or bulletins you will have to consult other guides.

Let us examine a typical library card (see p. 91).

1. 341.6–B977 is the call number, according to the Dewey Decimal system.
2. "Butler, Nicholas Murray, 1862–" tells you the author's name, last name given first; the date of his birth; and that at the time this card was made out he was still living.
3. "The path . . . 1930" tells you the title of the book and the subtitle; the author's name, written in the natural order; the place of publication; the name of the publisher; and the date of publication.
4. The fifth line tells you that the book has thirteen pages num-

bered in Roman numerals and 320 pages numbered in Arabic numerals, and that the height of the book is 19 centimeters.

5. The next two lines give you the subject references under which the book may be found listed in the card catalogue. You will find the book listed under: peace; renunciation of war treaty, Paris, Aug. 27, 1928; international law and relations; and under the title.
6. "Library of Congress" and "——— ——— Copy 2" tell you that the Library of Congress has two copies of the book.
7. "JX1952.B83" is the Library of Congress cataloguing symbol.
8. "30—28072" is the order number used by librarians in ordering cards.
9. "[31p5]" is the key to the printing of the card.
10. "341.6" is the class number under the Dewey Decimal system.
11. "Copyright A 29303" is the Library of Congress key to the copyright of the book.

341.6 **Butler, Nicholas Murray,** 1862–
B977
        The path to peace; essays and addresses on peace
        and its making, by Nicholas Murray Butler ...
        New York, London, C. Scribner's sons, 1930.

        xiii, 320 p.   19ᶜᵐ.

        1. Peace. 2. Renunciation of war treaty, Paris, Aug. 27, 1928.
        3. International law and relations.   I. Title.

                                                        30—28072
        Library of Congress   JX1952.B83

        —— ——— Copy 2.

        Copyright   A 29303   [31p5]   341.6

The card just examined is an author card. A title card is just like an author card, except that the title is typewritten at the top.

PE1075 Modern English in the making.
M3
    McKnight, George Harley, 1871–

    Modern English in the making, by George H. McKnight ... with the assistance of Bert Emsley ... New York, London, D. Appleton and company, 1928.

    xii p., 1 l., 590 p. front., illus., pl., facsims. 21^{cm}.

    1. English language—Hist. 2. English language—Grammar, Historical. I. Emsley, Bert, joint author. II. Title.

                                                      28—23547

    Library of Congress   PE1075.M3

    —— —— Copy 2.

    Copyright A 1054337   [35u2]

HC103 U. S.-Economic conditions
B57
    Bogart, Ernest Ludlow, 1870–

    ... Economic history of the American people, by Ernest Ludlow Bogart ... New York, London [etc.] Longmans, Green and co., 1930.

    xii p., 1 l., 797 p. illus. (maps) diagrs. 22½^{cm}. (Longmans' economics series)

    "First edition."
    "Bibliographical note" at end of each chapter.

    1. U. S.—Econ. condit. 2. U. S.—Indus.—Hist.

                                                         30—28303

    Library of Congress   HC103.B57

    —— —— Copy 2.

    Copyright A 29217   [33z3]   330.973

The descriptive line, "xii p., 1 l., 590 p. front., illus., pl., facsims. 21^{cm}." (see top of p. 92), tells you that there are twelve pages numbered in Roman numerals, one leaf printed on one side only, 590 pages of print, a frontispiece, illustrations, plates, and facsimiles. This specimen card also shows you that books are catalogued under the name of a joint author. All the other information you should be able to interpret for yourself.

A subject card (see bottom of p. 92) is an author card with the subject typed, usually in red, above the author's name at the top.

CALL NUMBERS

A "call number" is a symbol or group of symbols used by libraries to designate any particular book. The call number for any book is placed in the upper left-hand corner of the card-catalogue card, on the back cover of the book, and usually on the inside cover as well. Books are arranged on shelves according to their call numbers. Call numbers usually consist of two parts: the upper part is the classification number, and the lower part the author and book number.

For the ordinary undergraduate, a knowledge of the systems used in devising call numbers is relatively unimportant. To satisfy a natural curiosity on the part of many students and to make library work a little more interesting, the following brief explanation is given.

Two systems of classification are used by libraries in this country: the Library of Congress system and the Dewey Decimal system.

The Library of Congress system, found more frequently in college than in public libraries, uses the letters of the alphabet, followed by Arabic numerals or additional letters, as the basis of its classification.

A   General works
B   Philosophy—Religion
C   History—Auxiliary sciences
D   History and topography (except America)
E and F American history
G   Geography—Anthropology
H   Social sciences
J   Political science
K   Law
L   Education
M   Music
N   Fine arts
P   Language and literature
Q   Science
R   Medicine
S   Agriculture—Plant and animal industry
T   Technology
U   Military science
V   Naval science
Z   Bibliography and library science

The Dewey Decimal system, devised by Melvil Dewey, uses a decimal classification for all books. The entire field of knowledge is divided into nine groups, with an additional group for general reference books. Each main class and sub-class is shown by a number composed of three digits. Subdivisions of these classes are designated by numbers after a decimal point. In the following table the subdivision is shown under the class of natural science.

000 General works
100 Philosophy
200 Religion
300 Sociology
400 Philology
500 Natural science
       510 Mathematics
       520 Astronomy
       530 Physics
       540 Chemistry
       550 Geology
       560 Paleontology
       570 Biology
       580 Botany
       590 Zoology
600 Useful arts
700 Fine arts
800 Literature
900 History

THE REFERENCE LIBRARY

The reference library consists of all the general works, such as encyclopedias and dictionaries, and collections of pamphlets, bibliographies, guides, maps, pictures, and the like, which are to be consulted for some specific information rather than to be read in their entirety. Reference books ordinarily cannot be taken from the library. The following list of reference books should be a starting point for your explorations of the reference room of your library. Get acquainted with these books. Find out where they are shelved. Examine them, and examine others like them that you find on the shelves.

In the following list, the date given is usually the date of the latest revision.

The General Encyclopedias

Encyclopaedia Britannica, 14th ed., 24 vols., Encyclopaedia Britannica Company, London, 1937.

The authoritative articles deal with almost every field of human knowledge. The more important ones are signed with the initials of their authors; the index to the initials is found at the front of each volume. The subjects are arranged alphabetically; an index in volume 24 is an added convenience. Useful bibliographies follow many of the articles. There are also numerous illustrations, maps, figures, and diagrams.

Encyclopedia Americana, 30 vols., Americana Corporation, New York, 1936.

The articles in the *Americana*, usually shorter than in the *Britannica*, are written by authorities in the various fields. The various aspects of modern life—business, industry, science, government— are dealt with in reliable and compact essays. The historical studies are excellent. Like the *Britannica*, it has bibliographies, illustrations, and maps. The more important articles are signed in full.

New International Encyclopaedia, 25 vols., Dodd, Mead & Company, New York, 1922 (sup., 2 vols., 1925; 2 vols., 1930).

Although the *New International* is written from the American point of view, it is really international in scope. The 75,000 articles cover a wide field. Good bibliographies, maps, illustrations, and reading courses are included. The articles are unsigned, but the table of contents of each volume gives the authors of the more important articles.

The Special Encyclopedias

The Catholic Encyclopedia, 17 vols., Robert Appleton Company, New York, 1907-1922 (vols. 16-17 published by the Encyclopedia Press).

Although this work deals primarily with the accomplishments of Catholics, its scope is rather general. The signed articles are arranged alphabetically. It is useful not only for subjects relating to the Catholic Church but also for subjects relating to medieval history, art, literature, and philosophy.

The Jewish Encyclopedia, 12 vols., Funk & Wagnalls, New York, 1925.

This work contains articles (signed by initials) dealing with the history, traditions, customs, literature, and accomplishments of the Jewish people from the earliest times to the present.

Bailey, L. H., ed., Cyclopedia of American Agriculture, 4 vols., The Macmillan Company, New York, 1907-1909.

Signed articles are grouped under four heads: vol. 1, farms; vol. 2, crops; vol. 3, animals; vol. 4, farm and community. Bibliographies and illustrations are included.

Hastings, James, ed., Encyclopaedia of Religion and Ethics, 13 vols., Charles Scribner's Sons, New York, 1908-1928.

This work contains signed articles on various religions, systems of ethics, philosophies, religious customs and practices, persons important in religious history, and places famous because of religious associations.

Monroe, Paul, ed., Cyclopedia of Education, 3 vols., The Macmillan Company, New York, 1925.

This work contains articles dealing with various educational systems, noted educators, and colleges and universities.

Munn, Glenn G., Encyclopedia of Banking and Finance, 2 vols., Bankers Publishing Co., New York, 1935.

This is a manual of terms relating to banking, money, credit, trusts, foreign exchange, insurance, markets, securities, and the like.

Seligman, Edwin R. A., and Johnson, Alvin, eds., Encyclopaedia of the Social Sciences, 15 vols., The Macmillan Company, New York, 1930-1935 (reissued in 8 vols. in 1937).

The articles about sociology, political science, economics, ethics, philosophy, education, etc., are prepared under the sponsorship of ten national learned societies. Good bibliographies and an adequate index are included.

The Year Books

The World Almanac and Book of Facts, The New York World-Telegram, New York, 1868 to date.

This is the most widely used of the year books. It gives summarized and tabulated information about everything of importance that happens in the fields of science, finance, politics, medicine, sports, literature, current affairs, etc.

The American Year Book, now published by the American Year Book Corp., 1910 to date.

The articles for this year book are prepared under the direction of representatives of 45 national learned societies. They are classified under such headings as science, history, American government, etc. The articles are signed.

The Americana Annual, Encyclopedia Americana Corp., New York, 1923 to date.

This is the annual supplement to the *Encyclopedia Americana*.

The New International Year Book, now published by Funk & Wagnalls, New York, 1907 to date.

This is an annual supplement to the *New International Encyclopaedia*.

Statesman's Year-Book, The Macmillan Company, London, 1864 to date.

Information about governments, industries, resources, etc., is given by countries, the British Empire being listed first, followed by the United States, and then the other countries in alphabetical order.

Biographical Dictionaries

Dictionary of National Biography, 22 vols., Oxford University Press, London, 1921 to 1922.

This contains biographies of famous persons of the British Empire who are no longer living.

Dictionary of American Biography, 20 vols., Charles Scribner's Sons, New York, 1928 to 1936.

Prepared under the auspices of the American Council of Learned Societies, this is the American equivalent of the *Dictionary of National Biography*. This work contains the biographies of more than 15,000 men and women who have made some special contribution to our national life. Each biography is written by a recognized authority.

Who's Who, A. & C. Black, Ltd., London, 1849 to date.

This is an annual publication containing compact biographies of prominent living Englishmen and a few famous persons of other nations.

Who's Who in America, A. N. Marquis Co., Chicago, 1899 to date.

This is published every two years. It contains brief biographical sketches of famous living persons in the United States.

Dictionaries and Books of Synonyms

New English Dictionary, 10 vols. and sup., Oxford, Clarendon Press, 1888 to 1933.

This dictionary, also called the *Oxford Dictionary*, *Murray's Dictionary*, *N.E.D.*, and *O.E.D.*, is not for general use. Its purpose is to give the history of every word in the English language for the last 800 years. It contains many quotations illustrating meanings of words in various periods, full discussions of derivations and changes in meanings and spellings.

Webster's New International Dictionary, 2nd ed., G. & C. Merriam Company, Springfield, Mass., 1934.

This edition, published after ten years of preparation, is an entirely new book. It is the dictionary almost universally appealed to as the final authority in spelling, meaning, pronunciation, derivation, and usage.

New Standard Dictionary, Funk & Wagnalls, New York.

This one-volume unabridged dictionary is kept up to date through changes and editions with every printing.

Century Dictionary and Cyclopedia, 12 vols., The Century Company, New York, 1911.

This is a comprehensive work but now somewhat out of date. Each volume has a supplement of new words and phrases and new definitions. Hence it is often necessary to look for a word in two places in the same volume.

Volume 11, *Cyclopedia of Proper Names*, gives names from history, literature, biography, geography, mythology, art, etc.

The Roget Dictionary of Synonyms and Antonyms, G. P. Putnam's Sons, New York, 1931.

This is *Roget's Thesaurus*, revised and modernized, and completely rearranged in form. The revision is a decided improvement. Words are listed in dictionary order. The most important entries are followed by synonyms grouped as nouns, verbs, adjectives, and adverbs. Less important words are followed by a few synonyms and a reference to a major group.

Allen, F. Sturges, Allen's Synonyms and Antonyms, Harper & Brothers, New York, 1938.

The words, in alphabetical order, are followed by synonyms and antonyms but not by definitions. Usage labels, such as *affected*, *archaic*, *colloq.*, *formal*, *obs.*, etc., are helpful.

Crabb, George, Crabb's English Synonyms, Harper & Brothers, New York, 1934.

The words, in alphabetical order, are arranged by first word of groups of synonymous words, with explanations and examples of use. There are cross references and an index.

Fernald, James C., English Synonyms and Antonyms, Funk & Wagnalls, New York, 1938.

Under key words are synonyms and antonyms and correct use of prepositions, followed by discussions of differences between synonyms. There are questions for study and an index in part 2.

Fowler, H. W., A Dictionary of Modern English Usage, Oxford, Clarendon Press, 1926.

Although this is neither a dictionary nor a book of synonyms, it is an invaluable aid to every person who is interested in writing. No description can do justice to the wit and scholarship that went into the making of this little book. The index is the flower of true British reticence.

Gazetteers and Atlases

Lippincott's New Gazetteer, J. B. Lippincott Company, Philadelphia, 1906 (1931 with conspectus of 15th census).

A gazetteer is a geographical dictionary of the world, containing short descriptions of countries, rivers, cities, mountains, etc. This gazetteer needs to be brought up to date.

Rand McNally Commercial Atlas and Marketing Guide, 68th ed., Rand McNally & Company, Chicago, 1937.

This contains information about population, transportation, products, manufacturing, markets, steamship lines, and railroads. The maps are large and there is a good index.

The New-World Loose Leaf Atlas, C. S. Hammond & Company, New York, 1929.

This contains large maps—historical, economic, political, and physical. It is well indexed.

The Times Survey Atlas of the World, The Times, London, 1924.

There are 112 maps—political, commercial, racial, religious, etc. A pronouncing index and gazetteer are included.

Literature

Cambridge History of English Literature, 15 vols., The Macmillan Company, New York, 1933; Cambridge University Press, 1907-1927.

The chapters are arranged by periods and famous authors, each chapter being written by a specialist in that field. The bibliographies are extensive but not up to date.

Cambridge History of American Literature, 3 vols., The Macmillan Company, New York, 1933; 4 vols., G. P. Putnam's Sons, New York, 1917-1921.

This is similar in arrangement and plan to the *Cambridge History of English Literature.*

Guides to the Use of Libraries

Hutchins, Margaret, Johnson, Alice S., and Williams, Margaret S., Guide to the Use of Libraries, 5th ed., H. W. Wilson Company, New York, 1936.

Mudge, I. G., Guide to Reference Books, 6th ed., Am. Library Association, Chicago, 1936.

Literary Quotations

Bartlett, John, Familiar Quotations, 11th ed., Little, Brown & Company, Boston, 1937.

The quotations are arranged chronologically by the date of the author's birth. There is an index of authors in the front of the book. In the back of the book, the quotations are indexed by important words.

Hoyt, J. K., Hoyt's New Cyclopedia of Practical Quotations, Funk & Wagnalls, New York, 1922.

The quotations are arranged alphabetically by subjects, and then by authors under the subjects. Quotations represent English and foreign languages, both ancient and modern. The book is well indexed.

Stevenson, Burton, The Home Book of Quotations, Dodd, Mead & Company, New York, 1934.

About 50,000 quotations are arranged alphabetically by subjects. The authors are indexed, and quotations are listed by the important words in each quotation.

Mythology and Antiquities

Peck, Harry T., Harper's Dictionary of Classical Literature and Antiquities, American Book Company, New York, 1897.

This work deals with Greek and Roman history, literature, mythology, geography, biography, etc. The arrangement is alphabetical, with cross references.

Harvey, Sir Paul, The Oxford Companion to Classical Literature, Oxford, 1937.

This is an excellent new guide not only for the classical student but also for any person who wants to understand the classical allusions in his daily reading.

Smith, Sir William, A Dictionary of Greek and Roman Antiquities, 2 vols., John Murray, London, 1890-1891.

This is primarily for the classical scholar.

Gayley, Charles M., Classic Myths in English Literature and in Art, Ginn & Company, Boston, 1911.

This is a popular handbook.

INDEXES TO PERIODICALS AND NEWSPAPERS

In the reference room of the library you will also find a number of guides and indexes which enable you to find material published in magazines and newspapers. Although a little of the material which was originally published in magazines may be available in book form, most of it will never be republished. Some of it is too recent to be published elsewhere. Since in the study of any current question you must go directly to magazines and newspapers, you must acquaint yourself with the following guides:

Poole's Index to Periodical Literature, 1802-1881; supplements: 1882-1886, 1887-1891, 1892-1896, 1897-1901, 1902-1906.

This guide indexes about 590,000 articles in 12,241 volumes of 470 different American and English periodicals. To be able to use it intelligently, you must know that: it is a subject index only; it has no author entries; all articles having a distinct subject are entered under that subject; articles having no subject, like poems and stories, are entered under the first word of the title; no date is given, only volume and page, but not inclusive paging; the periodicals indexed are principally of a general nature.

Readers' Guide to Periodical Literature, 1900 to date.

This is a monthly publication, with annual and permanent cumulated volumes. Its special features are: the entries are under author, title, and subjects; it gives volume, inclusive paging, date; it indicates illustrations, portraits, maps, etc.; it indexes book reviews up to 1904; it has a list of 597 books in the second and third cumulated volumes.

Agricultural Index, 1916 to date.

This is a subject index, issued nine times a year and cumulated annually, except that every third year a three-year cumulation is published instead of the annual volume.

Experiment Station Record, 1889 to date.

This is a record and digest of current agricultural literature, so complete that it serves as an index to the periodical, bulletin, and report material on the subject.

Dramatic Index, 1909 to date.

This is an annual subject index to all articles on drama, the theater, actors and actresses, playwrights, and plays in about two hundred English and American periodicals.

The Education Index, 1929 to date.

This is an author and subject index. The field covered is obvious from the title.

The Art Index, 1929 to date.

This is an author and subject index.

Index to Legal Periodicals, 1908 to date.

This is an author and subject index, issued quarterly with annual cumulations.

Quarterly Cumulative Index Medicus, 1927 to date (Index Medicus, 1879-1926).

This is an author and subject index. It is a complete guide to more than 1,200 periodicals in the field of medicine. It indexes books, pamphlets, theses, as well as periodical articles.

Engineering Index, 1892-1906.

Engineering Index Annual, 1906 to date.

This is a classified subject index from 1906 to 1918, and an alphabetical index from 1919 to date.

Industrial Arts Index, 1913 to date.

This is published monthly with annual cumulations. It is a subject and title index.

International Index to Periodicals, 1907 to date.

This consists of current issues and cumulations in annual and permanent volumes. It is an author and subject index. The *International Index* deals with more scholarly journals than does the *Readers' Guide*. It is the best guide to articles in the foreign languages, especially in German and French.

New York Times Index, 1913 to date.

This is a monthly index of the pages of The New York *Times*, with annual cumulations. The references, arranged according to subject entries, are to date, section, page, and column. It may be used as an index to any daily newspaper over the United States, since the same news stories will probably be found in all daily papers on the day they appear in the *Times*.

THE RESEARCH PAPER

The research article, often called the investigative theme or the term paper, is an exposition which aims to present the results of careful and thorough investigation of some chosen or assigned subject. You will no doubt have occasion to write term papers based on laboratory experiments, or on questionnaires, or on your own critical reactions to something you have read; papers of that sort are organized and written like any other expository theme. The information given here applies primarily to papers based on published material. The problems treated here are those you will meet when you begin your investigations in a library.

The writing of a research paper is justified partly through what you produce and partly through the training you get in the process of writing it. If you produce a good paper, it will be, in one sense, a real contribution to knowledge. The paper may serve a reader by giving him in easily accessible form information which he would have difficulty in finding for himself. It may clarify or evaluate ideas and opinions. It may assemble and organize available materials as a basis for further investigations or for a new and original interpretation.

But the more immediate value, the one you will recognize and appreciate at once, lies in what it will do to you. You will become acquainted with the resources of your library. You will learn how to find information in books, periodicals, pamphlets, documents, and bulletins. You will learn how to take adequate and usable notes. You will get practice in assembling and organizing materials. Your thinking will be stimulated because you will have to reason from your assembled facts and because occasionally you will have to weigh contradictory opinions. And, finally, your judgment will be sharpened through practice in selecting and adapting material for some specific class of readers.

Since a research paper aims to gather and interpret facts for the use of some specific reader, it must be accurate, clear, and interesting. It must be accurate not only in the facts selected and presented but also in the emphasis given to different facts. The information must be based on the most recent studies. Clearness is partly a matter of understanding the purpose of the research and partly a matter of organization and composition. A good, though simple, outline helps to assure clearness. Adequate understanding of the subject matter usually results in greater clearness, since no writer can explain what he himself does not understand. A wide reading in the selected field is an aid to clearness, since it helps the writer to select and reject material wisely. Interest comes, first of all, from subject matter which is in itself interesting to the reader. Not even the most bungling writer can spoil that entirely. But interest may, and usually must, come from other sources—a new point of view, a new interpretation, the flavor of the writer's personality, a lively and enthusiastic attitude. A research paper should not—must not—be dull.

CHOOSING THE SUBJECT

As soon as the research paper is assigned, many students will almost instinctively ask themselves: "Now what subject do I know something about?" A major in English will want to investigate some author or literary movement. A student of forestry will want to write on conservation. A student of home economics will want to write on nutrition or antique furniture. In some ways this attitude is commendable; in other ways it is a mistake. A student should indeed be interested in the subject of his investigation, but his interest may as well bring the thrill of exploring a field entirely new to him. His choice of a field, however, must be limited by certain practical considerations. He cannot take a subject which is too technical for his understanding. No matter how far he explores into strange fields, he must never undertake to explain what he does not fully understand himself. Furthermore, he must limit himself to the resources of the college library. Since the project is designed to be the means of learning how to use library material, information secured by interviews, or through experiments, or from personal experiences, should be submitted only as a supplement to information found in the college reference library.

The following list of subjects should include something that will interest almost any type of student.

1. Food allergy
2. Endocrine glands
3. Migratory birds
4. Sir Basil Zaharoff
5. The Smithsonian Institution
6. The zeppelins
7. Advances in air conditioning
8. Canned blood
9. Stratosphere flights
10. The electric eye
11. The Golden Gate Bridge
12. The Florida Ship Canal
13. The civil war in Spain
14. Soil conservation service
15. Telephone progress
16. Social Security Act
17. The Davis cup
18. Diego Rivera
19. Modern American painting
20. The Olympic games
21. Archery
22. The National Geographic Society
23. The Metropolitan Museum of Art
24. Virus diseases
25. Insulin
26. Artificial fever
27. Irish Free State
28. The resources of Alaska
29. The McGuffey readers
30. Dust storms
31. American Medical Association
32. New roses
33. The American Legion
34. The Supreme Court
35. The American Bar Association
36. Butterflies
37. Arbor Day
38. Bee culture
39. Co-operative buying
40. Log cabins
41. The perennial border
42. Co-operative marketing
43. Modern Arabia
44. The Mayan civilization
45. Cartoons and cartoonists
46. Paul Cézanne
47. Folk dances
48. Deep sea explorations
49. Plant hormones
50. Lespedezas
51. Gargoyles
52. Disarmament
53. The rock garden
54. Farm tenancy

55. Greenland
56. Egg laying contests
57. Locusts
58. Land-grant colleges
59. The *Lusitania*
60. Mayan art
61. Stanley Baldwin
62. Why do birds migrate?
63. Boulder Dam
64. Cannibalism
65. Vitamins
66. Modern American music
67. The Suez Canal
68. Unemployment insurance
69. The Rome-Berlin axis
70. Ultra-violet rays
71. Old age pensions
72. The Isle of Man
73. Student self-government
74. Alpha rays
75. The Jewish state
76. Teaching as a career
77. The partition of Czecho-slovakia
78. Problem children
79. The Russian constitution
80. Music and citizenship
81. Automobile accidents
82. Colonial architecture
83. An efficient kitchen
84. Parent-teacher associations
85. Planning a small house
86. New anesthetics
87. Correspondence courses
88. Education of the feeble minded
89. How to make a lawn
90. Amplifiers
91. New uses for aluminum
92. Advertising mediums
93. The used-car problem
94. Automobile trailers
95. Public employment offices
96. Enzymes
97. Flood control
98. Uses of natural gas
99. New automotive fuels
100. Altitude flying
101. Model homes
102. Earthquakes
103. Glass brick
104. Holding companies
105. Prefabricated houses
106. Government housing projects
107. Dust diseases
108. Monel metal
109. Weather forecasting
110. Religion in Soviet Russia
111. First editions
112. Guaranty of bank deposits
113. A recreation room in the basement
114. Schools in Soviet Russia
115. The Soviet army
116. Highway illumination
117. How to treat burns
118. Tourist camps
119. Wood preservation
120. The Soviet theater
121. Color blindness
122. Adult education
123. What is communism?

185. Prospects of war
186. Preparedness for peace
187. The career of Gershwin
188. Strategy in football
189. Consumers' co-operatives
190. Racketeering
191. San Francisco Bay bridges
192. Control of poliomyelitis
193. The plays of Clifford Odets
194. The plays of Sean O'Casey
195. Shakespeare in motion pictures
196. Famous motion picture directors
197. Tap-dancing
198. The development of color films
199. Novels about China
200. Film censorship

Limiting the Subject

After you have indicated your general field of interest, you will, with the help of your instructor, select some part or aspect of it that can be effectively presented in the given space and time. If you are interested in literature, you may decide to write about Carl Sandburg. In a paper of about three thousand words you cannot tell everything about Sandburg. You may, however, choose to tell about his stories for children, or his glorification of industry, or his championship of the common man. Or if you are interested in the subject of industrial diseases, you might select some one disease, such as silicosis. In choosing your subject, always remember that you cannot narrow or limit a subject by excluding from it essential details. A research article should be interesting. Interest comes from the concrete details, the examples, or the imaginative touches that you can give your writing.

Before you make your final decision, it might be well for you to spend an hour or two browsing around in the library. Look in the card catalogue. Check through some of the periodical indexes to find out the extent of the published material in your field. Notice in what types of periodicals your information is found, and make a preliminary check, either through the general card catalogue or through a special index of periodicals, to see which of the sources are available in your library. After you have done that, you are ready to begin collecting your bibliography.

THE BIBLIOGRAPHY

A bibliography is an alphabetized list of books, articles, bulletins, or documents relating to a given subject or author. Bibliographies may be classified as either complete or limited.

A true bibliography consists of all the references relating to a given subject. It has nothing to do with the number of sources available in any given library or the number actually consulted in the preparation of any given research article. It is simply a directory. Like a city directory or a telephone directory, it is there to be consulted but not necessarily read from cover to cover when one wishes to locate an address or find a telephone number.

Most bibliographies are limited. The extent of the bibliography you will prepare will depend on the time you have or on the assignment made by your instructor. You should, however, attempt a fairly adequate guide to your subject. You should list many more references than you expect to use. Some of them will be worthless to you in your particular project; others you will not be able to get in your library. Always expect a certain amount of wastage of your materials. And, finally, remember that your bibliography is a convenience for your reader as much as an acknowledgment of the sources you have consulted.

If your instructor asks for only the sources actually used in the preparation of the paper, call it "a list of references," but not a bibliography. Acknowledgment of sources actually used is properly made through footnotes.

BIBLIOGRAPHY CARDS

Use 3 x 5 note cards for your bibliographic references, a separate card for each reference. Adopt a definite form for entries on your cards. Your bibliographic entries should be clear, uniform, complete, and accurate. Remember that three items of information are necessary for every reference: the author's name, the title, and the facts of publication. If you cannot find the author's name, start with the second item. In making out your cards, translate the forms used by guides to periodicals into more generally understood forms. Although you will find references in which Roman numerals are used, it is better for you to use Arabic numerals exclusively. The present tendency—and a welcome one—is to avoid Roman numerals altogether in all kinds of references. Never abbreviate the names of periodicals. Label the volume number and the page numbers; use *vol.* for *volume* and *pp.* for *pages.*

The following forms are recommended as being simple, usable, compact, logical, and practically foolproof:

References to Encyclopedias

For references to encyclopedias, copy:

1. The author's name, last name first, if you can find it (put a comma at the end of the line).
2. The title of the article (put quotation marks around it and a comma after it).
3. The title of the encyclopedia (underline it); the year or edition; the volume number; the pages (put a period at the end).

As soon as you have made out a card, give it a number. Write this above the line at the top—in the left-hand corner. This is your "code number" which you will use in the process of writing your theme. It will save you a great deal of useless copying of references; at the same time it is more accurate than any system of abbreviations that you could invent. Of course, when you copy the final draft of the paper, you will refer to the code numbers of the cards you have used, and copy, in correct form, every footnote, either page by page or all at the end of the paper. It does not matter what number you give to any card just so that you do not repeat numbers. And if you still do not understand what it is all about, try this scheme just the same. It is so childishly simple that most students who have not tried it expect it to be complicated and difficult.

---

[5]

- -

Thomas, Albert,

"The International Labor Organization,"

Encyclopaedia Britannica, 14th ed., vol. 12, pp. 517–520.

References to Books

For references to books, copy:

1. The author's name, last name first, exactly as it appears in the card catalogue (put a comma at the end of the line).
2. The title of the book (underline it to indicate italics and put a comma at the end of the line).

3. The publisher, the place and date of publication (put a period at the end).
4. The library call number (copy it in the upper left-hand corner).

```
┌─────────────────────────────────────────────────────────────┐
│                                                             │
│   [23]                                                      │
│   - - - - - - - - - - - - - - - - - - - - - - - - - - - -   │
│                                                             │
│   PE1075     McKnight, George Harley,                       │
│   M3                                                        │
│                 Modern English in the Making,               │
│                                                             │
│             D. Appleton and Co., New York, 1928.            │
│                                                             │
│                                                             │
│                                                             │
│                                                             │
└─────────────────────────────────────────────────────────────┘
```

References to Magazine Articles

For references to magazine articles, copy:

1. The author's name, last name first (if the article is unsigned, begin with the title).
2. The title of the article (in quotation marks).
3. The name of the magazine (underline it); the volume (use Arabic numerals); the pages; the date (in parentheses).

Punctuate this as you punctuated the reference to a book: a comma after the author line; a comma after the title line; a period at the end. Use this same form of punctuation in your footnotes and in your final copied bibliography. Every bibliographic entry thus becomes a single unit, divided into three parts by commas, closed with a period.

For example, let us assume that you find in the *Readers'*
Guide a reference like this one:

POUND, Arthur
    Industrial America: its way of work and
      thought. Atlan. 157:121–8 Ja '36

On your card the reference will appear, without confusing
abbreviations and symbols, like this:

---

[16]

- -

Pound, Arthur,

"Industrial America: Its Way of Work and
Thought,"

Atlantic Monthly, vol. 157, pp. 121–128 (January, 1936).

References to Government Bulletins

For references to government bulletins, copy:

1. The author's name (if the article is signed).
2. The title of the article (in quotation marks).
3. The publication (with correct references to volume, number,
   series, pages, date, and publisher).

Students in land-grant colleges and universities may have
occasion to use the card catalogue of the United States De-

partment of Agriculture (the USDA catalogue), which indexes all bulletins and magazines published by that department. Here is a sample card from the USDA catalogue:

HORSE–JUDGING

Reese, Herbert Harshman.
... How to select a sound horse. [By] H. H. Reese ...
Washington [Govt. print. off.] 1917

27p. illus. 23^{cm}. (U. S. Dept. of agriculture. Farmers' bulletin 779)

1. Horse [Judging] 1. Title.

Agr 17–332.

Library, U. S. Dept. of Agriculture   1A84f   no. 779

In using this catalogue remember that the facts of publication are all within parentheses in the descriptive line.

The reference to the same bulletin appears in the following form in the *Agricultural Index:*

> How to select a sound horse. H. H. Reese. il
> Farmers' B   779:1–26   '17

On your card this will appear as shown on the following page. Why use the USDA catalogue when the same references may be found in the *Agricultural Index?* The *Agricultural Index* was started in 1916; the USDA catalogue covers the whole range of publications of the Department of Agriculture. It is, moreover, arranged according to a subject classification, so that the student working with some one subject will find all his references conveniently grouped in one place.

```
[38]
------------------------------------------------

    Reese, Herbert Harshman,

    "How to Select a Sound Horse,"

    Farmers' Bulletin, No. 779, pp. 1-26 (1917),
    United States Department of Agriculture.




```

The bibliography card shown here should give you a key to the form that may be used for every kind of bulletin or pamphlet. Remember that three items are necessary for a complete reference: the author's name, the title, and the publisher. You will have no difficulty with the first two. If the article is unsigned, start with the title. For the third item get the name or title of that particular bulletin or series of bulletins, the number or numbers used to identify it, the date of publication, and the institution responsible for the publication. Verify every abbreviation by turning to the index of the guide you are using. Remember that a publisher may be a person, a department of a school, a college or a university, a department of state or national government, a business or industrial concern, a religious organization—in fact, the possibilities are infinite.

References to Newspapers

In copying references from the *New York Times Index* you must supply the year from the date of the volume you are using. The following references were taken from the 1936 volume. Notice that main subject headings are in capitals and subheads are in bold face

POLAND

France, Relations with

Foreign Min Beck comments on friendly relations, Ja 17, 7:2

Germany, Relations with

Germany considers Danzig settlement as showing that friendly relations have passed most serious test, Ja 26, 24:1

[15]

- -

"Foreign Minister Beck comments on friendly relations between Poland and France,"

The New York Times, January 17, 1936, p. 7, col. 2.

Bibliography: Final Form

Bibliography cards are for your own use. You need not hand them in unless your instructor asks for them. In spite of this, you should follow the prescribed form or style exactly down to the last period. If you do, you will memorize the correct form so that mistakes in your final bibliography or your footnotes will be impossible. Make out your cards in ink as you get your references. Do not copy a list of references on a sheet of paper and then type your bibliography cards. That procedure is a waste of time. The purpose of using cards is to save you time and useless work. You may have noticed that the models show the lower third of the card blank. That space is for your comments on the value or the thoroughness of your source. These comments are in no sense notes on reading. They are simply your estimate of the importance of the book, article, or bulletin, an estimate arrived at as a result of your preliminary examination of your source material. For example, your comments might be "Out of date," or "Accurate but brief," or "Too general."

The bibliography that you hand in with your research paper must be classified, alphabetized, and copied (preferably on a typewriter) on the same kind of paper that is required for your essay. Classify your bibliography under the following heads: 1. General reference works; 2. Books; 3. Periodicals and bulletins (which may be subdivided into "signed" and "unsigned" articles, bulletins, and newspaper reports).

Alphabetize within each division. Alphabetize unsigned articles according to the first letter of the title, disregarding *a*, *an*, or *the*. Start your entry at the margin on the left. Use single space between the parts of each reference and double space between references. Begin the second line of each reference about half an inch to the right of the margin. The following is a satisfactory form to use:

VITAMINS

BIBLIOGRAPHY

(General Reference Works)

Eddy, Walter H., "The Vitamines," *Encyclopedia Americana,* 1932, vol. 28, pp. 148–151.

Harden, Arthur, "Vitamins," *Encyclopaedia Britannica,* 14th ed., vol. 23, pp. 219–222.

(Books)

Harrow, Benjamin, *Vitamines, Essential Food Factors,* E. P. Dutton & Company, New York, 1921.

Plimmer, Robert H. A., *Food, Health, Vitamins,* 6th ed., Longmans, Green & Company, New York, 1933.

(Magazine Articles, Signed)

Ephraim, J. W., "Truth about Vitamins," *The American Mercury,* vol. 36, pp. 490–492 (December, 1935).

Holmes, H. N., and Corbet, R. E., "Crystalline Vitamin A Concentrate," *Science,* vol. 85, p. 103 (January 22, 1937).

Knight, H. G., "International Vitamin Standards," *Science,* vol. 77, p. 184 (February 17, 1933).

(Magazine Articles, Unsigned)

"Added Vitamins; Abstract," *American Journal of Public Health,* vol. 24, p. 161 (February, 1934).

"Chemists at Chapel Hill," *Time,* vol. 29, p. 61 (April 26, 1937).

"New Vitamin-analysis Method," *The Scientific American,* vol. 156, p. 131 (February, 1937).

(Bulletins)

Hoagland, Ralph, "Vitamin B in the Edible Tissues of the Ox, Sheep, and Hog," *Bulletin*, No. 1138 (1923), U. S. Department of Agriculture.

Smith, Sybil Laura, "Vitamins in Food Materials," *Circular*, No. 84 (1929), U. S. Department of Agriculture.

(Newspaper Articles)

"Comment on C Content of Lima Beans," The New York *Times*, April 18, 1937, sec. 12, p. 8, col. 4.

"Comment on Method of Standardizing A and D Content of Cod-liver Oil," The New York *Times*, March 14, 1937, sec. 12, p. 6, col. 4.

"Dr. R. R. Williams on B-1," The New York *Times*, April 13, 1937, p. 2, col. 4.

"Symposium by American Chemical Society," The New York *Times*, September 9, 1936, p. 23, col. 4.

FOOTNOTES

Footnotes have several uses. They may identify and acknowledge material used in the body of your paper. They may give additional information which does not fit into the text. They may quote in detail what has been merely referred to in the text. They may define or explain some term used in the text.

Although usage differs in regard to the correct style of footnotes, the following forms are acceptable. To indicate to the reader that a footnote is being used, place an Arabic numeral immediately after and a little above the material referred to. Place the same number before the footnote. Footnotes belong at the bottom of the page, not at the end of a chapter or in the appendix of a book. The styles used in numbering footnotes vary. Either you may number all your footnotes consecutively from the beginning to the end of your paper or you may begin numbering with number one on each page. Do whatever your instructor asks you to do.

There are three recognized ways of inserting footnotes on the page of the typewritten manuscript:

1. Place footnotes at the bottom of each page to which they have reference.[1]

[1] George H. McKnight, *Modern English in the Making*, D. Appleton & Co., New York, 1928, p. 67.

2. Place your footnote immediately below the material to which it refers in the text. Separate it from the text by two parallel lines.[2]

[2] Arthur Pound, "Industrial America: Its Way of Work and Thought," *The Atlantic Monthly*, vol. 157, p. 125 (January, 1936).

3. Place the footnote in brackets immediately after the material to which it refers in the text,[3] [[3] Thomas T. Craven, "Our Navy's Air Service," *Review of Reviews*, vol. 62, p. 402 (October, 1920).] and continue the text as if the footnote had not interrupted it.

To avoid copying the same footnote reference several times on the same page you may use the following abbreviations:

1. *Ibid.* (from the Latin *ibidem*, meaning "in the same place"), to show that the footnote refers to the same work as the footnote immediately preceding. It should be followed by an exact page reference.

2. *Op. cit.* (from the Latin *opere citato*, meaning "in the work cited"), with the author's name and page reference, to show that the footnote refers to a work already cited. It cannot, of course, be used when two or more works by the same author are being used. It should not be used when its use entails turning back a number of pages to discover what work is referred to.

3. *Loc. cit.* (from *loco citato*, meaning "in the passage just referred to").

The following example of footnotes is taken from a paper written by a college freshman in a course in English composition:

[1] Mrs. Barbara Armstrong, *Insuring the Essentials*, The Macmillan Company, New York, 1932, p. 46.
[2] *Ibid.*, p. 58.
[3] H. H. Hartman, *Should the State Interfere in the Determination of Wage Rates?* National Conference Board, New York, 1920, p. 21.
[4] Mrs. B. Armstrong, *op. cit.*, p. 65.
[5] *Ibid.*

For examples of footnotes used to identify sources, to give additional information, to direct the reader to different interpretations, and to comment in a manner that would not fit into the text, glance through the volumes of *The Cambridge History of English Literature*. Here is a sample from this work:

[1] See Hoadly's *Works*, vol. II, pp. 694–5, where he gives his reasons for not answering Law.
[2] For some of the side issues which were vehemently discussed by other writers see Leslie Stephen, vol. II, p. 157.
[3] *Works*, vol. I, letter I, pp. 6, 7.   [4] *Ibid.*, pp. 14, 15.
[5] So defined by Hoadly in his sermon *The Nature of the Kingdom or Church of Christ*, p. 7.
[6] *The Grumbling Hive*, first printed 1705, republished with explanatory notes under the title *The Fable of the Bees*, 1714.

Here is another sample from *The Cambridge History of American Literature*:

[1] See Book II, Chap. xv.
[2] Mention should be made here of Col. John W. De Forest (1826–1906), who has not deserved that his novels should be for-

gotten as they have been, even *Miss Ravenel's Conversion from Secession to Loyalty* (1867), which survives only in the thoroughly merited praise of W. D. Howells (*My Literary Passions*, 1895, p. 233), but which still seems strong and natural.

If you wish to examine some scholarly articles in which footnotes are used copiously, look up the *Publications of the Modern Language Association*. Here is a sample from that source:

[1] Cf. the Harvard, Oxford, Rolfe, and Temple eds. "A knot of ribbons worn by a knight, the gift of his lady."—Yale ed. etc.

[2] The *N.E.D.* (*favour*, 9.c. *Obs.*) cites this passage. Warburton's gloss was "countenance," Johnson's "features." Steevens argued, "I believe *favours* mean only some decoration worn by knights in their helmets, as a present from a mistress, or a trophy from an enemy. So, afterwards, in this play:

'But let my *favours* hide thy mangled face:'

where the Prince must have meant his scarf." Mason reaffirmed Steevens' note; Boswell reverted to Johnson's, citing *Richard II* to the same end.

NOTES ON READING

It is assumed that before you begin to take notes you have collected a fairly adequate bibliography. Take your bibliography cards with you to the library. Look up a few of the most promising of your references. You might start with the encyclopedia articles. Your purpose is to make a preliminary exploration of your field. Read for general information. Do not take notes, but indicate on your bibliography cards the merits or weaknesses of the sources you examine. While you are exploring, make a note of the most important topics that seem to be related to your particular project. These topics, properly arranged, will become your first rough outline. They will be the headings you will use on your note cards when you begin taking notes.

When you go to the library to begin work, you must have with you a generous supply of note cards. The 3 x 5 library or filing cards, like those you used for your bibliography, are most convenient. Larger cards may be used. If possible, get cards that have a space at the top marked off by a red line. This space you will use for your notation of the exact source from which you are taking your information.

After your preliminary exploration of your field you will be ready to construct a topical outline of your paper. This topical outline is to be based partly on what you have learned about your subject and partly on what any intelligent and mature person would want to be told if he were reading an article about your subject. Let us now experiment with two subjects. The first is "The Little Theater." You and I both know something about it. There is probably a little theater on the campus of our university. We have attended performances of plays there. What do we want to know about it? Or let us say, what is there that *can* be told about it in an hour's lecture? A few pertinent and interesting facts about, first, its origin and history; second, the leaders in the movement; third, some of the most famous little theaters; fourth, its influence on the professional theater; fifth, its value to the community; sixth, the opportunities it gives to unknown artists. Let us reduce these to outline topics:

The Little Theater

1. Origin and history
2. Leaders in movement
3. Famous theaters
4. Influence on professional stage
5. Value to community
6. Opportunities to unknown artists

These topics will be the headings under which you will gather your notes. As soon as you have found a book or article on which you are ready to take notes, copy in the space above the red line the code number of that reference from your bibliography card. After the code number write the exact page reference to your material. Let us suppose that your reference is an article in *Theatre Arts Monthly*. The number of your bibliography card to this article is 27. Write 27 in the upper left-hand corner of your note card. Just below the red line write one of the topics from your list. Fill the card with notes from that article relating to that topic.

Our next subject will be more technical—it will be "Diesel Engines." What do we know about Diesel engines? Well, we have read something about a mysterious passenger car equipped with a Diesel engine; we know that it burns crude oil; we know a few other things, most of them more or less indefinite. Here is what we should *like* to know:

Diesel Engines

1. Principles of structure
2. Advantages over other types
3. Difficulties to be overcome
4. Relation to fuel supply
5. Use in light passenger cars
6. Use in heavy trucks

As we read more extensively we may wish to modify our outline; that is part of the plan. The preliminary outline is just that—preliminary or experimental, subject to modification. But it will give us a guide for our note-taking.

Now as to the form which your notes should take: let us remember that although you will not take perfect notes, you can save much unnecessary waste by following a few well-defined principles. Here they are:

1. Take notes in the form of a condensed summary. Get what is essential and get it accurately, but do not waste words.

2. Do not copy your material in the form of direct quotations, unless you mean to use exact quotations in your paper. If you copy the exact words of the original, enclose them in quotation marks.

3. Let your first unbreakable rule be "One topic to a card." Do not include in your notes on the same card material relating to two or more topics. You may have as many note cards as you wish relating to the same topic, but you must label each card and give the exact source of your notes on each card.

4. Let your notes be so accurate and so complete that they will make sense to you when they become cold.

5. Use headings or topics which represent actual divisions of your outline, as closely as it is possible for you to anticipate the outline you will use. Avoid the unnecessary and confusing multiplication of topics and subtopics.

6. And, finally, remember that every note card must have three pieces of information:

   a. The exact source of your material.
   b. The heading or topic which shows where your information belongs.
   c. The information itself.

Your first attempts to take notes on your reading may result in a few scattered entries and much wasted time. But you will soon discover that your English composition course has taught you more than merely how to write a few themes. You begin to realize that at least half its value lies in what it has taught you about reading. You have learned to organize themes so that their contents may be comprehended by your reader easily, quickly, without confusion, without wasted effort. Those who write books, chapters, essays, or articles employ the same principles of writing that you have learned— so that *you* may get the information you want, easily, quickly, without confusion, without wasted effort. In a book you examine first the table of contents, the index, the chapter headings, and the topics of the minor divisions. In an essay or article you look for a formal statement of plan or purpose at the beginning of the selection. Then you glance through the essay, reading a topic sentence here, another one there, until you come to what you want.

You will also learn to use other signs indicating the value of your source. Look at the date of publication to see if it contains information recent enough for your purpose. Investigate the author, too. Is he an authority in his field? What is his reputation for scholarship or for honesty? If you are examining an article in a magazine, let the reputation of the magazine help you to determine the reliability of your author. Above all, beware of the mistake so often made by too many people—the mistake of assuming that anything in print is necessarily true.

THE OUTLINE

The outline is the literary architect's set of blueprints from which he builds his essay. That you know already. You know also that the common-sense method of beginning your planning is to ask yourself the same questions which your reader would ask if he had the chance to question you instead of merely reading what you have prepared. Your essay should satisfy your reader's legitimate questions. Put yourself in his place. Ask his questions. The answers to his questions should give you most of the main topics that you should discuss in your paper. Additional topics may have to be added, and some topics that at first appeared to be essential may have to be deleted as you work into your subject, but your main outline will probably remain much as it was at the beginning.

To show how this method of planning operates in actual practice, let us examine a number of preliminary outlines constructed in a freshman English composition class. Each student in the class asked five questions which he would like to have answered if he were reading an article on a given subject. These sets of questions were collected by the instructor, discussed briefly, and then assembled with the help of the class. Here are a few samples:

Grand Opera in America

1. What are some of the most famous grand opera companies in America?
2. What is the organization of a typical grand opera company?
3. Who were some of the greatest singers produced in America?
4. What were some of the notable performances in America?
5. How does American grand opera compare with European?
6. What has been the success of grand opera in English?
7. What is the outlook for the future of American grand opera companies?

(Topics)

1. Survey of background
2. Organization of typical company
3. Outstanding singers
4. Notable performances
5. Comparison with European
6. Grand opera in English
7. Outlook for the future

Rhodes Scholarships

1. How, when, and for what purpose were they established?
2. What is the method of selecting candidates?
3. What courses may a Rhodes scholar study at Oxford?
4. What opportunities for travel do these scholarships offer?
5. How does an Oxford education compare with the education a man can get at a good American university?
6. How good is the record made by American scholars at Oxford?

(Topics)

1. Origin and nature
2. Method of election
3. Opportunities at Oxford
4. Education through travel
5. Comparison with American universities
6. Record made by American scholars

Military Training in American Universities

1. When and under what conditions was it established?
2. What is the purpose of military training in state universities?
3. How efficient is this training?
4. Does it tend to teach the militaristic attitude?
5. Is it necessary as a measure of self-defense?
6. How strong is the sentiment against compulsory training?

(Topics)

1. Origin and history
2. Purpose
3. Efficiency of training
4. Dangerous influence
5. Need for self-defense
6. Sentiment against compulsory training

Beginning with the first tentative division of the main subject into parts, or topics, you will expand and elaborate—

and change where necessary—until you have a workable plan. Keep the details out of the plan; details belong in your finished manuscript. The following is an example of an outline as it developed from the first general questions through a topical outline to the final analytical form used by the student in writing his paper. It is not a perfect outline; it is rather the sort of outline which the average college freshman should be able to construct and use.

Wage Laws for Workers

Outline A

1. What is the history of wage legislation?
2. Are wage laws necessary for the people today?
3. Is the theory of wage laws sound?
4. What reforms may they bring about?
5. What experience have we to judge by?

Outline B

1. History of wage legislation
2. Conditions making laws necessary
3. Soundness of theory of wage laws
4. Expected benefits
5. Evidence of practicality

Outline C

I. History and background material
    A. Definition of a minimum wage
    B. Early attempts at wage laws
    C. Progress of wage legislation in the United States

II. Need for wage laws
    A. Wage conditions in the United States
    B. Effects of low wages
    C. Causes of low wages
    D. Relation of cheap products to cheap labor
    E. Attitude of sweat-shop employer

III. Theory of wage laws
    A. How wage must be set
    B. Ability of employer to pay
    C. Relation of efficiency to wage increase
    D. Violation of property rights

IV. Benefits of wage laws
    A. Raising standards of living
    B. Effect on unemployment
    C. Effect on society in general

V. Evidence from experience
    A. Status of workers in other countries
    B. Effect on wage level
    C. Administration and enforcement
    D. The experience under the NRA

Outline D

I. Starting with the first law in 1896, wage legislation has shown rapid progress in recent history.
    A. A minimum wage is understood to be the least wage that can be legally paid to any worker.
    B. Some of the early wage laws were moderately successful.
    C. The progress of wage legislation in the United States has been checked by decisions of the Supreme Court.

II. The deplorable condition of workers calls for wage legislation.
    A. A study of the situation reveals that many workers receive starvation wages.
    B. Low wages have had a devastating effect on American living conditions.
    C. Low wages are often caused by an over-supply of workers.
    D. Cheap products usually mean that cheap labor has produced them.
    E. The sweat-shop employer is concerned only with the money he makes.

III. The theory of wage laws is based on logical argument.
    A. Wages must be determined over a monthly or yearly period.

    B. Employers are generally able to pay higher wages.

    C. A wage rise means a corresponding rise in the efficiency of the workers.

    D. Property rights must not be held above personal rights.

IV. Wage laws would result in benefits to the nation.

    A. These laws would raise the general standard of the workers.

    B. Unemployment would be reduced by the stimulation of industry.

    C. America would generally become more prosperous.

V. Wage legislation has proved successful in actual practice.

    A. The status of workers in other countries has been improved by wage laws.

    B. The wage level has been raised in the countries having wage laws.

    C. Administration and enforcement would be made easier because of past experience with such laws.

    D. The NRA, although it was a much broader law, had a general beneficial effect in related fields.

Part II: A Handbook
of Writing and Revision

The lyf so short, the craft so long to lerne,
Th' assay so hard, so sharp the conquering.
—Chaucer.

GRAMMAR

PERIOD FAULT

1. Do not write part of a sentence as if it were a complete sentence.

A grammatically complete sentence must have a subject and a predicate. It must convey the meaning intended and give the reader or hearer a sense of completeness. A group of words lacking a subject or predicate or a complete thought but used as a sentence is called a *sentence fragment*. Placing a period after a sentence fragment is called a *period fault*.

Wrong: After I had shaved and dressed, I strolled down into the lobby of the hotel. Hoping but not expecting to meet Jane there.

Right: After I had shaved and dressed, I strolled down into the lobby of the hotel, hoping but not expecting to meet Jane there.

Right: After I had shaved and dressed, I strolled down into the lobby of the hotel. I hoped but did not expect to meet Jane there.

Wrong: There is always the hope that this dance may be different. That this evening may be enjoyable.

Right: There is always the hope that this dance may be different, that this evening may be enjoyable.

Some good writers use the sentence fragment occasionally in order to produce special stylistic effects. Others have developed the use of sentence fragments into an irritating mannerism. The fact that a good writer uses an incomplete sentence does not necessarily justify its use by an inexperienced writer. A sentence fragment may be used effectively, but it is better for you to avoid it until after you have mastered the possibilities of the complete sentence. After that you may experiment as you wish.

The point is that a sentence fragment used for effect may be good, but one written through ignorance is sure to be bad. If you care to observe what an experienced writer can do with sentence fragments, read the description of Gopher Prairie in chapter four of Sinclair Lewis's *Main Street*.

Modern literary custom, as well as ordinary common sense, sanctions the use of certain types of sentence fragments as complete sentences. In some of these either the subject or the predicate is understood; in others no amount of ingenious interpretation will supply a missing subject or verb. We must accept them for what they are—sentence fragments correctly punctuated as sentences.

    a. The command.

Right: Come.
       Open a window.
       At once!
       Please!

    b. The question.

Right: Too early?
       Not here yet?
       At the top of the page?
       How much?

    c. The exclamation.

Right: Splendid!
       How terrible!
       Well done!
       What a man!

d. Bits of dialogue.

Right: "Stop now? Glad to. Terrible heat, isn't it?"

"Impossible!" he objected. "Can't trust him. Never pays his bills. Never works. Never saves a cent. Just like his dad."

"How old are you?"
"Sixteen. Why?"
"Look young for your age, don't you?"

The following rules will call to your attention the faults most frequently committed by students:

1a. Do not write a dependent clause as a complete sentence.

Wrong: I let Ranger Bill pay for the coffee. As I did not want him to know I carried a hundred dollars in my pocket.

Right: Because I did not want Ranger Bill to know that I carried a hundred dollars in my pocket, I let him pay for the coffee.

Wrong: Their right halfback was edging in closer to the line. Which was being ripped to pieces by our attack.

Right: Their right halfback was edging in closer to the line, which was being ripped to pieces by our attack.

1b. Do not write a verbal phrase as a complete sentence.

Remember that the verbals—infinitive, gerund, and participle—are dependent forms of the verb. They cannot serve as predicates of complete sentences.

Wrong: I left school in time for the important work on the ranch. Repairing fences being the one labor I missed.

Right: I left school in time for the important work on the ranch, missing only the labor of repairing fences.

Wrong: The object being to save the wear on the larger and more expensive machines.

Right: The object was to save the wear on the larger and more expensive machines.

Wrong: To quit school now would be to disappoint my parents. To destroy the faith they had in me.

Right: To quit school now would be to disappoint my parents, to destroy the faith they had in me.

1c. Do not write an appositive phrase as a complete sentence.

Guard against this fault especially when the phrase is introduced by such words as *namely, for example, such as,* and the like.

Wrong: Now we come to the most important part of this discussion. The practice which the student must find time for in his hours of leisure.

Right: Now we come to the most important part of this discussion, the practice for which the student must find time in his hours of leisure.

Wrong: I have found one phase of college life truly stimulating. Namely, my contacts with my fraternity brothers.

Right: I have found one phase of college life truly stimulating, namely, my contacts with my fraternity brothers.

Wrong: My work in a CCC camp taught me several important virtues. Such as self-reliance, honesty, and loyalty.

Right: My work in a CCC camp taught me several important virtues, such as self-reliance, honesty, and loyalty.

1d. Do not write a sentence in which a part of the thought is left uncompleted.

Wrong: Too many stems and leaves mixed with the hops and you have to pick them over.

Right: If the picker has too many stems and leaves with the hops, he must pick them over.

Wrong: A moment of carelessness and your car will be skidding in the gravel or plunging into the ditch.

Right: A moment of carelessness on your part may send your car skidding in the gravel or plunging into the ditch.

A sentence of this sort is permissible if the punctuation indicates a sharp break in the thought.

Right: A moment of carelessness—and your car is skidding in the gravel or plunging into the ditch.

Wrong: Silent and lifeless, bleak desolation describes the desert of Arizona.

Right: Silent, lifeless, bleak, and desolate—these words describe the desert of Arizona.

EXERCISES

Exercise 1. Correct any examples of fragmentary sentences that you find in the following. Some of the word groups are complete sentences. You should be able to recognize them.

1. Boat racing is a dangerous sport. Especially near Astoria, since the Columbia River is often rough and treacherous.
2. The deck canvas and the rest of the boat are painted. The colors being of your own selection.
3. Success or failure in wheat farming depends, to a large extent, on rainfall. Over which, as I soon learned, not even the most scientific farmer has much control.
4. I registered for a course which included English literature, social science, sewing, archery, and golf. Believing that a broad, cultural education would be best for me.
5. After the first few days of wandering as if in a dream, we began to remember the location of some of the buildings.
6. Taking it for granted that it is possible to travel through interstellar space, it is interesting to imagine what one would find on a visit to one of the nearer planets.

7. One thing fraternity life does teach a man. Namely, a sense of social responsibility.
8. His knowledge of dancing, as I suspected, being confined to the waltz and the two-step.
9. Our valley is noted for its frequent showers. Especially during the winter months.
10. I enjoy the cool winds and the damp fogs that we often get on the coast. Although occasionally I like to get away from them. To bask in the sunshine of the inland deserts.

Exercise 2. Identify each of the following by stating whether it is a sentence, a dependent clause, or a verbal phrase.

1. An orange crate making a good nesting room for one pair of pigeons.
2. Although, of course, he was just pretending to be insane.
3. Her lovely singing caused much jealous comment.
4. That he had again forgotten the key was no surprise to his wife.
5. That being the only problem I had not attempted to solve.

COMMA FAULT

2. Do not run two sentences together with only a comma between them.

The comma fault, like the period fault, is assumed to be an infallible sign of illiteracy. Although the error may be more often the result of carelessness than of ignorance, it is serious enough to deserve your attention. Avoid it in one of the following ways:

(1) by using a period to separate the sentences:

Wrong: Cross-cut saws are used to cut the boards to the correct length, these saws are set in a table with the saw sticking out of the top.

Right: Cross-cut saws are used to cut the boards to the correct length. These saws are set in a table with the saw sticking out of the top.

(2) by using a semicolon in place of a comma, if the sentences are close enough in thought to be combined into a compound sentence:

Wrong: I knew that my brother would not be late, he was the most painfully punctual man I have ever known.
Right: I knew that my brother would not be late; he was the most painfully punctual man I have ever known.

(3) by inserting a simple co-ordinating conjunction after the comma:

Wrong: Don Morris is a very plausible man, he has no real depth of character, he cannot be trusted.
Right: Don Morris is a very plausible man, but he has no real depth of character. He cannot be trusted.

(4) by subordinating one of the two independent statements:

Wrong: To give him the chairmanship would be unwise, he has had no practical experience in student politics.
Right: Because he has had no practical experience in student politics, it would be unwise to give him the chairmanship.
Right: To give him the chairmanship would be unwise, for he had no practical experience in student politics.

Note, however, that usage sanctions the comma in compound sentences which consist of three or more clauses that are short, parallel in form, and closely connected in thought. The practice of using the comma in short sentences of two clauses, without a co-ordinating conjunction, although fairly common in journalistic writing, is still frowned upon in more serious and permanent writing.

Right: I came, I saw, I conquered.

He protested, he blustered, he stormed.

The leaves are turning to gold, squirrels are fattening, hunting time is near.

THE RUN–TOGETHER SENTENCE

3. Do not run two sentences together with no mark of punctuation between them.

The period fault, the comma fault, and the run-together sentence are probably all symptoms of the same infirmity—carelessness rather than ignorance of what constitutes a complete sentence. If you know what a sentence is, do not let slovenly carelessness mar your writing. After all, your writing is judged not by the knowledge you have but by the knowledge you use.

Wrong: He knows nothing about the problems of workingmen he never had to work for a living.

Right: He knows nothing about the problems of workingmen. He never had to work for a living.

Right: He knows nothing about the problems of workingmen; he never had to work for a living.

Right: Since he never had to work for a living himself, he knows nothing about the problems of workingmen.

EXERCISES

Exercise 1. Correct each of the following sentences by the method most appropriate to the thought.

1. They were suffering from the inevitable reaction, their rescuers had appeared so suddenly.
2. Mr. Turner will act as our financial adviser, he has had some experience in banking.

3. The wheat fields look brown and parched, we have had no rain since April.
4. Two virtues every dog trainer must have they are patience and gentleness.
5. One day a tramp appeared at our back door, Mother and Father were away I was so terrified that I just stared at him.

Exercise 2. Correct each of the following sentences by sub-ordinating one of the principal elements.

1. My favorite sport is basketball it is the one sport in which I excel.
2. Registration week was a nightmare to me I was lonely, confused, and homesick.
3. The new stadium will be finished this summer it will be the largest structure of its kind in the Middle West.
4. Unfortunately I do not like to write themes I have never had much practice in writing.
5. We drove through Texas last summer the dust storms were at their worst then.

Exercise 3. Correct each of the following sentences.

1. The world does not owe any person a living. Nor any institution.
2. Reformers come and go, the poor are always with us.
3. The urge to travel is perennial, it will overcome all obstacles.
4. Captain Conners directed the athletic program at our camp he had been a star football player at West Point.
5. Medicine or surgery I did not even consider I could never stand the sight of blood.
6. Dean Warrington believes that character rests on loyalty. Especially loyalty to one's ideals.
7. At most camps an extensive athletic program is attempted. Often including swimming, golf, baseball, boxing, and wrestling.
8. Some of the girls will be toasting marshmallows, others will be trying to harmonize one of the latest song hits.
9. Clothes make the man, this proverb is not always true.
10. I accepted his rebuke in silence, I did not have the courage to offer an explanation.

SUBJECT AND VERB

4. Make the verb agree in number and person with its subject.

4a. Do not let yourself be confused by a plural modifier that intervenes between a verb and its singular subject.

Wrong: The babble of so many shrill voices are irritating and confusing.

Right: The babble of so many shrill voices is irritating and confusing.

Wrong: A complete list of his plays are given in the appendix.

Right: A complete list of his plays is given in the appendix.

Wrong: One of his most unpleasant characteristics are his arrogance, his inability to see another person's point of view.

Right: One of his most unpleasant characteristics is his arrogance, his unwillingness to see another person's point of view.

4b. Use a plural verb with a compound subject joined by *and*.

Right: A horse and a cow are in the pasture.
       Courage, loyalty, and service constitute his code of life.
       Two officers and a private were killed in the skirmish.

When several singular subjects, however, represent the same person or thing, or when they form one collective idea, a singular verb is correct.

Right: Our friend and benefactor has come.
       The long and short of it is that I have no money.
       The sum and substance of his address was that our democratic system of government was in danger.

The tumult and the shouting dies.
The secretary and treasurer is Helen Thurston.

Notice also that when each of several singular subjects is considered separately, the singular verb is correct.

Right: The trifler, the athlete, the waster is not the typical college student.
Many a rascal and fool has prospered in times of public distress.

4c. Use a singular verb with singular subjects joined by *or* or *nor*, but when the subject is made up of both singular and plural substantives joined by *or* or *nor*, make the verb agree with the nearer subject.

Wrong: Either Margaret or her sister are coming with us.
Right: Either Margaret or her sister is coming with us.

Wrong: Neither the twins nor their nurse are ready.
Right: Neither the twins nor their nurse is ready.

When the subjects differ in person, it is correct to make the verb agree with the nearer subject.

Right: Either Don or I am responsible for the mistake.
Either I or Don is responsible for the mistake.
Neither my brother nor I am guilty.

Occasionally good writers will use the plural verb with *neither—nor*, since the subject is felt to be plural. You might even see a sentence like this: "Either Don or I is responsible." If you are in doubt as to the correct form, your prudence and good sense should advise you to dodge the problem by writing, "Either Don is responsible or I am."

4d. Do not let the addition of *as well as, together with, with, in addition to, except,* and *no less than* to the subject influence the number of the verb.

Right: Marion Jean, as well as the boys, enjoys fishing.

My purse, together with my gloves and keys, was taken from my locker last night.

The humblest workman, no less than our wealthy manufacturers, is affected by the new tariff.

A canteen of water, in addition to the usual supplies, is to be taken on the trip.

4e. Use the singular form of the verb after *each, every, each one, everyone, everybody, anybody, nobody, either,* and *neither.* Since these words are singular, they are also the antecedents of singular pronouns.

Wrong: Each of the men have contributed something valuable to the discussion.

Right: Each of the men has contributed something valuable to the discussion.

Wrong: Each one of them are dear to me.
Right: Each one of them is dear to me.

Wrong: Every loyal American must do their share.
Right: Every loyal American must do his share.

The plural form of the verb is sometimes used with *neither,* especially when the subject idea is felt to be plural. You are safe, however, in disregarding the exceptions.

4f. In *there is* and *there are* sentences, make the verb agree with the subject that follows it.

Wrong: There is, if I am not mistaken, a man and a dog under that juniper tree.

Right: There are, if I am not mistaken, a man and a dog under that juniper tree.

Wrong: There's a sandwich and a bottle of milk in your basket.
Right: There are a sandwich and a bottle of milk in your basket.

4g. With a collective noun use a singular verb when the group it names is regarded as a unit, and a plural verb when the noun is regarded as indicating the individuals of the group.

Right: After a short rest period, the class proceeds with its work. The class in modern history have finished their investigations.
The band are taking off their heavy overcoats. They are assembling in front of the speaker's stand.

4h. Make the verb agree with its subject, not with its subjective complement. If the difference in number between subject and subjective complement produces an awkward sentence, rewrite the sentence.

Wrong: His chief worry are his devoted but imprudent disciples.
Right: His chief worry is his devoted but imprudent disciples.

Wrong: The reason for my late theme are the many interruptions that kept me from my work.
Right: My theme is late because I was frequently interrupted in my work.

4i. Use a singular verb when the subject of the sentence is a title, the name of a book, a clause, or in general a group of words expressing a single thought.

Right: *Stones of Venice* is one of Ruskin's most famous books.
Amy Lowell's *Lilacs* is my favorite poem.
The *Times* is a reliable newspaper.

> That he was betrayed by his former friends is now evident.
> Everybody for himself and the devil take the hindmost is
> apparently the code by which he lives.

This rule applies to verbs used with nouns expressing quantity, distance, time, amount, etc., when the subject is felt to be a unit.

Right: Twelve years is a long time to spend in exile.
        Three hundred words is a good length for a paragraph.
        Thirty miles is a day's journey in these hills.
        Fifteen divided by three equals five.

4j. As a general rule, use a singular verb with nouns that are plural in form but singular in meaning.

When in doubt as to whether a noun is singular or plural in meaning, consult a good dictionary. Under the suffix *-ics*, *Webster's New International Dictionary* gives us the following helpful information: "As denoting a scientific treatise or its subject matter these plural forms are now construed as singular; but forms in *-ics* denoting matters of practice (gymnastics, tactics), activities (athletics), qualities (acoustics), are usually construed as plurals; but the presence of a complementary noun in the singular often causes such a form to be construed as a singular; as, dramatics is his hobby."

News, economics, physics, measles, ethics, and *mathematics* are construed as singular; *gymnastics, tactics, athletics, acoustics, tidings, scissors, riches,* and *trousers* as plural; *politics, alms, eaves, means,* and *lots of* as singular or plural.

Right: The news was received with loud applause.
        Mathematics is my favorite study.
        Athletics are his ruin.
        Ethics deals with the problem of moral duty.
        There's lots of life in her yet.

4k. With *none* use a singular verb if the meaning intended is singular, and a plural verb if the meaning is plural.

Right: None are so arrogant as those who have never suffered misfortune.

None (or *no one, nobody*) is jealous of his good fortune.

4l. Use a plural verb with a relative pronoun referring to a plural antecedent.

Right: Helen Hargrave is one of the women who have brought music to our city.

She is one of those women who believe that carrying matches is a sign of moral turpitude.

EXERCISES

Exercise 1. Correct the following sentences. Tell what rule applies.

1. The news you brought to us are indeed distressing.
2. The object of these exercises are to develop your speed and agility.
3. Mr. and Mrs. Brown and Helen is coming now.
4. The house, as well as the barns in which the fire started, were burned to the ground.
5. England expects every man to do their duty.
6. The purpose of my frequent questions are to keep you alert.
7. Each girl must bring their own blankets.
8. Physics are one of his most difficult studies.
9. There's no one who does their work more carefully than he.
10. A record of his losses were found among his private papers.

Exercise 2. Some of the following sentences contain errors. Point out each mistake that you find, correct the sentence, and tell what rule applies.

1. In this part of the boat is the motor and other mechanical equipment.
2. The knowledge of medicine and drugs in ancient times were very limited.
3. Now all that remains are charred walls and smoking timbers.
4. The courses which I must take in order to become a dietitian has been carefully selected.
5. Fifteen dollars is too much to pay for a hat.
6. The acoustics of the new auditorium is very poor.
7. Enthusiasm and willingness to work is very necessary.
8. We had an educational adviser in camp, but all he had to offer us were a correspondence course in Diesel engineering, a guitar-strumming course, and a few books.
9. During the last three years practically every automobile manu-facturer has adopted hydraulic brakes and added their own improvements.
10. The jury has reached a verdict.

PRONOUNS

5. Be careful to use the right form of the pronoun.

5a. Use the nominative case when the pronoun is the subject of a verb.

Determine the exact use of the pronoun; do not be con-fused by the position of the pronoun or by parenthetical expressions intervening between it and the verb.

Wrong: Dorothy is taller than me.
Right: Dorothy is taller than I [am].

Wrong: Whom did you say wrote *The Petrified Forest?*
Right: Who did you say wrote *The Petrified Forest?* (The expres-sion *did you say* is parenthetical. *Who* is not the object of *say;* it is the subject of *wrote.*)

Wrong: Give this package to whomever opens the door.
Right: Give this package to whoever opens the door. (*Whoever* seems to be attracted into the objective case by its position after the preposition *to*. But it is not the object of the preposition; it is the subject of the verb *opens*. The object of the preposition *to* is the entire clause *whoever opens the door*.)

Right: Captain Henry, than whom there is none more generous, at once offered to take Tom's place. (*Than whom* is an accepted idiomatic form.)

5b. Use the nominative case when the pronoun is a subjective complement (also called *predicate substantive, predicate nominative,* or *predicate word*) after a finite verb.

Right: It is I. It is she. It is they.
It was we whom you heard singing last night.
It was I who broke your window, Mrs. Casey.

Although the use of "It is me" in spoken English has been bitterly defended by some students of the language, the ordinary college student will do well to say "It is I." If he says *I* instead of *me* whenever he remembers to be correct, common human frailty will save him from being too noticeable among his fellows.

5c. Use the objective case when the pronoun is the direct or indirect object of a verb or verbal.

Right: I saw her at the game.
The traffic officer told her and me that the road was closed.
Our teacher gave Jim and me two books to read.
Who is the girl whom you met yesterday?
I heard of his inviting you and her to the dance.

5d. Use the objective case when the pronoun is the object of a preposition.

Wrong: Just between you and I, he is a hopeless dancer.
Right: Just between you and me, he is a hopeless dancer.

Wrong: For who was this remark intended?
Right: For whom was this remark intended?

Wrong: A number of we boys drove to Northfield yesterday.
Right: A number of us boys drove to Northfield yesterday.

5e. Use the objective case when the pronoun is the assumed subject or the complement of an infinitive.

Right: We want him to be our chairman.
            She thought Oswald to be me.
            Watch him run with the ball.
            A girl whom I believed to be her waved to me from a passing car.

5f. Use the possessive case when the pronoun expresses possession.

Right: Place your hand on his shoulder.
            Your friend is my friend.

Remember that the personal pronouns form the possessive without the apostrophe. The apostrophe is used with some of the indefinite pronouns, such as *somebody, anybody, nobody, other, one, someone, anyone, everyone.*

Right: Everybody's business is nobody's business.
            Someone's hat fell into the water.
            Was it your hat? I thought it was somebody else's. (See *else, adj.,* in *Webster's New International Dictionary.*)

5g. Use the possessive case when the pronoun introduces or modifies a gerund.

Right: Jimmie told us about his running away from home.
I cannot understand their staying so late.
The reason for his leaving the meeting was explained later.

The objective case is correct when the verbal is clearly a participle.

Right: We watched him trying to attract the girl's attention.
Just picture him running after a street car.

For a thorough discussion of the application of this rule to nouns as well as to pronouns, see George O. Curme's *Syntax*, pp. 485–491.

5h. Make a pronoun agree with its antecedent in number, gender, and person.

Be careful about words like *each, every, each one, everyone, everybody, anybody, nobody, either, person, type, sort,* and *kind.* These words are singular and therefore require singular pronouns. *Neither* is usually singular; some writers will occasionally use it in the plural sense. *None* is construed as either singular or plural.

Wrong: Every person in the room rose to their feet.
Right: Every person in the room rose to his feet.

Wrong: Nobody likes to have their name misspelled.
Right: Nobody likes to have his name misspelled.

Wrong: Every student should bring their dictionary to class.
Wrong: Every student should bring his or her dictionary to class.
Right: Every student should bring his dictionary to class.

5i. Use either a singular or plural pronoun to refer to a collective noun, depending upon whether the noun designates the group as a whole or the members of the group.

Right: The class took their places at the blackboard.
The band is playing its best selection now.
Corporal Jones wishes to report that the squad have rolled their packs and are ready to proceed.

5j. According to conservative, and especially British, usage, use *one*, not *he*, to refer to the indefinite pronoun *one*.

In other words, "when one unwarily commences *one-ing,* one is obliged to continue *one* to the end of one's sentence." But if you use *he*, you will be in the company of many good writers who have refused to be bound by this illogical and silly convention. For a full discussion of the convention, see: H. W. Fowler, *Modern English Usage*, pp. 403–404; Stuart Robertson, *The Development of Modern English*, pp. 520–522.

Doubtful: One never likes to have his name misspelled.
Preferred: One never likes to have one's name misspelled.

Doubtful: One must always think of his public.
Preferred: One must always think of one's public.

5k. In writing that is more or less formal, do not use the pronouns *you, they,* or *it* in the indefinite sense.

You is correct if you are speaking directly to your reader, giving him directions, explaining to him what he should do. It must not be used as a substitute for *a person, one, a student, a player*, or, if the reference is clearly established, for the pronouns *he*, *she*, and *they*. It is plainly absurd for a freshman to write to his English instructor: "Your roommate comes to you, downhearted and dejected. He pours his troubles into your receptive ear. You are a shoulder for him to weep upon." But it is correct for the instructor to say to the student: "Your theme shows the evidence of serious thought and careful preparation."

They and *it*, although not so often misused as *you*, also need to be watched.

Colloquial: If you are not careful, you will find yourself taking the fence alone.

Formal: If the rider is not careful, he will find himself taking the fence alone.

Colloquial: If you think only of yourself, you will never become popular.

Formal: A person who thinks only of himself will never become popular.

Colloquial: They do not allow hunting in the national parks.

Formal: Hunting is not allowed in the national parks.

Colloquial: It says in the morning paper that another revolution has broken out in Central America.

Formal: The morning paper reports the outbreak of another revolution in Central America.

Colloquial: They say that he beats his wife.

Formal: It is said that he beats his wife.

Colloquial: You can always recognize a clever woman by the expression on her husband's face.

Formal: A clever woman can always be recognized by the expression on her husband's face.

Colloquial: They do not allow dogs in Goochville.

Formal: Dogs are not allowed in Goochville.

5   GRAMMAR

EXERCISES

Exercise 1. Some of the following sentences contain errors in the use of pronouns. Correct the sentences and tell what rule applies in each case.

1. Salem will still be satisfied; they will retain the capital.
2. "Farmers have to watch the source of their income," I explained. "He can grow only one crop every two years."
3. Many women purchase goods with the intention of returning or exchanging it the next day.
4. One should never let one's emotions overcome one's judgment.
5. I do not think that Sarah is any prettier or brighter than me.
6. If anyone should ask me where to spend their vacation, I should tell them to go to Mount Rainier National Park.
7. It was he who first denounced the culprits.
8. The best course for you and I is to deny everything they say.
9. The watch will be awarded to whomever gets the most votes.
10. It was the same woman who we saw getting on the boat at Astoria.

Exercise 2. Correct every error in the use of pronouns. Give the rule which applies to each correction.

1. Before the patient went into my father's office, I asked their name and got their card from the file.
2. Anybody who thinks that making hay is all fun will soon change their idea.
3. Was it Roger who took you to the theater? Yes, it was him.
4. Everybody must keep their books closed until I give the signal.
5. Professor Childs told her and I that he did not assign a theme for Monday.
6. Every applicant for relief will have their case investigated without delay.
7. Who do you consider to be the best American poet?
8. The team will play its first game tomorrow.

9. One should never shirk one's obligations.
10. The dean told a number of we men that too many social rules were being ignored on this campus.

ADJECTIVES AND ADVERBS

6. Use the correct form of the adjective and adverb.

Adjectives and adverbs form the comparative degree either by adding -*er* to the positive or by using *more* or *less* with the positive degree. They form the superlative either by adding -*est* to the positive or by using *most* or *least* with the positive degree. Some adjectives and adverbs are compared irregularly.

Positive	*Comparative*	*Superlative*
strong	stronger	strongest
thin	thinner	thinnest
famous	more famous	most famous
good	better	best
fast	faster	fastest
rapidly	more rapidly	most rapidly
well	better	best

The comparison of adjectives which name absolute qualities is theoretically illogical, but with a total disregard for logic, modern usage, and especially colloquial usage, permits such forms as *most perfect, most complete*, etc. In formal writing, however, it is better to use such forms as *more nearly* or *most nearly perfect, most nearly complete, most nearly unique, more nearly black, whiter than before, more or less round*, etc. See Curme's *Syntax*, pp. 502–504.

Do not make the mistake of combining two forms to produce a comparative or superlative.

Wrong: His fame reached the more remoter districts of the country.
Right: His fame reached the more remote districts of the country.

Although a large number of adverbs have the distinctive ending *-ly*, do not assume that all adverbs must have this ending or that every word ending in *-ly* is an adverb. Certain adverbs have no distinctive form.

Examples: here, there, where, why, very, too, then, when.

Certain adverbs have the same form as the corresponding adjectives.

Examples:	(Adverb)	(Adjective)
close	Come close.	That was a close decision.
deep	Dig deep.	He dug a deep well.
early	Come early.	He was an early riser.
far	You are not far wrong.	He came from a far country.
fast	Run fast.	It was a fast game.
hard	Hit it hard.	The problem was hard.
high	Throw it high in the air.	He spoke in a high voice.
just	He just entered.	He is a just man.
late	He came late.	One student was late.
little	His work is little known.	I had a little sleep.
loud	Don't shout so loud.	His voice was loud.
low	Speak low.	I have a low opinion of him.
near	She came very near.	That was a near escape.
quick	Come quick.	He is a quick thinker.
right	Do it right.	That is the right answer.
slow	Go slow.	It is a slow train.
straight	He can't see straight.	Walk in a straight line.
well	He played well.	He is now a well man.

Some adverbs have two parallel forms. The distinctions between these forms must be learned by observing usage.

Examples:

late—lately	He came late.	Lately he has not been prompt.
high—highly	Aim high.	He was highly thought of.
near—nearly	Don't go near.	He is nearly there.
loud—loudly	Speak louder.	He protested loudly.
right—rightly	He did right.	He was rightly indignant.

Some adjectives have the *-ly* suffix which is characteristic of adverbs.

Examples: an early bird, a likely story, a lively kitten, a kindly person, a friendly community, an only child.

6a. Do not use an adjective in place of an adverb or an adverb in place of an adjective.

Ordinarily the meaning of the sentence will make it clear whether an adjective or an adverb should be used. Remember that an adjective names a quality or a condition; an adverb names the manner of an action.

Wrong: Mary did not take her study of grammar serious enough.
Right: Mary did not take her study of grammar seriously enough.

Wrong: I didn't do good in my last examination.
Right: I didn't do well in my last examination.

Wrong: We sure appreciated her kindness.
Right: We surely appreciated her kindness.

Wrong: Yes, I am doing fine.
Right: Yes, I am doing very well.

6b. After certain verbs like *become, appear, seem, prove, remain, look, smell, taste,* and *feel,* do not mistake the subjective complement for an adverb.

Wrong: This water tastes badly.
Right: This water tastes bad.

Wrong: The rose smells sweetly.
Right: The rose smells sweet.

Wrong: Lowell ranks highly as an essayist.
Right: Lowell ranks high as an essayist.

Wrong: You will be all right if you stay quietly for a few minutes.
Right: You will be all right if you stay quiet for a few minutes.

6c. Avoid illogical or misleading comparisons.

Wrong: Betty Jane is the prettiest of the twins.
Right: Betty Jane is the prettier of the twins. (Use the comparative form for two.)

Wrong: Seattle is larger than any city in the state of Washington.
(It cannot be larger than itself.)
Right: Seattle is larger than any other city in the state of Washing-
ton.
Right: Seattle is the largest city in the state of Washington.

Wrong: Bruce is the tallest of any man on the team.
Right: Bruce is the tallest man on the team.
Right: Bruce is the tallest of all the men on the team.
Right: Bruce is taller than any other man on the team.

6d. Use *very much* instead of *very* as a modifier of the past participle in a passive verb phrase.

Wrong: We were very surprised at her answer.
Right: We were very much surprised at her answer.

Wrong: He seemed very disgusted with the whole affair.
Right: He seemed very much disgusted with the whole affair.

But note that usage sanctions *very* or *too* when the past
participle is felt to be a pure adjective. It is correct to say:
"I am very tired. I am too tired to work longer."

6e. Although *due to, because of,* and *owing to* are coming to be felt as compound prepositions introducing prepositional phrases, the more careful writers still distinguish between the adjectival use of *due to* and the adverbial use of *because of.*

Wrong: Due to the stormy weather, the students came late.
Right: Because of the stormy weather, the students came late.

Wrong: We lost the game due to poor generalship.
Right: We lost the game because of poor generalship.
Right: The loss of the game was due to poor generalship.
Right: His illness, due to exposure and overwork, kept him in bed for a month.

See: Curme's *Syntax,* pp. 560–561; Fowler's *Modern English Usage,* p. 123; *Webster's New International Dictionary, due,* (*adj.*) 5. You might also notice the comment on *owing to* found in the *New International Dictionary:* "owing to. Because of; caused by;—used correctly either as an adverb or an adjective." A convenient rule, old but still serviceable, is: "Never begin a sentence with *due to.*"

EXERCISES

Exercise 1. In the following sentences, is the italicized word an adjective or an adverb?

1. After playing four sets of tennis I feel *good.*
2. Her voice sounds *loud* and *harsh* today.
3. Doesn't Homer Smith look *proud* and *pleased?*
4. I knew I had played it *wrong* as soon as I finished my swing.
5. The clouds are drifting in very *low* today.
6. That is a *likely* story.
7. It was a most *generous* and *friendly* act.
8. The *early* worm suffers a just punishment for getting up *early.*

9. *Lately* there have been several attempts to float the ship.
10. Marjorie, as usual, arrived *late* for the party.

Exercise 2. Correct the error in the use of the adjective or adverb in each of the following sentences.

1. Which is the oldest, Harry or George?
2. After life's fitful fever, he sleeps good.
3. They sure are hungry, aren't they?
4. The quarterback is usually smaller and lighter than any man on the team.
5. Due to her carelessness in heating the oven, the cake was spoiled.
6. Mr. Nelson thinks I am not taking my work serious enough.
7. You may not believe me, but I am real sorry that I said it.
8. Better move fastly if you want to get there by night.
9. So he is that muchly praised Texas fullback!
10. Wait for me, Bob; my theme is near finished.

Exercise 3. In each of the following sentences select the correct form.

1. I'm sorry, sir; I got up (late, lately) this morning.
2. The batter protested (loud, loudly) against the decision.
3. The teacher's comments made me feel (cheap, cheaply).
4. My uncle feels (some, somewhat) better.
5. Although my uncle seems to be in perfect health, he really has not felt (good, well) for a long time.
6. The trip cost (considerable, considerably) more than I had expected.
7. The room would have been pleasanter if she had arranged the furniture (different, differently).
8. The performance was postponed (due to, because of) the illness of the leading actress.
9. Do you realize how (bad, badly) things look for us?
10. My roommate can sing as (good, well) as I can.

VERB FORMS

7. Use the correct form of the verb. Be especially careful about the form of the past tense and the past participle.

Cultivate the habit of looking up troublesome verbs in a good dictionary. The following examples show the manner in which the principal parts of verbs are indicated in *Webster's New International Dictionary:*

rise; *past tense* ROSE; *past part.* RIS'EN; *pres. part. & verbal n.* RIS'ING.
raise; RAISED; RAIS'ING.
lie; *past tense* LAY; *past part.* LAIN; *pres. part. & verbal n.* LY'ING.
lay; LAID; LAY'ING.
sit; *past tense* SAT; *past part.* SAT; *pres. part. & verbal n.* SIT'TING.
set; *past tense & past part.* SET; *pres. part. & verbal n.* SET'TING.

Right: I usually rise at six o'clock.
Tom rose in order to raise the window.
The water has risen a foot since yesterday.
The coat is lying on the chair, where it has lain since yesterday.
Lay your coats on the bed.
The whistle blew just as I was laying down my tools.
Milly set the basket on the table and sat down.
Please sit down; I was just setting the table when you came in.

7a. Use the correct tense.

You know, of course, that present tenses refer to the present, past tenses to the past, and future tenses to the future. The following rules, however, will help you avoid errors where errors are most frequently made.

1. The verbs in a sentence must show the correct relation in time between the main verb and the subordinate verbs.

Right: George told me that he had written the theme.
I think that George has written his theme.

Ordinarily, common sense will tell you what tense to use in the subordinate clause; one part of the rule of sequence, however, needs special attention. The rule specifies that when a past tense form is used in the main clause, a past tense form should follow in the dependent clause.

Right: He says he will sing for us.
He says that he does not know this song.
He says that he has never sung this song before.

He said that he would sing for us.
He said that he did not know this song.
He said that he had never sung this song before.

An apparent exception to this fixed sequence is the present tense used in statements that represent something as habitual, characteristic, or permanently true.

Right: The speaker said that honesty is the best policy.
The county agent told my father that potatoes grow best in sandy soil.

2. Be careful to use the correct tense of infinitives and participles.

Wrong: I was delighted to have received your invitation.
Right: I was delighted to receive your invitation.

Wrong: He probably intended to have returned the book, but he forgot.
Right: He probably intended to return the book, but he forgot.

Wrong: Working hard all day, Jim was tired when evening came.
Right: Having worked hard all day, Jim was tired when evening came.

Notice in these examples that the time indicated by the verbal is always in relation to the time expressed by the main verb.

3. In telling a story, do not shift from the past to the present and from the present to the past unless there is a real change in time.

7b. Use the correct form of the subjunctive mood to express a condition contrary to fact or a wish.

The subjunctive mood in modern English, as an inflected form of the verb, need concern the average college freshman only through the two survivals *be* and *were*. There are, indeed, many other forms. The curious student, however, should read Curme's *Syntax*, pages 390–430. Through this courtesy call upon scholarship he may not be able to remember all that he reads about the labyrinthine subtleties of the subjunctive, but he certainly will pick up much interesting information about the growth of the English language.

Right: I wish that I were home in bed.
If he were heavier, he would be more useful to the team.
He looks as if he were sick.
If this be treason, then make the most of it.
Were he alive, he would be proud of his son.
The peace of quiet gardens be with you.

7c. Use the correct form of *shall* and *will.*

To some, the ritual of *shall* and *will* is as complex and quaint—and as futile—as a Japanese tea ceremony; to others it is a precious Nordic heritage, to be preserved at any cost. The college student who has the necessary fortitude may investigate the subject for himself. He will find excellent discussions in Curme's *Syntax*, pages 362–372, Curme's *Parts of Speech and Accidence*, pages 323–327, and Jespersen's *A Modern English Grammar on Historical Principles*, vol. 4, pages 235–352.

In colloquial speech most people use *will* and *would* for all persons. Careful usage still observes the following distinctions:

1. Use *shall* for the future tense in the first person, both singular and plural; use *will* for the future tense in the second and third persons.

Right: I shall go to New York. We shall eat dinner soon. You will find me at home. He will be twenty-one next June. She will come later. They will meet you at the station.

2. To express a promise, determination, or assurance, use *will* in the first person, and *shall* in the second and third persons.

Right: I will go to New York in spite of your warning. They shall not pass. You shall give me the money.

3. In asking questions, use the form which you anticipate in the answer.

Right: Will you return my book tomorrow? I will.
Shall he spoil our plans? He shall not.
Shall you be old enough to qualify for the position? I shall.

4. To express a habitual or customary action, use *would* in the first, second, and third persons.

Right: I would sit on the bank of a stream all afternoon.
He would go for long walks in the morning.
You would wander off when you knew your mother wanted you at home.

5. In conditional clauses, *shall* and *should* are correct in the first, second, and third persons.

Right: If we should have another rain, the hay would be ruined.
If he should come, please tell him I could not wait.
If they should be hurt, I would never forgive myself.

But notice the difference in the meaning of the sentence when *would* is correct: You could learn to play golf if you would only practice more often.

7d. Use the active voice unless you have a good reason for using the passive.

Weak: Your kind letter was received by me.
Better: I received your kind letter.

Weak: A fishing trip was suggested by my father.
Better: My father suggested a fishing trip.

EXERCISES

Exercise 1. With the help of your dictionary find the principal parts of the following verbs. Construct sentences in which you use the past tense of each of the verbs.

break	get	slay
bring	hang	spring
choose	lead	swim
do	lend	take
dive	prove	tear
drive	shake	throw
eat	sink	write

Exercise 2. Some of the following sentences contain incorrect forms of the verb. Correct the sentences.

1. I left it laying where it had lain all day.
2. The drouth will probably raise the price of wheat.
3. Have courage, young man; the whole world lays before you.
4. The murderer was hung at six o'clock yesterday morning.
5. I am tired; I have drove hard since early this morning.
6. All the refuse had rose to the surface of the pool.
7. When I heard that, you could have slayed me with a feather.
8. All the pears were shooken off the tree by the strong wind.
9. Please raise your voice if you want to be heard.
10. Have you wrote your theme yet, George?
11. No, I have took pains to do a good piece of work this time.
12. All right, George; I'll set down and wait until you finish it.
13. Jones will probably try to raise hogs on his farm.
14. He was so tired that he laid on the couch all evening.
15. I think you shouldn't have hanged that picture in this room.
16. You will catch cold if you set on the grass.
17. The principal asked me to set down just as I was raising to speak.
18. He was caught in the act of setting the garage afire.
19. When a hen cackles, the important question is, "Is she laying or lieing?"
20. Bobby was so frightened that his hair seemed to raise up.

Exercise 3. If you find any mistakes in tenses in the following sentences, make the necessary corrections.

1. They seemed pleased to be asked to go with us.
2. The doctor said that cancer is not a contagious disease.
3. I should have liked to have visited the Horner Museum.
4. We intended to have seen the Bonneville Dam on our way to Portland.
5. We were all surprised to have received the news of your marriage.
6. Having lost my job, I decided to enter the state university.

Exercise 4. Judging the following sentences according to the standards of literary usage, select the correct forms from those given in parentheses.

1. Professor Bowen (shall, will) be thirty on his next birthday.
2. The government is exerting every effort so that no one (shall, will) go hungry.
3. We (shall, will) be pleased to investigate your record.
4. I must insist that everyone (shall, will) have his theme ready by eight o'clock tomorrow morning.
5. Nancy (should, would) usually put off her work until it was too late to do it well.

Exercise 5. In the following sentences select the correct forms from those given in parentheses.

1. Mrs. Cummings acts as if she (was, were) very angry, but I know that she is really flattered.
2. If I (was, were) a man, you could not say that to me.
3. I wish it (was, were) possible to read the whole essay to you.
4. The senator moved that the motion (be, is) laid on the table.
5. May I ask that the consideration of my case (is, be) postponed until tomorrow?
6. I wish I (was, were) in San Francisco now.
7. If this (was, were) my dog, I (should, would) keep him locked up.
8. If I (was, were) they, I (should, would) feel flattered.
9. If I (was, were) the owner of half that dog, I (should, would) sell my half.
10. If Tom (was, were) my son, I (should, would) spank him.
11. If this (were, was) his first mistake, he could be forgiven.
12. I wish that my mother (was, were) here to help me.
13. He acts as if he (was, were) pleased, but I know that he is disappointed.
14. If I (were, was) the chaperon, I (should, would) ignore the entire incident.
15. We (will, shall) probably be late.

CONJUNCTIONS

8a. **Use the co-ordinating conjunction which will express the exact relationship between co-ordinate sentence elements.**

Every college freshman knows that *and, but,* and *for* are co-ordinating conjunctions—a bit of exact but fragmentary information which may actually hinder him in the development of variety and flexibility in writing. If you, the college freshman, become conscious of the monotonous series of *and's, but's,* and the colloquial *so's* in your themes, you may find help through a study of the following examples. The conjunctions *and, but,* and *for* are quite legitimate. You must not think that their use is an error. There are many other conjunctions, however, which may express more exactly what you mean. It does not matter at this moment that some of them are called conjunctive adverbs instead of conjunctions.

I can enjoy classical music *and* jazz.
I can enjoy *both* classical music *and* jazz.

Call your dog home, *or else* I shall notify the sheriff.

Sarah *and* I have not read the current best seller.
Neither Sarah *nor* I have read the current best seller.

He means well, *but* he is always unlucky.
He means well, *only* he is always unlucky.

Early apples, *such as* Gravensteins, do not keep well.

That new freshman can write poetry *and* play football.
That new freshman can write poetry *as well as* play football.

In that crisis he showed courage *and* resourcefulness.
In that crisis he showed *not only* courage *but also* resourcefulness.

These boys do not want to learn; *there* is the real problem.

I do not believe that they are lazy *and* ignorant.
I do not believe that they are lazy, *still less* that they are ignorant.

She is much older than I, *but* she fascinates me.
She is much older than I, *and yet* she fascinates me.

8b. Observe correct usage in punctuation with co-ordinating conjunctions.

The conjunctions *and, but, for, nor, or,* when introducing a co-ordinate clause within a sentence, require a comma before the conjunction, except when the clauses are short and closely related in meaning. The conjunctions *yet* and *so* usually take a comma.

The so-called conjunctive adverbs, *therefore, moreover, however, nevertheless, likewise, hence, also, besides, notwithstanding, accordingly,* require a semicolon before the conjunction if the conjunction stands at the beginning of the clause. Remember this, however: you will have to read several hundred pages of modern prose before you will find a sentence in which a conjunctive adverb begins a co-ordinate clause. In present-day expository prose the conjunctive adverbs are almost invariably tucked away within the clause.

The time-honored rule requiring a semicolon with conjunctive adverbs still holds good, since the clause with a conjunctive adverb tucked away in it usually begins without a conjunction.

Any of these conjunctive adverbs may be used to begin a sentence. They are frequently so used in modern writing.

Here are some of the connecting words which may be used for variety in sentence structure:

accordingly	in the first place
after all	in the second place
again	
also	later
and also	let alone
and moreover	likewise
and likewise	
and yet	meanwhile
as also	moreover
as well as	much less
at times	
all the same	namely
	nevertheless
besides	not to mention
but then	notwithstanding
conversely	only
	on the other hand
else	on the contrary
even	on that account
	or else
finally	
first	rather
firstly	
for all that	secondly
for that reason	still
further	still less
furthermore	still more
however	then
indeed	yet

8c. Do not use *like, except,* or *without* as conjunctions to introduce clauses.

Wrong: He acts like he was hungry.
Right: He acts as if he were hungry.

Wrong: Hold your club like your coach held it.
Right: Hold your club as your coach held it.

Wrong: They refuse to begin work, except you agree to raise their pay.
Right: They refuse to begin work unless you agree to raise their pay.

Wrong: I will not buy a ticket without you buy one too.
Right: I will not buy a ticket unless you buy one too.

9.   GRAMMATICAL TERMS

Absolute. An expression grammatically independent of the rest of the sentence. *The work having been finished,* we returned to the camp.

Adjective. A word used to limit or describe a substantive. The main classes of adjectives are:

1. Descriptive: a *new* hat, a *large* man, a *stern* father.
2. Pronominal: *my* hat, *her* man, *their* father.
3. Demonstrative: *this* book, *that* horse, *these* lessons.
4. Interrogative: *whose* book? *which* lesson?
5. Indefinite: *some* women, *any* teacher, *either* book.
6. Articles: *a* boy, *an* apple, *the* room.
7. Numeral: *one* apple, *five* cents, the *first* lesson.

Adjective clause. A subordinate clause used like an adjective. It modifies a substantive.

Our ranch, *which is small but well managed,* returned a profit last year.
George, *who is older than Sally,* spoke first.

Adverb. A word used to modify a verb, another adverb, or an adjective. Adverbs may indicate:

1. Place: Please remain *outside*.
2. Manner: He returned *quickly*.
3. Time: You may go *now*.
4. Degree: The dinner was *very* good.
5. Affirmation or negation: *Yes*, he is here. *No*, do *not* go.

Adverb clause. A clause used to modify a verb, an adjective, or an adverb. An adverb clause may indicate:

1. Time: *When he arrives*, give him this money.
2. Place: He worked best *where the difficulties were greatest*.
3. Cause: He left school *because he had to find a job*.
4. Purpose: He came to college *in order that he might meet the right people*.
5. Result: The troops rested *so that the supply train was able to overtake them*.
6. Condition: *If he asks questions*, deny the whole story.
7. Concession: *Although Father is old*, he is active and strong.
8. Manner: Try to dance *as Dorothy does*.
9. Comparison: Dorothy is more graceful *than you are*.

Adverbial objective. A substantive used adverbially.

He went *home*. He walked three *miles*.

Agreement. A correspondence between pronoun and antecedent in person, number, and gender; between subject and verb in person and number.

Antecedent. A word, phrase, or clause to which a pronoun refers.

England expects every *man* to do *his* duty.
He returned the money, which is the least he could do.

Appositive. A word placed beside another word and denoting the same person or thing.

Harold, the older *boy*, recommended *archery*, his favorite *hobby*.

Article. The words *a* and *an* are the indefinite articles; the word *the* is the definite article. Articles are used as adjectives.

Auxiliary. A verb is called auxiliary, or helping, when it helps to make a form of another verb. The auxiliary verbs are *be, have, shall, will, should, would, can, could, may, might*.

But I *do* know it. He *was* called. I *shall* return soon. He *might* like it.

Cardinal number. The numbers *one, two, three, four*, etc. See *ordinal numbers*.

Case. The relation, or the form indicating it, between nouns, pronouns, and adjectives and other words in the sentence. In English the three cases are nominative, objective, and possessive.

Clause. A group of words containing a subject and a predicate but used as part of a sentence. Clauses that make independent assertions are independent or co-ordinate. Clauses that depend on some other part of the sentence are called dependent or subordinate. Dependent clauses are used as nouns, adjectives, or adverbs.

Independent: The dogs barked, and the children shouted.
Dependent: Mary, *who is now fourteen*, attends junior high school.
If it rains, the game will be postponed.
What he planned to do will never be known.

Collective noun. A noun naming a collection of individuals by a singular form. Collective nouns are considered singular when the whole group is meant; they are considered plural when the individuals of the group are meant.

Examples: band, class, jury, assembly.

Comparison. The inflection of an adjective or an adverb to indicate degree. The three degrees are positive, comparative, and superlative. For examples see section 6.

Complement. A word used to complete the sense of a verb. A complement may be a direct object, an indirect object, a subjective complement, a double object, an objective complement, or a retained object. The first three in this list are the most common.

Direct object:	The pitcher threw the *ball*.
Indirect object:	Tell *me* your name.
Subjective complement:	Herbert is a good *boy*. (Noun.)
	Herbert is *weary*. (Adjective.)
Double objects:	Ask the *man* his *name*.
Objective complement:	They made him their *leader*.
Retained object:	They were given their *wages*.

Complex sentence. A sentence containing one independent clause and at least one dependent clause.

Compound sentence. A sentence containing two or more independent clauses.

Complex-compound sentence. A sentence containing two or more independent clauses and at least one dependent clause.

Conjugation. The inflectional forms of a verb.

Conjunction. See section 8.

Conjunctive adverb. See section 8.

Construction. The grammatical function of a word in a sentence.

Co-ordinate. Of the same rank; equal in rank; not subordinate.

Copula, copulative verb. A verb used to link subject with complement, to show the relation between subject and complement. It does not express action. The copulative or linking verbs are *is, was, were, seems, feels, tastes, smells, sounds,* and others like these. A linking verb does not take an object. It is followed by a subjective complement. The verb is, in effect, a sign of equality: it indicates that the subject either is the same thing as the complement or that it has a quality named by the complement.

Howard *was* a soldier.
The bread *is* very stale.
It *tastes* sour.
The air *smells* sweet.

Correlative conjunctions. Conjunctions that are used in pairs.

Examples: either . . . or, neither . . . nor, both . . . and, not only . . . but also.

Declension. The inflectional forms of nouns or pronouns.

Direct address. A construction in which a speaker or writer addresses a second person directly.

Father, let me have ten dollars.
In that case, *Mary,* I shall be delighted to take you home.

Direct discourse. The words of a speaker quoted exactly as they were spoken.

Ellipsis (elliptical expressions). The omission of words necessary to grammatical completeness. An expression in which some words are implied or understood.

She is taller than I (*am tall*).

Finite verb. A verb form capable of making a predication or an assertion, as distinguished from the nonfinite forms—the gerund, the participle, and the infinitive.

Gerund. A verbal used as a noun. A gerund, like the present participle, usually ends in *-ing*. A gerund, since it is partly a verb, may take adverbial modifiers and complements; since it is partly a noun, it has the functions of a noun and can be modified by an adjective.

Subject of verb: Driving a car is poor exercise. (Takes an object.)
Object of verb: I dislike aimless *walking* in the rain. (Modified by an adjective and by a phrase.)

Gerund phrase. A gerund with its complements and modifiers.

Idiom. An expression peculiar to a language. See section 30.

Examples: make a clean breast, take kindly to, make no bones about, do away with.

Infinitive. A verbal form usually preceded by the sign *to*. The sign is occasionally omitted. The infinitive has two tenses, present and perfect. Since the infinitive is partly a verb, it may take complements and adverbial modifiers. It may be used in the sentence as a noun, as an adjective, or as an adverb.

Noun: To work is *to pray.* (Subject and subjective complement.)
He wanted *to see* the game. (Object of verb and takes an object.)

Adjective: I have a right *to challenge* your statement. (Modifies *right.*)

Adverb: Harold came *to see* me. (Modifies *came.*)

With assumed subject: I wanted *him to succeed.*

Interjection. An exclamation, like *oh, alas, ah, fiddlesticks,* which is grammatically independent of the rest of the sentence.

Intransitive. See *verb.*

Mood or mode. The form of the verb which indicates the manner in which the action it denotes is conceived, as fact, assumption, volition, possibility, etc. The three modes in English are indicative, imperative, and subjunctive.

The indicative mode states a fact or questions it.

It is raining. Will it rain tomorrow?

The imperative mode is used for command or request.

Go at once.
Please do not return.

The subjunctive mode is used to express a condition contrary to fact, a wish, a supposition, a doubt. The subjunctive mode in modern English is being rapidly replaced by the indicative. See section 7.

I wish my mother were here.
If she were here, I would be happy.

Nominative absolute. See *absolute.*

Nonrestrictive clause. Clause which adds to the information about a word it modifies but does not help to point out or identify a certain thing or person or object. See section 20a.

Nonrestrictive: Our janitor, who is old and feeble, asked me to help him carry the package upstairs. (The clause does not help to point out any one janitor, or identify this janitor in a group of janitors.)

Restrictive: Janitors who are old and feeble should not be asked to carry packages upstairs. (This clause points out certain janitors—those who are old and feeble.)

Nonrestrictive clauses are set off by commas to indicate a greater degree of separation. Restrictive clauses are not set off by commas to indicate that they are close or necessary to the word they modify. As a rule, any adjective clause following a name or proper noun is nonrestrictive because the name identifies the person or thing sufficiently.

Noun. A word which names a person, object, quality, etc. A common noun names any one of the members of a class or group of persons, places, things, qualities, ideas, etc. Common nouns are not capitalized.

Examples: man, cat, dog, courage, city, advice, ocean, hat.

A proper noun names some particular person, place, or thing. Proper nouns are capitalized.

Examples: Clara Olson, Washington Avenue, Carleton College, New York, Civil War.

A collective noun names a group or collection by using a singular form.

Examples: class, jury, band, company.

An abstract noun names a quality or general idea.

Examples: service, loyalty, darkness.

A concrete noun names something that may be perceived by one of the senses.

Examples: finger, berry, tobacco, bread, table, napkin.

Noun clause. A dependent clause used like a noun.

Used as subject: Whatever he says seems to delight her.
Used as object: She understood *what I meant.*
Used as object of preposition: Give this to *whoever opens the door.*
Used as subjective complement: This is *what she said.*

Ordinal numbers. Numbers indicating order or succession, such as *first, second, third,* etc.

Parse. To explain the use of a part of speech in a sentence.

Participle. A verbal used as an adjective and occasionally as an adverb. A participle cannot be used to make a complete clause or sentence. Since it is partly a verb, it may take an object and be modified by adverbs. Since it is partly an adjective, it may modify a noun and be modified by adverbs. The participle has several forms:

Present active: Laughing and *shouting,* the children ran down to the stream.
Past: She was a badly *spoiled* child.
Perfect active: Having written his theme, John went to bed.
Present passive: The game just *being played* is the last of the series.
Perfect passive: The theme *having been written,* John went to bed.

Parts of speech. The classification of words according to the function they perform in the sentence. The parts of speech are noun, pronoun, verb, adverb, adjective, preposition, conjunction, interjection.

Person. Changes in the form of pronouns and verbs which indicate the speaker (first person), the person spoken to (second person), and the person spoken about (third person). Examples are: I am, you are, he is.

Phrase. A group of words, not containing a subject or predicate, but used as a single part of speech. The different kinds of phrases are:

Prepositional: Give this *to your teacher.*
Participial: *Having caught three large salmon,* we were very happy.
Gerund: *Playing with a radio set* is his recreation.
Infinitive: We took time *to explore the cave thoroughly.*

A verb consisting of several words is often called a verb phrase: *shall be going, should have read, might have lost,* etc.

Predicate. In a sentence, the verb and its modifiers and complements.

Predicate complement or subjective complement. See *complement.*

Preposition. The part of speech which shows the relation between a substantive called its object and some other word in the sentence.

Examples: about, across, around, beneath, for, in, to, up, with.

Principal parts of a verb. The forms of a verb from which the complete conjugation may be derived. The principal parts are: the present infinitive, the past tense (first person singular), and the past participle.

Examples:

begin	began	begun
drink	drank	drunk
slay	slew	slain

Pronoun. A word that takes the place of a noun. Pronouns are classified as follows:

Personal: I, you, he, she, it, they.
Demonstrative: this, that, these, those.
Relative: who, which, that, what, whoever, whatever.
Interrogative: who, which, what.
Indefinite: any, anyone, some, someone, nobody, each.
Intensive: myself, yourself, etc.

Restrictive clause. See *nonrestrictive clause.*

Strong verb. A verb that forms its principal parts by a change of vowel and not by the addition of *-ed*, *-d*, or *-t*.

Substantive. A general name for any word or group of words that may be used as a noun. Substantives are nouns, pronouns, gerunds, infinitives, and noun clauses.

Substantive clause. A clause used as a noun.

Syntax. The part of grammar which deals with the relationship of words to each other in a sentence.

Transitive verb. See *verb.*

Verb. A part of speech which asserts an action, a condition, or state of being. A verb may be either transitive or intransitive. A transitive verb is one that takes an object. An intransitive verb is complete without the addition of an object. The copula, or copulative verb, a special kind of intransitive verb, is followed by a subjective complement.

Transitive: He *hit* the ball.
  She *wore* a new hat.
  Mother *makes* good pies.

Intransitive: She *talks* in her sleep.
             Ducks *swim*.
             Flowers *grow* in her garden.
Copulative: He *is* an honest man.

Verbal. See *gerund, infinitive, participle.*

Voice. The characteristic of a verb, shown by its form, which tells whether the subject acts (active voice) or is acted upon (passive voice).

Weak Verb. A verb that forms its principal parts by adding *-ed, -d,* or *-t.*

Walk, walked, walked.

MECHANICS

THE MANUSCRIPT

10a. Use the kind of paper which is recommended by your English instructor.

Most English departments require composition students to use regulation typewriter paper (about 8½ x 11 inches in size), unruled if the themes are typewritten, ruled if the themes are handwritten.

10b. Write legibly.

If you use a typewriter, see that the ribbon is fresh and the type clean. If you write by hand, make your handwriting easy to read. Write with a good pen and use black or dark blue ink. Do not use red, violet, or green ink. Form all letters distinctly, especially those that might be confused with similar letters. Dot your *i's* and cross your *t's*. Do not decorate your letters with unnecessary loops or flourishes.

10c. Label your themes correctly.

Use the method of labeling themes that is recommended by your instructor. If the English department of your college collects all themes and files them in numbered boxes in a theme room, use the following system: In the upper right-hand corner of each page of your theme write your name, your file number, the number of the theme, and the number of the page. No other information is necessary to identify any page of any theme that you write. For example, the label on the first page of your fifth theme should read:

John K. Jones 893

5—1

Do not write the name or number of the course, the number of the section, the hour of recitation, the date, or your address.

All papers, unless you are otherwise instructed, are to be handed in flat. Do not fasten the sheets of manuscript together in any way. Do not twist, tear, or turn down the corners of the paper; do not use wire clips or other mechanical fasteners.

If your instructor asks you to fold your papers, fold them according to his directions. In the identifying label give him all the information he requests.

10d. Write the title on the first line of the first page, or about two inches from the top of the sheet.

Center the title on the page. Capitalize every important word in the title. Do not underline it or enclose it in quotation marks. Do not use a period after it, but you may use a question mark or an exclamation point if the sense of the title calls for either of these marks. Leave a space of about an inch between the title and the first line of the theme. Do not repeat the title on succeeding pages of the theme.

10e. Leave margins of an inch at the top and at the left of each page.

Do not crowd your words at the right or at the bottom of the page. Some instructors like a wide margin at the right as well as at the left of the page so as to have room for comments and corrections.

10f. Indent the first line of each paragraph.

Do not indent a line unless you are beginning a paragraph. If you are quoting verse in a paragraph, begin the first line following the quotation flush with the left margin. Do not leave a blank space at the end of any line except the last one in the paragraph.

10g. Draw a horizontal line through words which you want deleted.

Never use parentheses or brackets to delete or cancel a word. If you want to insert a correction in the text, mark the point of insertion with a caret and write the inserted material above the caret.

10h. In preparing copy for the printer follow the style manual of the publication for which you are writing.

Adequate general directions for the preparation of copy may be found on pages 1272 and 1273 of *Webster's Collegiate Dictionary*, fifth edition. A complete guide is the *Style Manual of the United States Government Printing Office*, which may be secured for a dollar from the Superintendent of Documents, Washington, D. C. Another widely used guide is *A Manual of Style of the University of Chicago Press*.

Very few students will have occasion to prepare copy for the printer. If you are fortunate enough to have some work of yours accepted for publication, remember that a theme good enough to be praised by your instructor is usually ready for the printer. Your copy is, of course, typed and double-spaced. Beyond that about all that you can do is to check spelling, punctuation, and capitalization.

TITLES

11a. Italicize titles of books, newspapers, periodicals, bulletins, and pamphlets. In manuscript, underscore once to indicate italics.

Some publishers use quotation marks with titles of books; a few set book titles in capitals. The most common practice, however, is to use italics. Quotation marks should be used to indicate chapter headings and titles of short stories and poems, especially when it is necessary to distinguish between the whole book and one of its parts.

Right: He spent the summer reading Woollcott's *While Rome Burns.*
I enjoyed reading W. Somerset Maugham's *East and West.*
The stories which I like best are "Rain," "The Letter," and "The Force of Circumstance."
We bought a copy of *Harper's Magazine.*

The name of a city which forms a part of the title of a newspaper is usually not italicized.

Right: We subscribed for the Minneapolis *Tribune.*

11b. A good title should be brief, accurate, and interesting.

Do not write long and involved titles. A title is not a topic sentence, nor is it a complete summary of what you have written. A good title should be truthful; that is, it should direct the reader's attention to what he may expect from the theme, but it must not promise more than the theme can deliver. A good title should be interesting; it should serve as a bait, a lure to interest the reader in the theme.

Poor: My Impressions of the Emotions of a College Freshman during the First Week of College; How I Would Feel If I Were Suddenly Told I Had Lost My Eyesight; Thoughts of a College Freshman on the Fickleness of Women.

Better: Six Days in a Daze; Lights Out; The Incredible Sex.

11c. Capitalize every important word in a title. The articles *a, an,* and *the* are capitalized when they begin titles.

Right: A Dictionary of Modern English Usage; A Comprehensive Guide to Good English; Modern Writers at Work; The Practice of Composition.

EXERCISES

Exercise 1. The following are titles of themes written in freshman English composition. Keeping in mind the three principles—brevity, truth, and interest—try to improve these titles.

1. Why I Like to Play Football
2. My Conception of an Ideal Roommate
3. A Description of an Interesting Character
4. Why I Like to Live in a Small Town
5. The Various Ways in Which Persons Commit Suicide
6. What I Expect To Get out of My College Education
7. How the Freshman English Course Could Be Improved

Exercise 2. Correct the following sentences by the proper use of capitals, italics, and quotation marks.

1. Her best short stories, three men and a girl, katinka, and the case of peter patchin, were first printed in the centerville journal.
2. After you left last night, I picked up O. Henry's roads of destiny and read the enchanted profile, the passing of black eagle, and friends in san rosario.

3 The current issue of the reader's digest gives in condensed form articles from such magazines as esquire, the saturday evening post, the american mercury, harper's magazine, and the yale review.

CAPITALS

12a. **Capitalize the first word of every sentence, of a group of words understood as a sentence, of a direct quotation, and of a line of poetry.**

Right: I admire patient women.
Do you think he will return?
Not now. Later, perhaps.
He said, "Try to get some sleep."
The question is, Shall the people rule?

And this same flower that smiles today
Tomorrow will be dying.

Do not capitalize the first word of an indirect quotation, of a direct quotation that is fragmentary or structurally a part of the sentence in which it stands, or of the part of a direct quotation which follows expressions like *he said* unless this begins a new sentence.

Wrong: He said that He would try to get some sleep.
He talked a long time about his comrades "Hid in death's dateless night."
"I believe you," the dean replied, "But I can do little for you."
Right: He said that he would try to get some sleep.
He talked for a long time about his comrades "hid in death's dateless night."
"I believe you," the dean replied, "but I can do little for you."

12b. Capitalize proper nouns and adjectives.

The following classes of proper nouns and adjectives are capitalized:

1. Names of persons and places: Joseph Conrad, Chicago, Harry, Dr. Jones.
2. Derivatives of proper names if used with a proper meaning: Miltonic, Macedonian Era, Russian literature, German poetry.
3. Names of races and languages: French, Latin, Jewish, Italian.
4. Names of political and geographic divisions if used in the proper sense: Dominion of Canada, Union of South Africa, the Middle West, the Orient.
5. Names of organizations: Elks, Masons, the Beavers, Bureau of Engraving and Printing.
6. Religious terms: Catholic, Protestant, the Almighty, Christianity.
7. Names of historic epochs and events: World War, Armistice Day, the Middle Ages.
8. Personifications: O wild West Wind, thou breath of Autumn's being.

12c. Capitalize any title when it is used preceding a proper name, or when it is used as a substitute for the proper name.

A title following a name is capitalized only when it is intended to indicate high respect or distinction.

Right: President Roosevelt; the President; King Edward; Dean Smith; Governor Martin; ex-President Hoover; Chairman Thomas; Captain Simms; the Governor; Cordell Hull, Secretary of State; Ralph Jones, chairman of the nominating committee; Theodore H. Busby, professor of mathematics.

Abbreviations after a name, such as *Esq., Jr., Sr., M.A., Ph.D., LL.D., D.D., F.R.S.*, are usually capitalized.

Right: Herbert Nelson, Esq., William Willoughby, Jr., James E. Stockton, Ph.D.

12d. Capitalize the points of the compass when they refer to specific geographical divisions, but not when they refer to direction.

Right: Prosperity has returned to the Middle West. The sun sets in the west. She has always lived in the East.

12e. Capitalize the pronoun *I,* the vocative *O* (but not *oh*), *B.C.* and *A.D.* *No.* (for *number*), *A.M.* and *P.M.* may be written in either capitals or small letters.

12f. Do not capitalize the names of studies unless they form a part of the name of a specific course. Do not capitalize the names of seasons, or the names of college classes.

Right: Lucy registered for mathematics, American history, and geology. I like Educational Psychology 113 better than any other course. He went to England in the spring and returned in the winter. The ideal student would have the intelligence of a senior and the enthusiasm of a freshman.

EXERCISES

Exercise 1. In the following sentences correct the errors in the use of capitals and supply capitals where they are necessary.

1. He registered for mathematics, latin, and english.
2. H. C. Brown, professor of french, returned to center college after a summer spent in the south.

3. "Golf is one of those games," remarked the chairman of the committee, "In which the score is often improved by a good lie."
4. The members of the Committee were dean Rogers, captain Holt, and colonel williamson.
5. Last Summer I took a short course in Psychology at the university of southern California.
6. My class in Psychology 232 meets every monday, wednesday, and friday at eight o'clock.

Exercise 2. Before each of the following statements write C if the statement is correct and W if the statement is wrong.

1. Capitalize the names of the seasons.
2. Capitalize the first word of an indirect quotation.
3. When in doubt as to correct capitalization refer to *Webster's New International Dictionary*.
4. It is a diesel engine but Macadam pavement.
5. A.M. and P.M. are preferred to a.m. and p.m.
6. Capitalize the points of the compass when they refer to directions.
7. Do not capitalize studies if they do not form part of the names of specific courses.
8. Always capitalize "Oh" but never "O."
9. Capitalize any title when it is used preceding a proper name.
10. Capitalize names of races and languages.

NUMBERS

13a. In formal writing spell out numbers that can be expressed in a few words, preferably in not more than two or three words.

Right: He earned sixteen hundred dollars last year.
Harry is only twenty-one years old.
Her story began in the late seventies.
The price was two and a half dollars.
He lived to celebrate his seventy-fifth birthday.
He moved the block not more than three-quarters of an inch.

13b. Do not begin a sentence with a figure.

Wrong: 27 students placed in the first decile.
Right: Twenty-seven students placed in the first decile.

13c. Use figures for dates. Do not use *st, nd, rd, th* with the day of the month.

Wrong: He was born on January sixth, eighteen hundred and seventy eight.
Wrong: He was born on January 6th, 1878.
Right: He was born on January 6, 1878.

13d. In ordinary writing do not express a sum in both figures and words.

Wrong: My father sent me ten ($10.) dollars.
Right: My father sent me ten dollars.

13e. Use a comma, for clearness and convenience, to separate thousands, millions, etc., in numbers of four or more digits except in dates, serial numbers, page numbers, and telephone numbers.

Right: The total number of ballots returned was 2,376,344. The contest closed October 15, 1937. Study the diagram facing page 1217. Please call Bryant 9944. Policy No. 332254.

13f. Use figures for: 1. street and room numbers; 2. page numbers; 3. divisions of a book; 4. decimals and percentages; 5. several numbers occurring in the same paragraph or section; 6. numbers not easily written out.

Right: Take this package to 244 West Second Street.
Read the discussion of gerunds in chapter 4, on page 231.
These systems are at distances ranging from 100,000 to

1,500,000 light years, their diameters range from 4,000 to 45,000 light years, and the total luminosities from 20 to 500 million times the luminosity of the sun.

Exercise 1. In the following sentences point out the numbers which should have been written out.

1. She paid $17.00 for her new hat.
2. On his 85th birthday he sold his business and bought a house at 235 Maple Street, where he lived until his death at the age of 90.
3. 4 years later he rented a small shop at 324 South Michigan Avenue.
4. My sister is only 2 years older than I but she is 6 inches taller.
5. The first bid was $3.50. Then in a spirited contest the bids were rocketed upward: $7.50, $10.00, $25.00, and finally $75.
6. During the three years that the camps have been in existence, over 100,000 men have been given employment.
7. Last summer I earned $350. Of that sum $75 went for tuition, $25 for books, $50 for clothes, and the rest will have to take care of my board and rent for the next 3 months.
8. There are 6 brothers and 2 sisters in my family.
9. On the 3rd day of November a heavy snow blocked all roads in the valley.
10. About 2000 students responded to the appeal.

ABBREVIATIONS

14a. **Avoid the use of abbreviations in formal writing.**

The following abbreviations are permissible: *Mr.* (*Mister*), *Mrs.* (*Mistress*), *Messrs.* (*Messieurs*), *M.* (*Monsieur*), *Mme.* (*Madame*), *Mlle.* (*Mademoiselle*), used before proper names; *Dr.* (*Doctor*), *Col.* (*Colonel*), *Rev.* (*Reverend*), *Hon.* (*Honorable*), used before names in informal writing; *Jr.* (*Junior*), *Sr.* (*Senior*), *Ph.D.* (*Doctor of Philosophy*), *D.D.* (*Doctor of Divinity*),

LL.D. (*Doctor of Laws*), and other titles, used after names; *A.D.* (*Anno Domini*), *B.C.* (*before Christ*), used with dates only when necessary for clearness; *No.* (*number*), used with numerals; *i.e.*, *e.g.*, *viz.*, *cf.*, *etc.*, used in informal writing, but written out when a more formal effect is desired: *that is, for example, namely, compare, and so forth.*

Remember that the words *reverend* and *honorable* must not be used with surnames alone. They should be followed by the first name, or initials, or the appropriate title. If preceded by *the*, these words are usually not abbreviated.

Formal: The Reverend George M. Donaldson, the Reverend Dr. Donaldson, the Honorable Elihu Root.
Less formal: Hon. Elihu Root, Rev. George M. Donaldson.

In student themes be on your guard against such abbreviations as: *lab., prof., doc., lit., ag., convo., libe., chem., phys. ed., stenog., soph.*

For a complete list of abbreviations and their meaning, consult any good dictionary. Use the same authority in determining the correct punctuation and use of capitals with abbreviations.

14b. In ordinary writing, except in footnotes, bibliographies, addresses, and tabulations, spell out:

1. Names of countries and states.
2. Names of months and days of the week.
3. *Number, volume, chapter, page, and, street, avenue, manufacturing, company, mountain, Christmas.*
4. Christian names.

Wrong: My chem. class meets every Mon., Wed., and Fri.
Wm. & Chas. found jobs with a mfg. concern on Union Ave.
The U.S.A. was not represented at the peace conference.

Our cabin faced snow-covered Mt. Shasta.
The Co. for which I worked has a branch office on a st. near the docks.
I shall go home Xmas and return in Feb.

Right: My chemistry class meets every Monday, Wednesday, and Friday.
William and Charles found jobs with a manufacturing concern on Union Avenue.
The United States of America was not represented at the peace conference.
Our cabin faced snow-covered Mount Shasta.
The company for which I worked has a branch office on a street near the docks.
I shall go home Christmas and return in February.

EXERCISES

Exercise 1. Correct the errors in the use of abbreviations in the following sentences.

1. Henry Lawler, prof. of chemistry, Dr. I. M. Jones, Ph.D., and Rev. Stockman represented the U of Oregon at the dedication ceremonies.
2. My roommate registered for two lab courses in chem this term.
3. At the first convo of the year the entertainment was provided by a committee representing the soph class.
4. The war began in 1914, A.D.
5. Our leader was Mister Howard, a graduate of the U of Wisconsin.

Exercise 2. What do the following abbreviations mean?

1. AAA	9. CCC	17. TVA
2. A.E.F.	10. D.A.	18. S.P.C.A.
3. anon.	11. D.S.C.	19. RFC
4. A.W.O.L.	12. f.o.b.	20. U.S.S.R.
5. B.L.	13. F.R.S.	21. U.P.
6. B.P.O.E.	14. I.O.O.F.	22. TNT
7. B.T.U.	15. G.A.R.	23. Sc.D.
8. cm.	16. dial.	24. l.c.

SYLLABICATION

15a. Avoid dividing a word at the end of a line.

Never divide words of one syllable. In writing by hand or in typewriting it is usually unnecessary to divide short words of two syllables.

15b. If you find it necessary to divide a word, make the division between syllables, and place a hyphen at the end of the line, not at the beginning of the next line.

15c. Never divide the last word of a paragraph or of a page.

EXERCISES

Exercise 1. Determine which of the following words can be divided into syllables. Indicate the proper division. When in doubt, consult your dictionary.

1. hour	7. pleasure	13. theatrical
2. idler	8. educate	14. children
3. science	9. master	15. extraordinary
4. curiosity	10. architecture	16. through
5. logical	11. procedure	17. azure
6. ranger	12. lighthearted	18. used

Exercise 2. Determine which of the following are divided correctly.

1. comp-li-cat-ed	5. rhyth-mi-cal	9. real-ize
2. com-mit-tee	6. de-sic-cate	10. re-al-ly
3. rhy-thm	7. in-noc-u-ous	11. rar-e-fy
4. rhyth-mic	8. i-noc-u-late	12. pre-pos-i-tion

ITALICS

To indicate that a word should be italicized, draw a single straight line under it.

16a. Italicize titles of books, plays, newspapers, magazines, musical compositions, works of art, and names of ships and aircraft.

Do not italicize chapters of books, titles of short stories, or titles of articles in magazines.

Right: Richard Boleslawski's *Way of a Lancer*, H. W. Fowler's *A Dictionary of Modern English Usage*, John Galsworthy's *The Silver Box*, the Minneapolis *Tribune*, *Theatre Arts Monthly*, *Harper's Magazine*, Corot's *Orpheus and Eurydice*, the *Spirit of St. Louis*, the *Titanic*.

16b. Italicize unnaturalized foreign words and phrases.

It may be difficult for you to know whether or not a certain foreign phrase has been Anglicized. A dictionary will help you. In *Webster's Collegiate Dictionary*, for instance, you will find parallel bars before foreign words that are used frequently in English but which are not completely Anglicized. Look up *au revoir* and *laissez faire*. Which would you italicize?

16c. Italicize words, letters, or figures when they are referred to as such.

See also section 24e and exercise 2 under section 24h.

Right: He used *infect* in place of *inflict*. Dot your *i's* and cross your *t's*. You have used too many *and's* in your theme. Do you think that *liquefy* is a difficult word to spell correctly?

16d. Italicize a word or phrase to which you wish to give particular emphasis.

The use of italics for emphasis is a privilege that must be resorted to circumspectly.

If you want to examine a sample of an older style, look up an old edition of Poe or Carlyle. It was once the fashion for an author to shout and scream at the reader in capitals and italics. At present it is permissible to use italics for emphasis only when the sentence would not be immediately clear without italics. The following sentences are not examples of bad writing; they are merely illustrations of an older fashion.

Great is the combined voice of men; the utterance of their *instincts*, which are truer than their *thoughts:* it is the greatest a man encounters, among the sounds and shadows which make up this World of Time. He who can resist that, has his footing somewhere *beyond* Time.—Thomas Carlyle.

But, as *you* draw near, the woman raises her wasted features. Would Domrémy know them again for the features of her child? Ah, but *you* know them, bishop, well! Oh, mercy! what a groan was *that* which the servants, waiting outside the bishop's dream at his bedside, heard from his labouring heart, as at this moment he turned away from the fountain and the woman, seeking rest in the forests afar off. Yet not *so* to escape the woman, whom once again he must behold before he dies.—Thomas De Quincey.

17   BIBLIOGRAPHY

A bibliography is a list of writings relating to a given subject or author. It may be a complete directory of all published information relating to a subject, or a selected list of books or articles which the ordinary reader might find useful, or simply a list of the printed sources which the writer has used. A true bibliography is not necessarily a list of the sources used, since a student may compile a bibliography without ever intending to write an essay based on the source material he has collected.

For information dealing with the construction of a bibliography consult the section dealing with the preparation of the research paper, pages 113–123.

17a. Arrange and classify bibliographic items logically.

The arrangement of items in a bibliography depends on the purpose of the list. Ordinarily it will be satisfactory to classify items under the following heads: 1. General reference works; 2. Books; 3. Magazine articles, signed; 4. Magazine articles, unsigned; 5. Newspaper articles; 6. Bulletins.

17b. Select a simple form and use it consistently.

The following examples illustrate an acceptable form:

For general reference books:

Melville, F. J., "Philately," *Encyclopaedia Britannica*, 14th ed., vol. 17, pp. 713–715.
"Philately," *Encyclopedia Americana*, 1932, vol. 21, pp. 736–739.

For books:

Greenough, James Bradstreet, and Kittredge, George Lyman, *Words and Their Ways in English Speech*, The Macmillan Company, New York, 1901, 1923.
Yeats, William Butler, *Collected Poems*, The Macmillan Company, New York, 1933.

For magazine articles, signed:

Green, Z. E., "English Literature in the Rural High School," *Peabody Journal of Education*, vol. 12, pp. 270–275 (May, 1935).
Pardee, J. T., "Appalachians Offer Gold Possibilities," *Engineering and Mining Journal*, vol. 136, p. 183 (April, 1935).
Watkins, S. B., "Climbing Roses," *Queensland Agricultural Journal*, vol. 36, pp. 116–119 (July, 1931).

For magazine articles, unsigned:

"New Swiss Oil Recovery Process," *Chemical Industries*, vol. 34, p. 48 (January, 1934).

For newspaper articles:

"Comment on C Content of Lima Beans," The New York *Times*, April 18, 1937, sec. 12, p. 8, col. 4.

For bulletins:

Munn, M. T., "Quality of Vegetable Seeds on Sale in New York in 1932," *Bulletin*, No. 618 (1933), New York State Agricultural Experiment Station.
Rubinow, Isaac Max, "Russia's Wheat Trade," *Bulletin*, No. 65 (1908), Bureau of Statistics, U. S. Department of Agriculture.
Tracy, Samuel Mills, "Grape Growing in the South," *Farmers' Bulletin*, No. 118 (1900), U. S. Department of Agriculture.

18 FOOTNOTES

Footnotes are used to identify and acknowledge material used in the body of the essay, to give additional information which does not fit into the text, to quote in detail what has been merely referred to in the text, or to define or explain some term used in the text.

To identify footnotes place an Arabic numeral immediately

after and a little above the material referred to. Place the same number before the footnote. Number all of your footnotes consecutively from the beginning to the end of your essay or begin numbering with number one on each page. Either method is acceptable.

18a. For your footnotes use a form which is brief but absolutely clear.

A footnote which refers to a source used is like a bibliographic item with two minor changes: (1) the author's name is usually given in the normal order; (2) the exact page reference is added.

There are three ways of inserting footnotes on the page of a typewritten manuscript.

1. Place the footnotes at the bottom of each page to which they have reference.[1]

[1] Carl Van Doren, *Contemporary American Novelists*, The Macmillan Company, New York, 1922, p. 93.

2. Place your footnote immediately below the material to which it refers in the text. Separate it from the text by two parallel lines.[1]

[1] Edna St. Vincent Millay, *Wine from These Grapes*, Harper & Brothers, New York, 1934, p. 12.

3. Place the footnote in brackets immediately after the material to which it refers in the text [1] [[1] Stuart Robertson, *The Development of Modern English*, Prentice-Hall, Inc., New York, p. 258.], and continue the text as if the footnote had not interrupted it.

18b. Use abbreviations in footnotes whenever you can do so without sacrificing clearness.

The following abbreviations are permissible in footnotes:

Ibid., in the same place.
Op. cit., in the work referred to.
Loc. cit., in the place mentioned.
Id., the same.
p., pp., page, pages.
vol., vols., volume, volumes.
l., ll., line, lines.
ff., following (pages).
cf., compare, see.

Ibid. (or *ibidem*) may be used to show that the footnote refers to the same work as the footnote immediately preceding. If the reference is not to the same page as in the preceding footnote, *ibid.* must be followed by the exact page reference.

Op. cit. is used with the author's name and the page reference to show that the footnote refers to a work already cited but not to the one immediately preceding. Of course it cannot be used if more than one work by that author has been mentioned.

Loc. cit. is used under practically the same conditions as *op. cit.* In a reference to a printed source, the distinction between *work* and *place* is so fine as to be negligible.

In ordinary writing it is better to use English words in place of the abbreviations of their Latin equivalents. Write *for instance* or *for example* instead of *e.g.*, *that is* instead of *i.e.*, *and so forth* instead of *etc.* In footnotes, however, abbreviations are convenient.

PUNCTUATION

The purpose of punctuation is to help make clear the meaning of written or printed language. In learning how to punctuate correctly, you must not forget two guiding principles. The first of these is that correct punctuation depends upon an understanding of the grammatical relation of the parts of the sentence. The other is that punctuation rules are a set of conventions, which, like the conventions of social etiquette, of play, or of business, make communication between people easy and natural. If punctuation marks are to facilitate understanding of what is written, the same marks must always be used for the same sort of sentence construction. In other words, the reader must understand at once what each mark is doing in the sentence. The following rules represent the most widely accepted practice in ordinary writing.

PERIOD, QUESTION MARK, EXCLAMATION POINT

19a. Use a period after a declarative or an imperative sentence, or after an indirect question.

Right: Revenge is a kind of wild justice.
Do not hold up your hand.
Please leave the room quietly.
Our teacher asked us how many books we had read.

19b. Use a period after an abbreviation.

For a list of abbreviations permissible in ordinary writing see section 14. Use the period after such common abbreviations as *Mr., Mrs., Dr., St., Ave., Jr., Sr., p.m., a.m., A.D., B.C.* Do not use a period after the letters standing for certain recently created governmental agencies: *TVA, CCC, RFC, NRA;* nor after *MS* (manuscript).

19c. Use periods or dots (usually three within a sentence, four at the end of a sentence) to indicate the omission of words from a quoted passage, or pauses and hesitations in dialogue.

The souls of emperors and cobblers are cast in the same mould. . . . The same reason that makes us wrangle with a neighbour causes a war betwixt princes.—Montaigne.

"You think I go about staring at nothing," she remarked. . . . "Not a bit of it! I have been planning all sorts of things. . . . I have been thinking how I could get to Germany. . . . Or one might catch them in Switzerland. . . . I've had all sorts of plans. They can't go guarded for ever. . . ."
From H. G. Wells, Mr. Britling Sees It Through.

19d. Use a question mark after a direct question.

Right: Can you understand him? Did he say anything to you?
Who said we couldn't win this game?
And what satisfaction can I get from failure?

A question mark may be used to end each of a series of elliptical phrases or clauses which may be read as a single sentence.

Right: How much have you spent for books? for clothes? for entertainment? Will he respond to your arguments? or your threats? or your tears?

A single question mark is used after a double question, that is, a quoted question following a question.

Right: Did he say, "How many?"
Who said, "When do we eat?"

A question mark within parentheses may be used to indicate doubt or uncertainty as to the preceding figure or fact.

Right: Lucien Botha was born in 1779 (?) and died in 1859.

The use of a question mark to indicate irony is not sanctioned by reputable practice. It should be avoided in serious writing.

Poor: We returned from a most enjoyable (?) hunting trip.

19e. Use an exclamation point after an expression of strong feeling.

Use the exclamation point with caution and discretion. Your tendency will be to use it too often. Words like *yes, no, oh, well, alas, surely,* and the like, when beginning a sentence, are usually followed by a comma. If *oh* introduces an expression of strong feeling, put the exclamation point at the end of the expression. And never use more than one exclamation point after an exclamation.

Right: Come here this very minute!
"Great guns!" he shouted in consternation.
He actually said that!
Oh, this is unspeakable!
No, I don't think it will rain.
Well, what do you think we should do now?
"No!" he shouted. "You can't stop me now!"

THE COMMA

The best way to master the uses of the comma is to learn and to apply the rules. But the student who expects a rule for every possible use of the comma is like the boy who buys a handbook of correspondence in order to find out what he should write to his sweetheart. Comma rules should be interpreted with the aid of a little common sense. Rules are good as far as they go. They are guides for the learner—dependable guides, it is true, but they cannot take the place of good sense and an understanding of the function or purpose of punctuation. The primary function of punctuation, let us repeat, is to make clear the meaning of written language. Most of the possible uses of the period, the question mark, the exclamation point, quotation marks, and even the semicolon are definitely determined by custom. Most of your punctuation may be done by rule. But punctuation may have another function—a rhetorical one. The comma—and, to a certain extent, the semicolon—may be used to indicate subtle differences in meaning, degrees of pause or emphasis in reading, or the rhetorical balance or contrast of ideas.

The important fact still remains, however, that the student who hopes to make punctuation an artistic resource must first learn the rules.

20a. Use commas to set off nonrestrictive clauses. Do not use commas to set off restrictive clauses.

If the distinction between restrictive and nonrestrictive clauses is not already clear to you, think of restrictive clauses as "identifying" or "pointing-out" clauses. A restrictive clause helps to locate or identify its antecedent. It says to the reader, "I mean this particular person, object, or thing, and no other." It is close to its antecedent in meaning, so close that it cannot be separated from it by a comma. A nonrestrictive clause does not identify or point out. It merely gives additional information about its antecedent.

Restrictive clauses:

The boy *who has a hobby* will never be lonely.

The student *who works hard* will succeed.

The teacher *who demands accuracy and thoroughness* will always be popular.

Please bring me the book *which you see lying on my desk.*

The girl *who spoke to us as we passed* is my new roommate.

Nonrestrictive clauses:

My English teacher, *who invariably closes his eyes when he lectures,* told me to speak more directly to my audience.

Astronomy, *which is the study of the heavenly bodies,* is a fascinating subject.

We were introduced to Ben Ross, *who asked us to go salmon fishing with him.*

My father, *who had not heard the question,* shook his head in silence.

Old Pop Lawler, *who is a superstitious fellow,* will not walk under a ladder.

20b. Use a comma to separate co-ordinate clauses joined by *and, but, for, nor, or,* except when the clauses are short and closely related in meaning.

Right: I could look back into America and see its beginnings, but I could also see other beginnings that never grew, and then I thought I saw why it was so lonely and lopsided and aggressive.—John Hyde Preston.

I went up to my room with a heavy heart, for I was bowed under the weight of the first lie I had ever told to my mother.

After a time a farmer offered to help us, and we went into his machine shed to get a chain.

He explained that he was sorry, but he found that he could think better if he walked about the room.

20c. Use commas to separate words, phrases, or clauses in a series.

Right: The nation increased in wealth, numbers, and power every year.
A university is not made up of a stadium, a library, science laboratories, and recitation halls.
The thief pried open a window, entered my bedroom, and stole my watch and purse.
Everywhere you may see the same nearly flat country, the same fields and crops, the same rough wooden fences, and the same solitary farmhouses.

20d. Use commas to separate consecutive adjectives preceding the noun they modify when the adjectives are co-ordinate in meaning.

Right: A wet, hungry, tired group of boys awaited her.
Bones was a surly, treacherous, cruel fellow.
Henry was a lazy old fellow.

The comma is correct only when the adjectives are co-ordinate—that is, when each of the adjectives refers directly to the noun. When an adjective modifies the whole idea that follows it, it is not separated from it by a comma. If you can substitute *and* for the comma, the comma is correct. It would be natural and correct, for instance, to say "a surly and treacherous and cruel fellow," but it would be unnatural to say "a lazy and old fellow."

Right: It was a raw, blustery winter night.
He stood under the spreading chestnut tree.
She wore an old sport suit.

20e. Use the comma to separate words and phrases that might be incorrectly joined in reading.

Right: Instead of a few, hundreds attended the rally.
Before starting to eat, Father bowed his head in prayer.
Above, the sun burned a dull red; below, the sand radiated heat like a furnace.

20f. Ordinarily, use the comma to set off a modifier which precedes a main clause, especially when the introductory phrase or clause is long and not closely connected with the main clause in meaning.

Right: Although the candidate is honest and patriotic, we do not believe he is practical enough.

In so far as the school can rely upon the genuine merits of America, there is no need to associate the teaching of American patriotism with the inculcation of false standards.

But in the modern period of intense mobility and widespread mechanization, there is every reason to encourage the growth of the richest and finest type of personalities.

The excitement being over, the students returned to the room.

In punctuating modifiers that precede the main clause you must depend on your good sense as well as on rules. You must decide whether or not the sentence will be clearer with the introductory modifier set off. Length of clause alone will not tell you when to use a comma and when not to use it. Frequently very short clauses are set off for emphasis. Adverbial phrases, as a rule, are not set off, partly because they are shorter than clauses, and partly because they are closer in meaning to the main clause. But remember that punctuation groups words not only for clearness but also for rhetorical effect.

Right: When I go to the theater I want to be entertained.
If his letter had stopped at this point, he would have been spared much grief and humiliation.
After the game we all went to Jim's room.
There, at the end of the street, one sees a majestic pile of grey marble.
In the first place, all that war proves is that one side is stronger.
On his head rested a ridiculous green cap.

If you want to find out how good writers actually punctuate, ask your teacher to select for you three or four essays by contemporary writers of recognized ability. Go through these essays carefully, copying the beginning of every sentence that starts with a phrase or clause. What do you learn about punctuation? How frequently do good writers begin sentences with adverbial phrases or clauses?

20g. Use commas to set off words, phrases, or clauses used to explain, or to qualify, or to emphasize.

Right: The Smiths, by the way, did not accept our invitation.
Our interpretation of his motives is, I think, totally unfair.
In such organizations, whatever their name, the ambitious student may learn lessons of social conduct.
This, I suppose, is the essence of morality.
No teacher can give you an education; he can only, as it were, point in the direction of it.

This rule applies to expressions which serve as directive, transitional, and summarizing sentence modifiers. Some of these expressions are: *in the first place, finally, therefore, on the other hand, broadly speaking, when all has been said.*

20h. Use commas to set off appositives.

Right: Mr. Walker, the grocer, came to the door.

Her language, a terrifying mixture of bad grammar and slang, irritated and fascinated her teachers.

The three boys made the hazardous journey down the Snake River canyon, an exploit which called for unusual courage and resourcefulness.

20i. Use commas to set off substantives used in direct address.

Right: George, let me tell you what I did last night.

Come here, my child, and talk to me.

"Please change places with me, Helen," I requested.

20j. Use commas to set off mild exclamations and interjections.

Right: Well, I don't know what to tell him.

Oh, it does not matter.

20k. Use commas to set off absolute phrases.

Right: The guests having departed, we returned to the kitchen.

To tell the truth, he did not need much urging.

Our work finished, we went in search of fun and excitement.

Everything being considered, you are really fortunate to escape a more severe punishment.

20l. Use commas to set off an explanatory clause like *he said* when it breaks into a sentence of dialogue.

Right: "All the same," she said, "it is just as well to be on the safe side."
"No," said the teacher, "you cannot leave the room now."
My father answered, "Throw it away, then."
"It is a rough trail," the guide explained. "Walk slowly, and watch out for falling rocks."
"I am sorry," replied Baker; "I did not mean to be rude."

20m. Use a comma between a statement and a short question dependent on it.

Right: You brought the coffee, didn't you?
This is the house, isn't it?

20n. Use a comma to indicate a contrast between sentence elements.

Right: The mistakes of our opponents, not our organization or planning, won the election for us.
The teacher, even more than the poet, must be an individualist.

20o. Use commas to set off items in dates and addresses.

Right: Barbara Lee was born on Friday, September 13, 1908.
Send the package to Harry Tweed, 67 Stark Street, Yorktown, Nevada.

20p. Use commas to set off transposed or inserted sentence elements, or modifiers placed after the words they modify.

Right: With good intentions, hell proverbially is paved.
Inequality, by arousing jealousy and envy, provokes discontent.

The losing team, battered and discouraged, limped off the field.

Our plan, sound in principle and proved in practice, will bring greater prosperity to our community.

There he stood, stiff and self-conscious in his new clothes.

They were like a ballet of spinsters, elderly but flippant, standing in affected attitudes with the simpering graces of a bygone age.

20q. Do not use unnecessary commas. Avoid the following common mistakes in the use of the comma.

1. Do not use a comma to separate a subject from its verb.

Wrong: That our candidate was fighting a losing battle, was only too evident.

Right: That our candidate was fighting a losing battle was only too evident.

2. Do not use a comma to separate a verb from its complement.

Wrong: My favorite sports are, fishing, golf, and swimming.
Right: My favorite sports are fishing, golf, and swimming.

3. Do not place a comma between an adjective and the noun it modifies.

Wrong: The scout was a tall, cadaverous, ungainly, fellow.
Right: The scout was a tall, cadaverous, ungainly fellow.

4. Do not put a comma after a co-ordinating conjunction.

Wrong: A war to save democracy was fought twenty years ago, but, democracy is still in danger.

Right: A war to save democracy was fought twenty years ago, but democracy is still in danger.

5. Do not put a comma before a co-ordinating conjunction joining two words or two phrases.

Wrong: From his pocket he fished out an old pipe, and a pouch of tobacco.

Right: From his pocket he fished out an old pipe and a pouch of tobacco.

Wrong: Before she left the room she stopped to powder her nose, and to pat her hair.

Right: Before she left the room she stopped to powder her nose and to pat her hair.

6. In an indirect quotation do not put a comma between a word like *said* and the clause which is its object.

Wrong: The principal announced, that a new election was to be held.

Right: The principal announced that a new election was to be held.

7. Do not put a comma between a substantive and its restrictive modifier.

Wrong: Mrs. Booth is a woman, who enjoys looking on the dark side of life.

Right: Mrs. Booth is a woman who enjoys looking on the dark side of life.

8. Do not put a comma between an intensive pronoun and its antecedent.

Wrong: The hostess, herself, did not remember the name of her guest of honor.

Right: The hostess herself did not remember the name of her guest of honor.

EXERCISES

Exercise 1. Punctuate each nonrestrictive clause in the following sentences.

1. Chess which most of the other boys considered to be a form of mild insanity was his favorite recreation.
2. We looked up at the blue clusters of wild grapes which hung among the foliage of the elms.
3. I fancied that my father who was a country doctor was a sort of medieval knight going about on errands of mercy.
4. Through my bedroom window which was left open all summer I caught the faint breath of orange trees in blossom.
5. The play was written by A. A. Milne who is also the author of some delightful stories for children.
6. Naturally I addressed myself to the man who was seated next to me.
7. A good hunting dog which every boy in town aspired to possess could be purchased for a few days of hard work in the harvest fields.

Exercise 2. In the following sentences you will insert commas where they are necessary. What rule governs the punctuation in these sentences?

1. It is only as we become older mellower less violent and more tolerant that we begin to value the art of conversation.
2. The battle raged all over the bathroom until Moppet was finally washed dried brushed and perfumed.
3. All her life she had been petted humored and spoiled.
4. She gloried in her reputation of being the most untamable unpredictable and generally impossible girl in Philomath.
5. It was all a part of her dream invisible intangible inaudible yet there.
6. With a sigh she dropped the package into the cold murky swirling waters.
7. They regretted the colorful pageantry of football contests the festive evenings in fraternity houses and the stimulation of

human contacts which they had learned to enjoy in college days.

8. A tall gaunt moody-looking negro at the door bared his teeth in a mechanical grin.
9. Their scientific knowledge was devoted to making guns poison gas bombing planes and submarines for the purpose of killing their fellow men.
10. No one could understand how this motley group of third-rate artists futile poets and frustrated esthetes had accepted him so completely as one of their kind.

Exercise 3. Supply every missing comma and tell what rule governs its use.

1. A crackling cheerful fire awaited us.
2. Mr. Brown who is our next-door neighbor is very ill.
3. Although the boy could neither read nor write English his diction was surprisingly cultured and dignified.
4. My aunt lives at 230 University Avenue Southeast Minneapolis Minnesota.
5. I knew that the game had started for I heard the students cheering.
6. Tall slender girls should not seek the company of short fat men.
7. Before starting to work Father carefully removed his coat folded it and laid it on a stump.
8. Lillian Foster the girl with the red hair spoke to me just as we left the room.
9. Close the door Mary if you want to keep warm.
10. Becoming tired of fighting the boys suddenly found a victim in Styx a big white cat who belonged to our neighbor.

Exercise 4. This exercise is additional drill for you in the use of commas. Punctuate by rule. Tell what rule governs every comma that you use.

1. According to the proverb the best things are the most difficult.
2. Be not careless in deeds nor confused in words nor rambling in thought.

3. The robins have returned but there is still snow on the ground.
4. He is a pig a rat and a coward.
5. Having devoured the ice cream and cookies the boys bashfully shuffled out eager to engage in affairs more important to boys.
6. Before putting the dog inside Father gave him a bone to comfort him.
7. A tall stately lady approached our booth.
8. The president of our class George Turner called me that same afternoon.
9. The truth is usually unpleasant isn't it?
10. Jane gathered the flowers for her mother was busy making an apple pie for dinner.
11. Oswald who could not remain quiet for more than two minutes finally slipped from his chair and ran out of the room.
12. Before starting to clean the maid shook out the dust mop.
13. He swam rode and hunted but his vacation was still not a success.
14. Universal's stupendous colossal million-dollar four-star production was a complete failure.
15. Part of his nervousness I dare say arises out of his feeling of superiority to us.
16. He is of course a poet himself.
17. If I should be asked for examples of short-sighted policy I should mention these three.
18. He has no solution for unemployment low wages long hours unsanitary conditions and general discontent among the workers.
19. We shall always remember those rambling discussions of books love music politics religion and women.
20. We were amused of course by his transparent pose of bewilderment.
21. That was Mr. Burgess the mayor of Center City wasn't it?
22. My mother who likes to read popular novels asked me about the college course in contemporary literature which I was taking.
23. After the game the students tore down the goal posts broke them into small pieces and took the pieces home for souvenirs.
24. This is your fifth cup of coffee isn't it?

THE SEMICOLON

21a. Use a semicolon between the clauses of a compound sentence when they are not joined by one of the co-ordinating conjunctions.

Right: Crime cannot be hindered by punishment; it will always find some shape and outlet, unpunishable and unclosed.
—Ruskin.

He was bred to no profession; he never married; he lived alone; he never went to church; he never voted; he refused to pay a tax to the state; he ate no flesh, he drank no wine, he never knew the use of tobacco; and, though a naturalist, he used neither trap nor gun.—Emerson.

We have, during this time, learned many things; we have become acquainted with college routine; we have become an integral part of a new society.

The college is primarily not a place of the body, nor of the feelings, nor even of the will; it is, first of all, a place of the mind.—Alexander Meiklejohn.

21b. Use a semicolon between the clauses of a compound sentence joined by a co-ordinating conjunction when the clauses are long and when they contain other punctuation, or when you desire a more distinct pause than the comma would give.

You should interpret this rule in terms of sentences written by professional writers. The following examples will give you an idea of what is meant by "clauses that are long."

Right: But whether St. Mark was first bishop of Aquileia or not, St. Theodore was the first patron of the city; nor can he yet be considered as having entirely abdicated his early right, as his statue, standing on a crocodile, still companions the winged lion on the opposing pillar of the piazzetta.—Ruskin.

The old view of government as the natural field of an hereditary aristocracy has been definitely relegated to the museum of historic antiquities; and it is certainly difficult not to feel that the scale of life today is for the average man ampler than at any previous time.—Harold J. Laski.

21c. The semicolon may be used to show balance or contrast between co-ordinate sentence elements.

Right: The world embraces not only a Newton, but a Shakespeare; not only a Boyle, but a Raphael; not only a Kant, but a Beethoven; not only a Darwin, but a Carlyle.—John Tyndall.

At the same time there must be great emphasis upon truth and honesty; upon Aristotle's four great humanist ideals, temperance, fortitude, wisdom, and justice; and upon consideration for those with whom one shares this earth in common.—Frank Snowden Hopkins.

The older men speak of their teachers with more affection; the younger, with more respect.—Arthur Hobson Quinn.

21d. Use a semicolon between co-ordinate clauses joined by one of the conjunctive adverbs: *therefore, however, hence, accordingly, then, thus, still, moreover, nevertheless, furthermore, consequently.*

The practical value of this rule is limited by the fact that contemporary writers avoid beginning the second of two co-ordinate clauses with a conjunctive adverb. These connectives are used frequently, it is true, but they are placed at the beginning of a sentence or tucked away neatly in the second clause. See section 8.

Exercise 1. Look through a collection of essays recommended by your instructor and bring to class ten sentences in which semicolons are used. Try to determine the reason for using each semicolon. Would commas have served the purpose just as well? Why were not commas used?

Exercise 2. Imitating the examples given here, or others that you collect from the works of good modern essayists, construct ten sentences in which you use semicolons.

THE COLON

22a. Use the colon to introduce a long and formal quotation, an enumeration or a list of particulars, or a formal explanation.

Right: Clearing his throat, the speaker began as follows: "We look before and after, and we see, through the half-drawn folds of time . . ."

His faults are these: an uncontrollable temper, inexperience, and a lack of interest in his work.

22b. Use the colon between two clauses if the second supplements, amplifies, or interprets the first.

Right: They can insist with unanswerable force that this is absurd: that the great mass of men must be guided by rules and moved by symbols of hope and fear.—Walter Lippmann.

22c. Observe the following special uses of the colon: after a formal salutation of a letter; between the hour and minute figures of clock time; between the title of a book and the subtitle; in Biblical references.

Right: Dear Madam:
     At 8:35 a.m.
     English Fundamentals: A Handbook and Practice Leaves.
     Luke 4:5–13.

EXERCISE

Exercise 1. Get a copy of *Harper's Magazine* or *The Atlantic Monthly.* Copy five sentences in which colons are used and bring them to class for discussion. Try to determine why the colon was used in each case.

THE APOSTROPHE

23a. **Use an apostrophe and *s* to form the possessive of a noun, singular or plural, which does not end in *s*.**

Right: A man's hand, men's suits, a child's hat, children's shoes, a horse's neck, my mother-in-law's house, George's books, Nolan and Clark's store, Sears and Roebuck's catalogue.

23b. **Use the apostrophe alone to form the possessive of a plural noun ending in *s*.**

Right: Foxes' tails, boys' clothes, ladies' hats, the Smiths' house.

23c. **Use the apostrophe with *s* to form the possessive of singular nouns ending in *s*, if the resultant form is not unpleasant or difficult to pronounce; otherwise use the apostrophe alone.**

Right: Keats's poems, Jones's office, James's hat, for goodness' sake, Demosthenes' orations, Jesus' words.

23d. Use an apostrophe with *s* to form the possessive of indefinite pronouns.

Right: One's, another's, everybody's, nobody's, anybody's.

For *somebody else's* and *somebody's else*, see *else* in *Webster's New International Dictionary*, second edition.

23e. Use an apostrophe to indicate the omission of letters or figures.

Right: Doesn't, isn't, o'clock, the class of '37, I'll, it's (it is).

23f. Use an apostrophe and *s* to form the plurals of figures, letters, and words referred to as words.

Right: You haven't dotted your *i*'s or crossed your *t*'s.
Your *m*'s, *n*'s, and *u*'s look alike.
He used too many *and*'s, *so*'s, and *but*'s in his theme.
Be careful not to make your *3*'s look like *8*'s.

Many present-day writers, however, omit the apostrophe in some of these forms.

EXERCISES

Exercise 1. Insert apostrophes wherever they are necessary in the following sentences.

1. At seven oclock the doors of the boys dormitory swung open, and a crowd of noisy youngsters trooped out.
2. Sallys coat and Donnas gloves had disappeared.
3. Its still anybodys game.
4. If its not too much to ask, will you remember to bring your roommates dictionary to class?
5. I agreed with the deans remark that ones religion was ones own private affair.

6. Everybodys business is usually nobodys business.
7. Its two oclock; Ill be late for the meeting of the class of 27.
8. The Joness dog killed one of the Davises chickens.
9. Your theme is full of *buts* and *ands*.
10. He received three weeks pay and left the camp.

Exercise 2. Write the possessive singular and the possessive plural of the following.

Example: girl   girl's   girls'

1. cat
2. woman
3. attorney
4. reader
5. contributor
6. Smith
7. Jones
8. Powers
9. creditor
10. soldier

QUOTATION MARKS

24a. Use double quotation marks to enclose a direct quotation.

Right: "I did not hear you," Dorothy replied. "I was in the other room."
George said, "I saw him enter this building."

Do not leave out one set of quotation marks. Quotation marks come in pairs, one set at the beginning and one set at the end of every quoted part.

Wrong: "Oh, how can I tell? he objected. What's the good of asking me that now?"
Right: "Oh, how can I tell?" he objected. "What's the good of asking me that now?"

If a quotation consists of several sentences, place quotation marks at the beginning and at the end of the entire quotation. Do not enclose each sentence in quotation marks.

Right: George replied: "Yes, that is his weakness. I have pleaded with him; he only laughs at me. I have appealed to his sense of honor, but he is too selfish to see the rights of others."

24b. If a quotation consists of several paragraphs, begin each paragraph with quotation marks but place them at the end of the last paragraph only.

In writing dialogue, use a separate paragraph for every change of speaker. Short descriptive, narrative, or explanatory passages may be paragraphed with dialogue, especially if they are placed between sentences of dialogue spoken by the same person.

Right: "Good morning, Mr. Lovett. I came to find out what you propose to do about my son." Her manner conveyed the impression that she expected him to bluster, perhaps to use bad language.

       Professor Lovett smiled mechanically. "Good morning," he replied. "Your son? I am afraid I do not understand."

       "I think you do understand," she said meaningly. "You failed my son in your course in Shakespeare."

24c. Do not put quotation marks around an indirect quotation.

Wrong: The teacher asked "how many had their themes ready."
Right: The teacher asked how many had their themes ready.

24d. Use single quotation marks to enclose a quotation within a quotation.

Right: Mary replied, "The dean said to me, 'No report has reached this office.' "

24e. Use quotation marks to enclose words spoken of as words or slang expressions used in formal writing, to call attention to a word used in a special sense, or to set off phrases borrowed from other writers and used in your own work.

For the more commonly used method of indicating words spoken of as words, see section 16c. See also exercise 2 at the end of this section.

Right: Gertrude thought I should have written "preying" mantis instead of "praying" mantis.

"Style" and "form" are not separate qualities that can be thrown over "content" like a raincoat.

National greed has disguised itself in mandates to govern "inferior" races.

Mrs. Henderson politely asked where one could find women "living their own lives."

He is the sort of person who wears "galluses" and smokes a pipe.

Avoid sprinkling your writing with quotation marks. Remember that quotation marks do not justify or excuse slang. If you are sure that some slang expression is more vivid or more eloquent than respectable English, use it, by all means, but use it without shame or apology. And do not use quotation marks for proverbs or for phrases so familiar that they have become common property.

24f. Place the comma and period inside the quotation marks.

Right: "Yes," she repeated. "Marriage is not a word; it is a sentence."

Louis Untermeyer once said that "violet," "laughter," and "willow" are three of the most musical words in the English language.

24g. Place the question mark, the semicolon, the colon, and the exclamation point inside the quotation marks if they belong to the quoted part; if they do not, place them outside the quotation marks.

Right: Did you hear him say, "I won't go"?

"Well, I like that!" she exclaimed in anger.

"It is as much a trade," says La Bruyère, "to make a book as it is to make a clock"; in short, literature is largely a matter of technique.—Irving Babbitt.

24h. For introductory or explanatory phrases (like *he said*) with dialogue use the marks of punctuation which the structure of the sentence calls for.

Right: "Sister," she replied sweetly, "did you ever hear of Cleopatra?"

Shouts of "Turn out, Americans! Turn out!" and the sound of many running feet rang through the lanes.

She continued breathlessly: "They are going to fight. I heard them shouting and cursing at each other. Please do something, Father . . ."

"But you said—" she began, but suddenly turned aside in confusion.

Mr. Bromley bowed, "An honor, sir."

"Howard!" a voice called from the garden.

"The price is not a matter of profit," he said, stiffly; "it is a matter of principle."

Exercise 1. Look through an issue of some magazine of the better kind and bring to class five examples of unusual uses of quotation marks. Look for broken or elliptical sentences and for sentences which are part quoted matter and part not quoted.

Exercise 2. Find an essay about language or words. Your instructor may save you time by directing you to one. Bring to class five examples of words referred to as words, or of slang expressions enclosed in quotation marks. You may find that in one essay words referred to as words are always italicized; in another essay they are always enclosed in quotation marks. What do you find to be true in the essay you examine?

Exercise 3. Point out the incorrect uses of quotation marks in the following sentences.

1. "The message is important—in a way, Dorothy replied. Let us try the Western Union office at the hotel."
2. He departed for the country from which "no traveler returns."
3. "Where are you going"? she shouted.
4. It was his luck to find all thrilling episodes "continued in our next," until he began to feel like a tramp peering into the back windows of college life.
5. "I want to take my hair down, she said, and have a heart-to-heart talk with myself."
6. "I wonder who that man is," he mused. "He seemed hurt by what I said."
7. The speaker inquired "how many had voted the Republican ticket at the last election."
8. A college man who wants to "be in the swim" must "work up a line."

9. "Santa Barbara is a charming place," I replied. The most beautiful place in California.

10. "Tolstoy was lost in the creative mood when he made 'Natasha,' 'Pierre,' and 'Anna,'" said John Galsworthy in an address entitled "On Expression."

THE DASH

25a. Use the dash to indicate a sudden, abrupt break in thought or structure.

Right: This song—how many remember it?—once swept the country.

He said—how could he?—that he was tired of me.

He asked me—but I cannot repeat his words.

The break in the structure of the sentence may be caused by an explanatory or parenthetical phrase or clause, by an appositive, or by a summary.

Right: "The West"—there were successively many of them—unlike the colonial America, was of almost limitless extent and wealth.—James Truslow Adams.

And New Orleans—or rather the Creole quarter of New Orleans, for the rest of the city is commonplace—is delicious, suggesting old France and Spain, yet a France and Spain strangely transmuted in this new clime.—James Bryce.

The American frontier is sharply distinguished from the European frontier—a fortified boundary line running through dense populations.—Frederick Jackson Turner.

Directly we go wrong—directly, that is to say, we cease to act in a way of which society approves—conscience begins to nag.—C. E. M. Joad.

That train of reasoning is what logicians call a syllogism, and has all its various parts and terms—its major premise, its minor premise, and its conclusion.—Thomas Henry Huxley.

25b. Use the dash to indicate hesitation or uncertainty in speech, or a speech abruptly broken off.

Right: "I wish—I wish you'd let him know—please do—it was an accident."
"I don't know whether she would like—"

THE HYPHEN

26a. Use hyphens with two or more words forming a compound adjective before a noun.[1]

Right: A worn-out metaphor, a heaven-sent blessing, a double-bottomed boat, a red-hot poker, a foul-smelling pipe, a long-delayed answer, a heart-to-heart talk, an old-fashioned woman, a wide-open door, the dark-blue sea, the well-known scientist, in up-to-date condition, a ten-foot pole, a six-by-eight sheet, a two-thirds majority.

Do not hyphenate compound modifiers used in the predicate; compounds consisting of two proper nouns; compounds in which an adverb ending in *-ly* is used.

Right: The poet was well known. His information was up to date. The horse responded to the softly spoken command. He is a United States citizen. He inspected several New Jersey schools.

26b. Use hyphens with compound numbers from twenty-one to ninety-nine.

Right: Fifty-five men, twenty-seven dollars, seventy-three cents. One hundred and twenty-nine.

[1] Dictionaries and other authorities often disagree about the use of the hyphen.

26c. Use a hyphen at the end of a line to mark the division of a word when the remainder of the word is carried to the next line. See section 15.

26d. Use a hyphen with the following classes of words:

1. With the prefixes *ex-*, *self-*, but rarely with other prefixes: ex-president, ex-convict, self-starter, self-adornment.
2. To avoid doubling a vowel or tripling a consonant: pre-existence, re-enter, re-echo, semi-independent, semi-invalid, shell-leaf, skill-less, thrill-less, bell-like, co-operative, co-ordination.
3. With groups making or containing prepositional phrases: son-in-law, father-in-law, man-of-war.
4. To prevent confusion with similar words: re-form (*cf. reform*), re-cover (*cf. recover*), re-create (*cf. recreate*).

When in doubt as to the correct form of a compound word, consult a good dictionary. You will find, however, that dictionaries and style manuals do not always agree.

EXERCISE

Exercise 1. With the aid of a dictionary determine which of the following words are written solid, which with a hyphen, and which separate.

1. all right	9. anti typhoid
2. all American team	10. air driven pump
3. all inclusive examination	11. air base
4. any body	12. base ball
5. any how	13. book store
6. any time	14. by pass
7. any more	15. by law
8. anti Fascist	16. dining room

17. drug store
18. every body
19. every thing
20. every time
21. every where
22. eye opening answer
23. eye shade
24. foot ball
25. full back
26. good night
27. good by
28. half crazed animal
29. half intoxicated man
30. half back
31. half cousin
32. in as much as
33. note book
34. north east
35. one armed paper hanger
36. out doors
37. post office
38. quarter back
39. re written theme
40. score board
41. score card
42. some thing
43. some body
44. sharp tempered
45. text book
46. un balanced
47. under graduate
48. upper class man
49. week end trip
50. well chaperoned dance

PARENTHESES, BRACKETS

27a. Use parentheses to enclose material that is supplementary, explanatory, or interpretive.

The general principle to follow in the use of parenthetical marks is that commas set off material which is fairly close to the thought of the sentence; dashes set off material which is more loosely connected; and marks of parenthesis are used to indicate the most distant parenthetical relation. This principle is not observed by all writers. A study of a group of modern essays will probably reveal that some writers seldom use parentheses, others use them frequently but logically, and still others use them when the mood comes upon them. But the privilege of being moody and irrational in punctuation is denied to young writers.

Right: Houston was born in Cairo (Illinois, not Egypt) in 1897.

　　　　She brought with her a reputation for originality, or eccentricity, or downright willfullness (whatever one wished to call it).

　　　　There is really nothing (except the salary) that attracts me to my present occupation.

　　　　The pruned rose plant (see fig. 7) will have more under ground than above.

If other marks of punctuation are necessary with parentheses, place the comma, the semicolon, or the period after the second parenthesis; place a question mark or an exclamation point before it.

Right: Your opinion is as good as mine (theoretically at least).

　　　　Everyone listened attentively (imagine falling asleep during one of his sermons!).

　　　　When George brought me the orchids (it was George, wasn't it?), I realized that my destiny had arrived.

Do not use parentheses to show that you want to cancel or delete any part of your writing. Draw a line through the part you want to cross out.

27b. Use brackets to enclose corrections, interpolations, and supplied omissions added to a quotation by the person quoting.

Right: Santayana says: "Religion lay on him [Dickens] like the weight of the atmosphere, sixteen pounds to the square inch, yet never noticed nor mentioned."

　　　　The President [Harding] offered him an appointment in the diplomatic service.

　　　　The battle began on the 6th [5th] of August, 1916.

EXERCISES

Exercise 1. Look through a copy of a good magazine and bring to class five sentences in which parentheses or brackets are used. Try to determine the exact reason for the presence of these marks.

Exercise 2. Write five sentences of your own in which you use parentheses.

Exercise 3. Are parentheses correctly used in the following sentences?

1. It is their resentment, not their judgment (if they have any), that speaks this language.
2. I missed his kindness, and I missed his crossness, and wished him to be alive again, to be quarreling with him (for we quarreled sometimes), rather than not have him again.
3. Soon after this another sociable little pilgrim (*motacilla domestica*, house wren) also arrives from the south.
4. Man was made to stay at home (why else are there so many millions born who never dreamt of stirring from it?)—to vegetate, to be rooted to the earth, to cling to his local prejudices, to luxuriate in the follies of his forefathers.
5. George Sand says neatly, that "Art is not a study of positive reality" (*actuality* were the fitter word), "but a seeking after ideal truth."

SPELLING

Let us extend a word of encouragement to the poor spellers: The inability to spell is not an inherited disease. It is not due to malnutrition, or to improper functioning of one of the ductless glands. It is indeed a curse, but the curse can be lifted by proper incantations—one is almost tempted to say by the use of proper spells! If you are a bad speller, you must begin by refusing to admit defeat. Spelling can be learned. You can learn it.

You can learn how to spell by observing the following directions:

1. Memorize the spelling rules and use them constantly.

2. Whenever your attention is called to a misspelled word, look it up in a good dictionary and learn to pronounce it by syllables. Some of your trouble with spelling comes from an incorrect pronunciation of words. Keep a list of the words that you misspell. Review this list frequently.

3. Whenever you look up a word in a dictionary, copy it carefully, forming each letter as plainly as you can. Some of your trouble with spelling comes from your bad handwriting. It is possible that you have used illegible handwriting as a shiftless substitute for learning how to spell.

4. After you have tried to photograph the word on your mind, write it from memory on a sheet of paper. Check your spelling with the correct spelling.

5. Whenever you misspell a word, look through the spelling rules to see what rule might have helped you to remember the correct spelling.

PRONUNCIATION

28. Pronounce words correctly.

The following is a brief list of words often misspelled because of incorrect pronunciation:

Right	*Wrong*	*Right*	*Wrong*
accidentally	(accidently)	literature	(liteture)
athlete	(athelete)	occasion	(ocassion)
athletics	(atheletics)	optimistic	(optomistic)
arctic	(artic)	particular	(paticular)
barbarous	(barbarious)	perform	(preform)
boundary	(boundry)	perseverance	(perserverance)
candidate	(canidate)	perspiration	(prespiration)
disastrous	(disasterous)	practically	(pratically)
dissatisfied	(disatisfied)	probably	(probally)
February	(Febuary)	quantity	(quanity)
formerly	(formally)	recognize	(reconize)
government	(goverment)	representative	(represenative)
hindrance	(hinderance)	sophomore	(sophmore)
history	(histry)	strictly	(strickly)
interesting	(intresting)	surprise	(supprise)
introduce	(interduce)	temperament	(temperment)
laboratory	(labratory)	tragedy	(tradegy)

FINAL –E

29. A word ending in silent e generally drops the e before a suffix beginning with a vowel, but it retains the e before a suffix beginning with a consonant.

Drop -e

arrange	+	ing	=	arranging
arrive	+	ing	=	arriving

Drop -e

admire	+	ation	=	admiration
admire	+	able	=	admirable
allure	+	ing	=	alluring
believe	+	ing	=	believing
care	+	ing	=	caring
come	+	ing	=	coming
deplore	+	able	=	deplorable
dine	+	ing	=	dining
desire	+	ous	=	desirous
explore	+	ation	=	exploration
fame	+	ous	=	famous
imagine	+	ary	=	imaginary
imagine	+	able	=	imaginable
love	+	able	=	lovable
lose	+	ing	=	losing
move	+	able	=	movable

Retain -e

arrange	+	ment	=	arrangement
care	+	ful	=	careful
force	+	ful	=	forceful
hate	+	ful	=	hateful
like	+	ness	=	likeness
move	+	ment	=	movement

But after *c* or *g*, if the suffix begins with *a* or *o*, the *e* is retained to preserve the soft sound of *c* or *g*.

advantage	+	ous	=	advantageous
change	+	able	=	changeable
courage	+	ous	=	courageous
notice	+	able	=	noticeable
outrage	+	ous	=	outrageous
peace	+	able	=	peaceable
service	+	able	=	serviceable

There are a number of exceptions: hoeing, shoeing, toeing (to guard against mispronunciation); dyeing, singeing (to distinguish from dying, singing); duly, argument, truly, awful, abridgment, acknowledgment, judgment.

IE OR EI

30. In words with *ie* or *ei* when the sound is long *ee*, use *i* before *e* except after *c*.

i before e

achieve	cashier	piece	shriek
apiece	field	pierce	siege
belief	fierce	priest	thief
believe	frieze	relieve	wield
brief	grief	retrieve	yield
besiege	niece	reprieve	
chief	pier	shield	

except after c

ceiling	conceive	deceive	receipt
conceit	deceit	perceive	receive

Exceptions: either, neither, financier, weird, species, seize, leisure.

These may be remembered by arranging the words in a sentence: "Neither financier seized either species of weird leisure."

FINAL CONSONANT

31. In words of one syllable and words accented on the last syllable, ending in a single consonant preceded by a single vowel, double the final consonant before a suffix beginning with a vowel.

Examples:

drop (word of one syllable) + *ed* (suffix beginning with a vowel) = dropped.
control (accented on the last syllable) + *ed* (suffix) = controlled.
benefit (not accented on the last syllable) + *ed* (suffix) = benefited.
confer (accented on the last syllable) + *ed* (suffix) = conferred.
confer (notice the shift in accent) + *ence* (suffix) = conference.

Where the dictionary gives two forms, such as *canceled, cancelled*, notice that the preferred form, given first, always follows the rule. See *Webster's New International Dictionary*, second edition, page lxxix, note at the bottom of the first column.

Suffix begins with a vowel
(One syllable)

brag	— bragging		man	— mannish
cram	— cramming		plan	— planning
drag	— dragging		snap	— snapped
din	— dinning		sin	— sinning
drop	— dropped		stop	— stopped
cut	— cutting		quit	— quitting
bid	— bidding		rob	— robbed
flag	— flagged		stab	— stabbed
get	— getting		whip	— whipped
clan	— clannish		glad	— gladdest

(Accent on last syllable)

admit	— admitted		equip	— equipped
begin	— beginning		commit	— committee
commit	— committed		occur	— occurrence
concur	— concurring		submit	— submitted
confer	— conferring		compel	— compelled

(Not accented on last syllable)

prefer	— preference		benefit	— benefited
refer	— reference		profit	— profitable
happen	— happened		marvel	— marvelous

Suffix begins with a consonant

glad	— gladness	sin	— sinful
fat	— fatness	equip	— equipment
man	— manhood		

FINAL –Y

32. A noun ending in y preceded by a consonant forms the plural in *ies;* a verb ending in y preceded by a consonant forms its present tense, third person singular, in *ies.*

Examples:

(Ending in *y* preceded by a consonant)

baby, babies	sky, skies	fairy, fairies
marry, marries	copy, copies	fly, flies

(Ending in *y* preceded by a vowel)

attorney, attorneys	valley, valleys	delay, delays
destroy, destroys	enjoy, enjoys	chimney, chimneys

SIMILAR FORMS

33. Learn the distinction between certain words similar or identical in sound.

accept, except	breath, breathe
accent, ascent, assent	canvas, canvass
advice, advise	capital, capitol
affect, effect	coarse, course
all ready, already	cite, site, sight
all together, altogether	complement, compliment
altar, alter	choose, chose
berth, birth	consul, council, counsel

dairy, diary	peace, piece
desert, dessert	plane, plain
decent, descend, descent	precede, proceed
device, devise	presence, presents
dining, dinning	principal, principle
formally, formerly	quiet, quite
forth, fourth	respectfully, respectively
hear, here	right, rite, write
instance, instants	shone, shown
irrelevant, irreverent	stationary, stationery
its, it's	staid, stayed
knew, new	straight, strait
know, no	statue, statute, stature
later, latter	their, there, they're
lead, led	threw, through
lose, loose	till, until
of, off	to, too, two
past, passed	weather, whether

SPELLING LIST

34. The following is a list of words often misspelled by college students. Memorize ten of these words every day.

1. abbreviate	11. accustom
2. absence	12. achievement
3. absorption	13. acknowledge
4. absurd	14. acquaintance
5. accept	15. acquitted
6. accidentally	16. across
7. accommodate	17. additionally
8. accomplish	18. address
9. accompanying	19. affect
10. accumulate	20. aggravate

21. all right
22. alley
23. allies
24. always
25. almost
26. although
27. altogether
28. alumna (ae)
29. alumnus (i)
30. amateur

31. among
32. amount
33. analysis
34. analyze
35. angel
36. angle
37. annual
38. answer
39. apartment
40. apology

41. apparatus
42. apparent
43. appearance
44. appropriate
45. arctic
46. argument
47. arising
48. arithmetic
49. arrangement
50. artillery

51. ascend
52. association
53. athlete
54. athletics
55. attendance

56. audience
57. auxiliary
58. awkward
59. bachelor
60. balance

61. balloon
62. banana
63. barbarous
64. battalion
65. becoming
66. beggar
67. begging
68. beginning
69. believing
70. benefited

71. biscuit
72. boundaries
73. brilliant
74. Britain
75. Britannica
76. bureau
77. burglar
78. business
79. busy
80. cafeteria

81. calendar
82. candidate
83. can't
84. capital
85. capitol
86. career
87. carburetor
88. cemetery
89. certain
90. changeable

91. changing
92. chaperon
93. characteristic
94. chauffeur
95. choose
96. chose
97. clothes
98. coarse
99. column
100. coming

101. commission
102. committed
103. committee
104. comparative
105. compelled
106. competitive
107. complement
108. compliment
109. compulsory
110. concede

111. conceivable
112. confidently
113. confidentially
114. conference
115. conferred
116. connoisseur
117. conqueror
118. conscience
119. conscientious
120. conscious

121. consciousness
122. continuous
123. controlled
124. convenient
125. courteous

126. criticism
127. criticize
128. curiosity
129. cylinder
130. dealt

131. debater
132. deceive
133. describe
134. description
135. desperate
136. desert
137. dessert
138. develop
139. development
140. dictionary

141. difference
142. dilapidated
143. dining room
144. disagree
145. disappear
146. disappoint
147. disastrous
148. discipline
149. dissatisfied
150. dissipate

151. divide
152. doctor
153. dormitory
154. during
155. ecstasy
156. eighth
157. eligible
158. eliminate
159. embarrass
160. eminent

161. emphasize
162. employee
163. encouraging
164. engineer
165. enthusiastic
166. equipped
167. equivalent
168. erroneous
169. especially
170. exaggerated

171. exceed
172. excellent
173. except
174. exceptionally
175. exhaust
176. exhilarate
177. existence
178. experience
179. explanation
180. extraordinary

181. extremely
182. familiar
183. fascinate
184. February
185. fiery
186. finally
187. financier
188. foreign
189. forestry
190. formally

191. formerly
192. forty
193. fourth
194. frantically
195. fraternities

196. friend
197. gauge
198. ghost
199. generally
200. government

201. governor
202. grammar
203. grievous
204. guard
205. guidance
206. handkerchief
207. harass
208. having
209. height
210. hindrance

211. hoping
212. humorous
213. hypocrisy
214. illiterate
215. imaginary
216. imagination
217. immediately
218. impromptu
219. incidentally
220. incredible

221. independence
222. indictment
223. indispensable
224. inevitable
225. infinite
226. ingenious
227. ingenuous
228. innocence
229. innocuous
230. inoculate

231. instance
232. instants
233. intellectual
234. intelligence
235. intentionally
236. intercede
237. interesting
238. irrelevant
239. irresistible
240. itself

241. judgment
242. knowledge
243. laboratory
244. laid
245. legitimate
246. liable
247. library
248. lightning
249. likely
250. liquefy

251. literature
252. loneliness
253. loose
254. lose
255. lying
256. maintain
257. maintenance
258. maneuver
259. marriage
260. mathematics

261. mattress
262. meant
263. merely
264. millionaire
265. miniature

266. minute
267. mischievous
268. misspelled
269. murmuring
270. muscle

271. naive
272. naturally
273. necessary
274. neither
275. nevertheless
276. ninety
277. ninth
278. noticeable
279. nowadays
280. oblige

281. obstacle
282. occasion
283. occasionally
284. occur
285. occurred
286. occurrence
287. omitted
288. omission
289. oneself
290. opportunity.

291. optimistic
292. origin
293. original
294. outrageous
295. paid
296. pamphlet
297. parallel
298. paralysis
299. parliament
300. participle

301. particularly
302. partner
303. pastime
304. peaceable
305. perceive
306. perform
307. perhaps
308. permissible
309. perseverance
310. personal

311. personnel
312. perspiration
313. physically
314. picnicking
315. planned
316. pleasant
317. politics
318. possession
319. practically
320. prairie

321. precede
322. precedence
323. preceding
324. preference
325. preferred
326. prejudice
327. preparation
328. presence
329. presents
330. prevalent

331. principal
332. principle
333. privilege
334. probably
335. proceed

336. professor
337. pronunciation
338. propeller
339. prove
340. quantity

341. questionnaire
342. quiet
343. quite
344. rarefy
345. really
346. receive
347. recognize
348. recommend
349. reference
350. referred

351. regard
352. religious
353. repetition
354. representative
355. respectfully
356. respectively
357. restaurant
358. rhythm
359. rhythmical
360. ridiculous

361. sacrilegious
362. sandwich
363. saxophone
364. schedule
365. secretary
366. seize
367. sense
368. separate
369. sergeant
370. severely

371. siege
372. similar
373. simultaneous
374. soliloquy
375. sophomore
376. specifically
377. specimen
378. speech
379. stationary
380. stationery

381. statue
382. stature
383. statute
384. stopping
385. stretch
386. strictly
387. studying
388. successful
389. superintendent
390. supersede

391. surprise
392. syllable
393. temperament
394. temperature
395. their

396. there
397. they're
398. thorough
399. throughout
400. together

401. tragedy
402. tries
403. truly
404. Tuesday
405. unanimous
406. undoubtedly
407. unnecessary
408. until
409. using
410. usually

411. vilify
412. village
413. villain
414. weather
415. weird
416. whether
417. writing
418. wholly
419. women
420. you're

WORDS

USE OF THE DICTIONARY

Every college student should own a good desk-size dictionary. When he has occasion to consult an unabridged dictionary, he should use either the *Webster's New International* or the Funk and Wagnalls *Standard*. Copies of these are usually to be found in the reference room of the college library.

For desk use the following dictionaries are usually recommended: *Webster's Collegiate*, the Funk and Wagnalls *College Standard*, the *Winston Simplified*, and *Macmillan's Modern Dictionary*.

35a. Use the dictionary to help you determine the exact meaning of a word.

In *Webster's Collegiate:* [1]

1. The order of definitions is that of the historical order of development of the meanings; that is, the earliest are given first, and the present-day meanings are given last.
2. Heavy-faced Arabic numerals are used to number definitions when a word has several different meanings.
3. Heavy-faced letters are used to group definitions that are closely related to each other.
4. Synonyms are given at the end of the entry.

[1] Quotations and illustrations from *Webster's Collegiate Dictionary* are reprinted by permission of the publishers of *Webster's Collegiate Dictionary*, fifth edition, copyright, 1936, by G. & C. Merriam Co., Springfield, Mass.

In the Funk and Wagnalls *College Standard:* [1]

1. The order of definitions is the order of usage, in which the most common meaning is given first.
2. Synonyms are given at the end of the entry.

In the *Winston Simplified:* [2]

1. The order of definitions is the order of usage; that is, "the meaning which is now most commonly and immediately attached to the word defined" is listed first.
2. Synonyms are given at the end of the entry.

In *Macmillan's Modern Dictionary:*

1. If a word may be used as different parts of speech, the definitions follow the proper label indicating the use of the word.

35b. Use the dictionary to find the correct spelling of a word.

In *Webster's Collegiate:*

1. When two permissible spellings are given side by side, the preferred one is given first:

> among, amongst
> program, programme

2. When two spellings are given in different places in the vocabulary, the preferred form carries the etymology and definitions:

> gauge, gage

In the Funk and Wagnalls *College Standard:*

1. When a word is spelled in two or more ways, the simpler form is preferred.

---

[1] Quotations and illustrations from the *College Standard Dictionary* are reprinted by permission of Funk and Wagnalls Company, publishers.

[2] Quotations and illustrations from the *Winston Simplified Dictionary* are reprinted by permission of The John C. Winston Company, publishers.

2. The simplified spellings recommended by the American Philological Association and the Philological Society of England are marked by a superior (^{P}):

du′ra-bl(e^P ; phos′phate, fos′fate^P.

3. The simplified spellings recommended by the Simplified Spelling Board are marked by a superior (^{S}):

de-serv(e^S ; phos′phor-us, fos′for-us^S.

In the *Winston Simplified:*

1. When a word is spelled in more than one way, each form is listed in its proper alphabetical place.
2. The etymology and definition appear with the preferred form.
3. A brief definition appears with the permissible form.
4. The definition of the permissible form is followed by "Also" and the preferred form, marked *Pfd. S.* (preferred spelling):

gage . . . See gauge, *Pfd. S.*

In *Macmillan's Modern Dictionary:*

1. When two permissible spellings are listed side by side, the preferred form is given first.
2. When two spellings are listed in different places in the vocabulary, the definitions are given with the preferred form.

esthete, esthetic, *see* aesthete, aesthetic, etc.

35c. Use the dictionary to find the correct pronunciation of a word.

In *Webster's Collegiate:*

1. The pronunciation is given, in parentheses, after the word.
2. The word is respelled in the Webster phonetic alphabet.
3. A brief key to this alphabet is printed at the bottom of every two pages facing each other; a full key is given in the guide to pronunciation.
4. When two or more pronunciations are given, the one given first is preferred.

In the Funk and Wagnalls *College Standard:*

1. The pronunciation is given, by respelling in two different ways, following the word.
2. The first respelling uses the Revised Scientific Alphabet.
3. The second respelling uses the Textbook Key.
4. The key words which explain the sounds used in both keys are given at the top of every two pages facing each other; a complete guide to pronunciation is given in the introductory pages.
5. When two differing pronunciations are given, both are sanctioned by usage.

In the *Winston Simplified:*

1. The pronunciation is given, in parentheses, after the word.
2. The word is respelled according to a phonetic key which is printed at the bottom of every two pages facing each other.
3. If two pronunciations are given, the alternative pronunciation is given second.

In *Macmillan's Modern Dictionary:*

1. The pronunciation is given in parentheses after the word.
2. The phonetic spelling used to indicate pronunciation is explained in a "Key to Pronunciation," pp. xi–xii.
3. A short key is printed at the bottom of every two pages facing each other.
4. Where two pronunciations are permissible, both are indicated; the preferred one is given first.

suave (swäv; swāv)

35d. Use the dictionary to find the source or etymology of a word.

In *Webster's Collegiate:*

1. The etymology is given, in brackets, before the definition.
2. In the etymology the words in italic type are those from which

the word is derived; the definitions of the italicized words are in roman type.

3. The history of a word is generally traced back as far as it can be with certainty:

> Nice. . . [OF., ignorant, fool, fr. L. *nescius* ignorant, fr. *nescire* to be ignorant, fr. *ne-* not + *scire* to know.]

In the Funk and Wagnalls *College Standard:*

1. The etymology is given, in brackets, after the definition.
2. In the etymology the words in italic type are those from which the word is derived; the definitions of the italicized words are in roman type.
3. The history of the word is traced back as far as possible:

> nice. . . [F., < L. *nescius*, ignorant, < *ne*, not, + *scio*, know.]

In the *Winston Simplified:*

1. The etymology is given, in heavy brackets, before the definition.
2. Source words are printed in italics; definitions of the italicized words are in roman type.
3. Words are traced to their source:

> nice. . . [M.E. = stupid < O.F. < Lat. *nescius*, ignorant, < *ne*, not + *scire*, to know].

In *Macmillan's Modern Dictionary:*

1. The etymology is given in brackets after the definitions.

> desiccate. . . [L. *dēsicco* < *de-* + *siccus*, dry.]

35e. Use the dictionary to find the correct accent.

In *Webster's Collegiate:*

1. A heavy accent mark ['] is placed after the syllable on which the chief stress falls; a light accent mark is placed after the syllable on which there is a secondary stress:

> co'in·cide'

In the Funk and Wagnalls *College Standard:*

1. The single accent mark ['] indicates the chief or primary accent;
   the double accent mark ["] indicates the secondary accent:

co"in-cide'

In the *Winston Simplified:*

1. The principal stress is indicated by a single accent mark [']
   placed after the syllable; the secondary stress is indicated by a
   double accent mark:

co-in-cide (ko"in-sid')

In *Macmillan's Modern Dictionary:*

1. The principal stress is indicated by a heavy accent mark ['] at
   the end of the syllable.
2. The secondary stress is indicated by a light accent mark ['].

en-cy'clo-pe'di-a

**35f. Use the dictionary to find how a word is correctly
divided into syllables (to find where a word can be
broken at the end of a line).**

In *Webster's Collegiate:*

1. Syllabic divisions of a word are marked by: a centered period
   after an unaccented syllable; an accent mark, without a centered
   period, after an accented syllable; a hyphen between hyphenated
   words.

nev'er · the · less'
gen'tle · man-at-arms'

In Funk and Wagnalls *College Standard:*

1. Syllabic divisions of a word are marked by: a single hyphen after
   an unaccented syllable; an accent mark, without the hyphen,

after an accented syllable; a double hyphen between hyphenated words.

nev''er-the-less'
gen'tle-man=at=arms''

In the *Winston Simplified:*

1. In the vocabulary, a light hyphen is used to mark division into syllables; in the pronunciation, the light hyphen is omitted wherever an accent is used, and a long hyphen, retained with an accent, is used in compound words.

nev-er-the-less
fa-ther—in—law

In *Macmillan's Modern Dictionary:*

1. Syllabic divisions of a word are marked by: a hyphen after an unaccented syllable; an accent mark, without a hyphen, after an accented syllable; a long hyphen between hyphenated words.

beau'ti-fi-ca'tion
fa'ther—in—law'

35g. Use a dictionary to find whether a word is in good use.

Examples from *Webster's Collegiate:*

1. pinch: 4. *Slang.* A theft; arrest; raid.
2. burgle: *Humorous.* to burglarize.
3. gent: *Vulgar.* Shortened form of GENTLEMAN.
4. burn: *Chiefly Scot. & Dial.* A brook; a rivulet.

Examples from the *College Standard:*

1. pot: [Slang] A person of consequence.
2. aroint: [Archaic or Poet.] To betake out of the way.
3. square: 8. [Colloq.] Solid; full; satisfying.

Examples from the *Winston Simplified:*

1. dicker: *U.S.Colloq.*, to barter or trade on a small scale.
2. shiner: *Colloq.*, . . . 2, a black eye.
3. cracksman: *Slang*, a burglar.

Examples from *Macmillan's Modern Dictionary:*

1. girl: sweetheart (*colloq.*).
2. jack: (*slang*) money.

35h. Use the dictionary to find out whether a compound is to be written solid, hyphenated, or separate.

Examples from *Webster's Collegiate:*

1. quarterback, self-confidence, drugstore, notebook, note paper, X-ray, all right.

Examples from the *College Standard:*

1. quarter-back, self-confidence, drug-store, note-book, note-paper, X-rays, backboard, housekeeper, house-fly.

Examples from the *Winston Simplified:*

1. quarter back, self-confidence, drug store, notebook, note paper, X ray, housekeeper, house fly.

Examples from *Macmillan's Modern Dictionary:*

1. quarter back, quarter-back, drugstore, note-book, note paper, housefly.

35i. Use the dictionary to find synonyms for a word.

Examples from *Webster's Collegiate:*

1. Courage: daring, fearlessness, audacity, mettle, pluck.
2. Financial: fiscal, monetary, pecuniary.

Examples from the *College Standard:*

1. House: abode, building, cabin, cot, cottage, domicil, dwelling, dwelling-place, edifice, habitation, hall, home, hovel, hut, manor, mansion, palace, residence, shanty, villa.
2. Discover: ascertain, descry, detect, discern, disclose, expose, ferret out, find, find out, invent.

Examples from the *Winston Simplified:*

1. Courage: intrepidity, fortitude, valor. (See bravery.)
2. Reply: rejoinder, repartee, retort, answer, response.

Examples from *Macmillan's Modern Dictionary:*

1. Synonyms are given among the definitions, as, for example: **courage,** bravery, fearlessness; **mishap,** evil hap or chance, ill luck, misfortune.

35j. Use the dictionary to get information about correct idioms.

Examples from *Webster's Collegiate:*

1. Fight shy of.
2. Hang together.
3. Leave off.
4. Lay by the heels.
5. Lay hold of.
6. Take stock.
7. Take the floor.
8. Touch up.
9. Wash one's hands of.
10. Work one's passage.

Examples from the *College Standard:*

1. To go to the wall.
2. To go under.
3. To eat humble pie.
4. To eat one's words.
5. To put heads together.
6. To take after.
7. To take to heart.
8. To strike a balance.
9. To strike dumb.
10. To hit off.

Examples from the *Winston Simplified:*

1. To get along.
2. To take after.
3. With a grain of salt.
4. To spread the table.
5. To be struck with pity.
6. To try one's hand at something.
7. To lend a hand.
8. To go bail.
9. They struck into the woods.
10. To fall flat.

Examples from *Macmillan's Modern Dictionary:*

1. Go in for.
2. Get one's back up.
3. Lay hold of.
4. Lead off.
5. Sing the same song.
6. Go west.
7. Get the hang of.
8. Lead to the altar.
9. Show the cloven hoof.
10. Turn the scale.

35k. Use the dictionary to get information about plurals of nouns and the principal parts of verbs.

In *Webster's Collegiate:*

1. Inflectional forms are given when they are irregular or present difficulties of spelling or pronunciation.
2. Examples are:
   > index, *pl.* INDEXES, INDICES
   > deer, *sing. &° pl.*
   > ox, *pl.* OXEN, *rarely* OX
   > brother-in-law, *pl.* -ERS-IN-LAW

   > blow, BLEW; BLOWN; BLOWING
   > dive, DIVED; DIVING. *Colloq. past, chiefly*
   > *U.S.,* DOVE

In the *College Standard:*

1. Inflectional forms are given where they are not formed regularly.
2. Examples are:
   > appendix [-DIXES or -DICES]
   > deer [DEER, *pl.*]
   > ox [OXEN, *pl.*]

hang [HUNG or HANGED; HANGING]
dive [DIVED or (*Colloq.*) DOVE; DIVING]

In the *Winston Simplified:*

1. Inflectional forms are given whenever they are in any way irregular.
2. Examples are:

    mouse [*pl.* mice].
    deer [*pl.* deer].
    brother-in-law [*pl.* brothers-in-law].

    swim [*p.t.* swam or *Archaic*, swum, *p.p.* swum, *p.pr.* swimming].
    dive [*p.t.* and *p.p.* dived, *p.t. Colloq.* or *Archaic*, dove, *p.pr.* diving].

In *Macmillan's Modern Dictionary:*

1. Inflectional forms are given when they are irregular or present difficulties in spelling or pronunciation.
2. Examples are:

    appendix, *pl. E.* -dixes; *L.* -dices.
    phenomenon, *pl.* -ena.
    good (*comp.* better; *superl.* best).

    go, (went, gone, going).
    dive, (dived, diving).
    hang, (hung, hanged, hanging).

351. Use the dictionary to find out to what part of speech a word may belong.

The part of speech of each word is given by the appropriate abbreviation. In all four dictionaries the abbreviation follows the pronunciation.

35m. Use the dictionary to get information about famous persons, dead or living; about Biblical or literary characters; about characters from mythology.

In *Webster's Collegiate:*

1. The Pronouncing Biographical Dictionary lists the names of famous persons, living or dead, and gives brief information about dates, occupations, reputation, pronunciation, and the spelling of their names.
2. Names of characters from the Bible, from literature, and from mythology are listed in the main vocabulary.

In the *College Standard:*

1. All biographical information is given in the main vocabulary.

In the *Winston Simplified:*

1. Information about famous persons, living or dead, is given in Appendix IV.
2. Information about literary and Biblical characters and characters from mythology is given in the main vocabulary.

In *Macmillan's Modern Dictionary:*

1. All biographical information is given in the main vocabulary.

35n. Use the dictionary to get information about places.

In *Webster's Collegiate:*

1. Information about places is given in the pronouncing gazetteer.

In the *College Standard:*

1. Information about places is given in the main vocabulary.

In the *Winston Simplified:*

1. Information about places is given in Appendix IV.

In *Macmillan's Modern Dictionary:*

1. Information about places is given in the main vocabulary.

35o. Use the dictionary to learn the correct form of abbreviations.

In *Webster's Collegiate:*

1. A list of abbreviations used in the book is given in a special section in the explanatory notes.
2. A complete list of abbreviations used in writing and printing is given in the appendix.

In the *College Standard:*

1. A complete list of abbreviations used in writing and printing is given in the main vocabulary.

In the *Winston Simplified:*

1. A list of abbreviations used in the book is given in Section IV of the explanatory notes.
2. A list of abbreviations used in Appendix IV, Names of Persons and Places, is given in a special section preceding Appendix IV.
3. A complete list of abbreviations used in writing and printing is given in the main vocabulary.

In *Macmillan's Modern Dictionary:*

1. A list of the abbreviations used in the book is given on page xiii.
2. A complete list of abbreviations used in writing and printing is given in the main vocabulary.

EXERCISES

Exercise 1. Look up the meaning of each of the following words. In what different senses is each of these words commonly used?

aggravate	fellow	nice
homely	irony	curious
criticize	hobby	minute

Exercise 2. Check the preferred spelling of each of the following words.

theater or theatre	judgement or judgment
good-by or good-bye	advisor or adviser
to-day or today	mould or mold
enrolment or enrollment	dramatize or dramatise
honor or honour	chlorin or chlorine
sulfur or sulphur	colour or color

Exercise 3. Determine the preferred pronunciation of each of the following.

either	coupon	decile
neither	italics	precedence
suite	adult	column
literature	vehement	vagary

Exercise 4. What interesting information can you find about the origins of the following words?

curfew	lunacy	bedlam
calico	saxophone	mob
boycott	macadam	vandal

Exercise 5. Use the dictionary to determine the correctness— or, rather, the appropriateness—in formal writing of each of the italicized words.

1. Instead of listening to symphonic music he preferred going to a *show* at the local motion-picture theater.
2. Each candidate is required to pass a comprehensive *exam* before he is admitted to the university.
3. The local merchants appreciated their *patronage*.

4. He preferred to *hang around* his fraternity house.
5. They were told to *sit tight* when they were being questioned.
6. The older men did not *take kindly* to the new restrictions.
7. In daring to lecture on the subject of religion, he knew that he would have to *skate on thin ice* most of the time.

THE RIGHT WORD

36a. Use the right word.

The right word for you—and for every writer—is the word which does exactly what it has been told to do. Every word that you write is, in a way, an accredited ambassador sent from your mind to the mind of another person. It has an obligation placed upon it, but, at the same time, it must serve you under many handicaps. Since it is but a word—a symbol, a coin, and not the concept or sense image that is in your mind—it cannot *convey* what is in your mind to the mind of another. It has merely the power to suggest, or call forth, something which is already in his mind. Once a word goes out as your messenger, it begins to function independently. You lose control over it. It does its work in terms of its own reputation, its family history, its background. Its reputation, moreover, like the reputation of a person, is not something it carries with it like a halo. It exists in the mind of the person to whom it delivers your thought. Let us illustrate. "What that man writes is poetry," you say. "Ah—poetry!" thinks your reader. "That means exaltation of the spirit, melody, nobility of sentiment, beauty!" "Oh—poetry!" thinks another. "That means he is confused, inflated, high flown, hard to understand!" You see how important it is that you know something about the powers and weaknesses of these messengers that go from your mind to the minds of others.

We speak of certain attributes of words—their denotation and connotation. The **denotation** of a word is its actual, literal meaning. The word "mother" means "a female parent, especially one of the human race." "Bread" is "dough made from the flour or meal of grain, moistened, raised, kneaded, and baked." But when you see the word "mother" on this printed page, does it mean the same to you as "a female parent"? When you say, "Give us this day our daily bread," are you actually thinking of "dough or meal, moistened, raised, kneaded, and baked"? The difference lies not in the words themselves, since they mean different things to different persons, but in their power to call up associations and experiences. This power to suggest associated images or emotions we designate by another label—**connotation.** What the word "mother" calls up in your mind we cannot know exactly; nor can you foretell, when you use the word, what it will call up in the mind of any of your readers. You cannot foretell *exactly*, yet you do know, by drawing upon the fund of common human experience, that the word "mother" ordinarily suggests love, unselfish devotion, a home, warmth, kindness—all pleasant associations. There are other words, like "rat," "snake," "traitor," which ordinarily call up unpleasant associations. But "a female parent"—these are cold, sterilized words.

Choose your words with care, with due regard for their literal as well as for their associated meanings. Your dictionary, through the definitions, the synonyms, and the illustrations of correct use, will help you find the exact meanings of words. What the dictionary cannot tell you, you must learn through reading and living.

Study the synonyms that a dictionary lists under a word. You want to convey the impression, let us say, that your father is a *kind* man. Do you mean that he is *gentle, humane, affectionate, amiable, charitable,* or *friendly?* You want to say that aviation demands young men with a certain quality of character—shall it be *courage, fearlessness, audacity, pluck, boldness,* or *fortitude?* Or you are trying to say that your roommate looks *depressed;* might he not be, more accurately, *dejected, sick at heart, crestfallen, disconsolate, cowed, despondent, scowling, moping, dispirited, morose, gloomy, sulking,* or *long-faced?*

EXERCISES

Exercise 1. Find the synonyms which the *Roget Dictionary of Synonyms and Antonyms* gives for the following words: work, handsome, beautiful, dull, strenuous, keen, large, interesting.

Exercise 2. You may play a little game with words. Pronounce each of the following words in turn. First try to determine whether your general reaction is pleasant or unpleasant. Then tell what mental images, what experiences or associations come to your mind when you speak the word. In this manner you will come close to understanding what is meant by the connotation of a word.

1. snake	13. book	25. smoke
2. rain	14. cowboy	26. letter
3. cheap	15. Hollywood	27. mirror
4. father	16. blanket	28. cows
5. uniform	17. love	29. dog
6. drink	18. radical	30. lady
7. face	19. cat	31. war
8. countenance	20. catty	32. red
9. Sunday	21. hospital	33. flag
10. beer	22. shepherd	34. altar
11. teacher	23. earth	35. foreigner
12. heart	24. fire	36. garden

36b. Use words that are in keeping with the subject of your theme, with the occasion, and with the readers you are addressing.

Whenever possible use the simple, the familiar, or the homely word in preference to the bookish, the learned, or the pretentious word. In ordinary writing it is pretentious and affected, for instance, to speak of a horse as a "steed," a lie as a "prevarication," a home as a "domicile."

EXERCISE

Exercise 1. In the following groups of words try to determine which word in each group would be most appropriate in ordinary informal writing.

1. Apparel, garb, raiment, clothes, attire, habiliment.
2. Repast, nutriment, food, sustenance, grub, victuals.
3. Marriage, matrimony, nuptials.
4. Adversary, foe, antagonist, enemy.
5. To imbibe, to carouse, to drink, to quaff, to tipple.
6. Discourse, conversation, colloquy, talk, parley.
7. Cogitation, thought, rumination, meditation, cerebration.
8. Soak, drench, saturate.
9. Procrastination, dilatoriness, delay.
10. Sagacity, sapience, wisdom, rationality, erudition.

36c. Distinguish carefully between words that are easily confused because they are similar in form or related in meaning.

EXERCISE

Exercise 1. Study the meanings of the following words. Use each one correctly in a sentence.

ability—capacity
accept—except
admittance—admission
advise—inform
affect—effect
all ready—already
all together—altogether
allusion—illusion
altar—alter
alternate—alternative
among—between
anxious—eager
apt—likely—liable
balance—rest
can—may
canvas—canvass
capital—capitol
censor—censure
cite—site—sight
claim—maintain
complement—compliment
consul—council—counsel
contemptible—contemptuous
continual—continuous
coarse—course
credible—credulous

desert—dessert
detract—distract
disinterested—uninterested
effective—effectual
expect—suspect
fewer—less
forceful—forcible
formally—formerly
happen—transpire
healthful—healthy
infer—imply
ingenious—ingenuous
instance—instants
judicial—judicious
later—latter
leave—let
lose—loose
locate—settle
passed—past
practical—practicable
principal—principle
proposal—proposition
respectfully—respectively
sensual—sensuous
stationery—stationary
statue—stature—statute

IDIOMS

37a. Use the correct English idiom.

An idiom is an expression peculiar to a language. An idiom may be (it is not always so) irrational, untranslatable, even ungrammatical. How can one, literally, *pick a quarrel* with a person who is *beside himself with anxiety?* How can one translate "How do you do?" into French or German? Be-

cause idioms are created out of the day-to-day living of ordinary men and women, they are themselves alive, pungent,
racy. They are truly the heart of the language. But it is
highly misleading to say, as has often been said, that idiomatic
speech is that used by cultivated Englishmen. Many idioms
border on slang; many of the idioms now accepted as part
of the language were roundly denounced by cultivated but
squeamish English gentlemen of a former day.

You must not think that the study of English idiom concerns itself with a few illogical phrases like those just mentioned, or with a score or so of verbs that must always be
used with certain prepositions. Vizetelly and De Bekker in
Idioms and Idiomatic Phrases [1] list 498 pages of idioms. You
cannot memorize all the idioms in the English language. At
best you can cultivate a different attitude toward idiomatic
speech—an attitude of curiosity and understanding.

Many idiomatic phrases have grown up around the verbs
of everyday living—to go, to do, to get, to make, to take.
Notice the following idioms. Some of these are still restricted
to speech or informal writing; some of them are correct in
any kind of writing.

To do:

I am *done for.*
We shall *do away with* poverty.
He *did* himself *proud.*

To make:

She *made faces* at her mother.
He *made free* with my money.
He *made good.*
He *made off* with the jewels.

[1] Funk and Wagnalls Company, New York, 1923.

I cannot *make out* what he is saying.
Please *make sure* of it.

To go:

He *goes in for* gardening.
He'll *go to the dogs*.
It *goes without saying*.

To take:

He was *taken aback*.
Take it from me.
She *takes after* her mother.
Take hold of the rope.
Take him *in hand*.
Take him *down a peg*.

To get:

She will *get along*.
The dean will *get wind of* it.
The fish *got away*.
He will *get on with* mother.

A study of the following list will help you avoid a few common mistakes in the use of idiom. The expressions in the first list are all under suspicion for some reason or other. Some of them are almost in good standing, but not one of them enjoys unquestioned respectability at the present time.

Under suspicion	*Preferred in formal use*
all-around	all-round (*still colloq.*)
all the farther	as far as
all the faster	as fast as
anyplace, anywheres	anywhere
blame it on him	blame him for it
cannot help but laugh	cannot help laughing
complected	complexioned
different than	different from
equally as bad	equally bad

Under suspicion	*Preferred in formal use*
feel of it	feel it
in back of	behind
inside of a year	within a year
near enough that	near enough to
no doubt but that	no doubt that
nowhere near enough	not nearly enough
off of	off
out loud	aloud
over with	over
remember of	remember
stay to home	stay at home
tend to the sick	tend the sick
try and get it	try to get it
very interested	very much interested
want in (off, out)	want to come in, to get off, to go put
where are we at?	where are we?

EXERCISES

Exercise 1. Look up the following subjects in H. W. Fowler's *A Dictionary of Modern English Usage*, "Cast-Iron Idiom."

entertained to a dinner	entertained at a dinner
on his own accord	of his own accord
contented himself by saying	contented himself with saying
get the better hand	get the upper hand
to a great measure	in a great measure
promoted to a professor	promoted to a professorship
rise equal to the occasion	rise to the occasion

Exercise 2. With the help of several dictionaries find the idioms listed under the following words:

have	eat	run
pick	stand	hang
mouth	head	foot
hand	heart	word
home	horse	dog

37b. Use the correct prepositions after verbs, participles, adjectives, and nouns.

The following list will not take the place of an unabridged dictionary. It will serve merely as a check list to put you on your guard. Consult the dictionary for more complete information.

abhorrence of
abhorrent to
absolve from
abstain from
accede to
accommodate to (to conform)
accommodate with (to furnish, oblige)
acquiesce in
acquit of
addicted to
adept in
adequate for
adhere to
admit into (a place)
admit of (to permit)
agree to (a thing)
agree with (a person)
agree in (opinion)
agreeable to
angry with (a person)
angry at (a thing)
apprehensive of (danger)
apprehensive for (one's safety)
authority on
averse to
capable of
careless of, about

center in, at, upon
characteristic of
coincident with
collide with
compare to (for illustration)
compare with (to examine qualities)
concerned for (troubled)
concern in (be interested)
concerned with (involved)
concur in (an opinion)
concur with (agree with a person)
conducive to
confide in (entrust a secret)
confide to (entrust)
conform to, with
consist in, of
contend for (to argue)
contend with (opposition)
contrast with
conversant with
desire for
desirous of
desist from
devoid of
differ about
differ from (things)

differ with (a person)
difference between
different from
disagree with
disdain for
dissent from
distaste for
empty of
engage in
envious of
expert in
foreign to
guard against
hint at
identical with
independent of
in search of
infer from
initiate into
inseparable from
interest in
involve in
jealous of
laugh at, over
liable to, for
mastery of (a subject)
mastery over (self)
meddle in, with
monopoly of
need of, for
negligent of
obedient to
oblivious of
part with, from
peculiar to
plan to
prefer to

preparatory to
prerequisite to
prior to
prodigal of
proficient in
profit by
prohibit from
protest against
reason with
reconcile to, with
regret for
repent of
repugnant to
resemblance between, to
responsible for, to
revel in
rewarded for, with, by
sensible of
sensitive to
separate from
subscribe to, for
substitute for
superior to
sympathize with
tamper with
treat of, with
trust in, to
try to
unconscious of
unmindful of
variance with
vexed at, with
vie with
view of
wait for, on
weary of
worthy of

GOOD USE

38. In formal writing avoid the frequent use of colloquialisms; in any kind of writing avoid all crude, trite, or dull slang, and all the various errors which rhetoricians list under such titles as *vulgarisms, improprieties, barbarisms,* and *archaisms.*

Your choice of words is governed by certain standards of good taste. A word is said to be in good use if it is in present use, in national use, and in reputable use. It is in good use if it belongs to our time and age, not to the past; if it is accepted and used throughout the entire country; if it is recognized and accepted by educated men and women.

The following definitions and discussions may help you to decide what kinds of words you want to use and what kinds to avoid. Better still, read some of the books on the subject of English usage which are listed at the end of this section.

Slang has been defined as a kind of made-to-order language, characterized by extravagant or grotesque fancy or humor. Greenough and Kittredge, in *Words and Their Ways in English Speech,* speak of it as "a peculiar kind of vagabond language, always hanging on the outskirts of legitimate speech, but continually straying or forcing its way into the most respectable company." But they also add, "in fact, slang may almost be called the only living language, the only language in which these processes [growth of the language] can be seen in full activity."

The following expressions are labeled slang in *Webster's New International Dictionary: savvy, hooey, in the neck, to neck, to take a rap, scram, a bull* (policeman), *a gat, what do they stick you for a meal.*

Colloquialisms are not wrong in themselves. They are expressions correct in conversation, in informal speeches or writing, or in familiar letters, but not in formal writing. There has been much pedantic nonsense taught college students about colloquialisms. As Professor Kittredge has pointed out, every educated person uses colloquial English, and, what is very important to remember, he uses it correctly if he uses it appropriately. He uses formal English correctly when formal English is more appropriate, when he dresses up in his literary clothes, as it were. Your practical problem will be to determine when an occasion is formal and when it is informal. Some of your themes will be formal; many of them will be informal. It might be a safe rule for you to guard against too free and informal a style, to err a little on the side of formality and dignity. And then it is just possible that your written English is stiff, prosy, and barren because you are afraid to use the language that is natural to you. If that is true, remember that it is better to write forcefully and informally than to write with stiff and ineffective formality.

Here are a few expressions marked *colloq.* in *Webster's New International Dictionary:*

to go in for, to go west (to die), *to get ahead of* (to surpass), *to fix one's hair, to get away with* (to carry off, to defeat), *to fire* (to eject forcibly), *a fish story, to make no bones about, to take a brace, to take the road, to walk into* (to attack), *to set one's cap for, I'll, haven't, shan't, exam, lab, dorm, thusly.*

Provincialisms, often called localisms or dialectal expressions, are to be avoided in formal writing because, theoretically, these words run the risk of not being understood outside their native district. The warning against provincialisms has become a bit of traditional futility, since newspapers, magazines, the radio, and the motion pictures have made known the speech of even the most isolated and backward regions. We may not ourselves use *I reckon, out of kilter,* or *you-all,* but we certainly know what these expressions mean. The provincialisms which are not generally understood very few college students will be tempted to use.

A word is **obsolete** if it is no longer in use. A word is archaic if it is too old-fashioned to be generally used. Here are a few examples of words or special meanings that have fallen by the wayside: *consecute* (to follow closely), *whilom* (formerly), *smug* (a blacksmith), *sim* (to simmer), *homespun* (a rustic person), *to face* (to brag), *a fellow* (a partner). The average college freshman will find little occasion to worry about archaic words in his vocabulary.

Words that are in some way twisted out of their proper use and form are given such names as **vulgarisms, barbarisms,** and **improprieties.** Fortunately enough for the student who is more interested in effective writing than in linguistic classifications, these terms, perhaps having succumbed to the diseases they sought to cure, are now more or less obsolescent. One dictionary, for instance, uses the words *impropriety, neologisms, obsolete, provincial* in a definition of *barbarism,* and quotes *burgle, undoubtably,* and *lab* as examples. Then in the vocabulary it labels *burgle* as *humorous, undoubtably* as *obsolete* except as *dialectal* and *illiterate,* and *lab* as *colloquial.*

Any student who is interested in words will find it profitable to look through some of the following books:

Barfield, Owen, *History in English Words,* George H. Doran Company, New York, 1924.
Fowler, H. W., *A Dictionary of Modern English Usage,* Oxford, at the Clarendon Press, 1926.

Greenough, James B., and Kittredge, George Lyman, *Words and Their Ways in English Speech*, The Macmillan Company, New York, 1901, 1923.

Herbert, A. P., *What a Word!* Doubleday, Doran and Company, New York, 1936.

Kennedy, Arthur G., *Current English*, Ginn and Company, Boston, 1935.

Krapp, George Philip, *The Knowledge of English*, Henry Holt and Company, New York, 1927.

McKnight, George H., *English Words and Their Background*, D. Appleton and Company, New York, 1923.

Robertson, Stuart, *The Development of Modern English*, Prentice-Hall, Inc., New York, 1934.

Smith, Logan Pearsall, *Words and Idioms*, Houghton Mifflin Company, Boston, 1925.

Smith, S. Stephenson, *The Command of Words*, Thomas Y. Crowell Company, New York, 1935.

CONCRETENESS

39. Use the concrete and specific word in preference to the abstract and general.

Abstract and general words, it is true, are necessary in a language; we must have them to express abstract qualities and general ideas. The principle, however, will serve you well, as your danger will be the too frequent use of general words. And even when you are expressing a general idea or an abstract concept, you can make it clearer by means of a concrete example or illustration. To illustrate—*fuel* is a general term; *coal* is more specific. *Virtue* is an abstract term. So is *courage*, although it is more specific than *virtue*.

But if you say, "At the risk of his own life, Herbert rescued the child from the burning house," you are giving a concrete example of courage.

EXERCISES

Exercise 1. Find specific words for the following general words:

tree	clothing	animal
building	bird	weapon
furniture	ship	vehicle
road	grass	flowers
speak	to move	to play
to hit	to oppose	to laugh

Exercise 2. Construct sentences in which you give concrete examples of the following abstract terms:

thoughtfulness	modesty	loyalty
fear	hope	pleasure
horror	delight	speed
dullness	gratitude	friendliness
humility	thoroughness	efficiency

Exercise 3. Try to determine which word in each of the following groups is the most specific.

1. Bird, ptarmigan, grouse, large bird.
2. Rodent, animal, small animal, rat, pack rat.
3. Ship, vessel, sailing ship, schooner, merchant ship.
4. Bad, depraved, wrong, sinful.
5. Superior, good, healthful, adequate.

Exercise 4. Rewrite the following sentences, making them more specific and concrete.

1. Various objects littered the table.
2. Three articles of furniture almost filled the small room.

3. Her features were unattractive.
4. The man was armed with a dangerous weapon.
5. The bright-colored shrubs contrasted with the dark foliage of the trees.
6. My sister expressed her displeasure.
7. The morning air was sweet with the songs of many birds.
8. A moving vehicle passed him at high speed.
9. As he passed the house, a dog barked at him.
10. He seated himself upon the nearest article of furniture.

VIVIDNESS

40. Select words which give life and freshness to your style.

If you avoid dull, colorless, and trite expressions, if you avoid worn-out slang, if you avoid general and abstract words, you may have, instead of a vigorous and lively style, a head full of negative rules that will keep you from saying anything at all. Mere avoidance of dullness does not create a vivid style. But you do have positive and practical aids as well as negative cautions:

1. Use nouns which are exact and which call up definite sense images. This is just another way of saying that specific words are better than general words. When you say, "I heard a bird singing," your words may call up a definite sense image in the mind of your reader, but you do not know what that image is. If instead of "bird" you say "meadow lark" or "hermit thrush," your reader will at least make an effort to recall the song of the meadow lark or the hermit thrush. Whenever you use a specific noun, you make it easy for your reader's mind to create a specific image. You do more than suggest images by your words; you direct the picture making that goes on in your reader's brain.

2. Use adjectives that are bold, vital, alive—adjectives that carry their heads high and strut as if they were proud to be on your pages. You may overwrite, it is true, but overwriting is a sin that may, in time, lead to a freer style. Your teacher can prune luxuriant eloquence, but what can he do for you if you offer him merely a few spindly, anemic plants? What are some of these anemic adjectives in your vocabulary? You say, "That was a *good* lecture," when you mean that it was *witty, stimulating, eloquent, instructive, informative,* or *entertaining.* You say, "She is a *nice* girl," when you mean that she is *friendly, sympathetic, generous, vivacious, modest, talented,* or *conventional.* What adjectives can you find that are more vivid than *pleasant, dull, swell, big, easy, hard?* A book of synonyms will help you find them.

3. Use verbs that carry in themselves the descriptive force of a modifying adverb. A verb-adverb group may often be replaced more effectively by a single verb. Study the following examples:

He ran quickly. (He fled, sprinted, trotted, rushed, surged.)
He was breathing rapidly. (He was panting, blowing, wheezing, puffing, gasping.)
He cut through it. (He pierced it, sliced it, tore it, split it.)
He threw it down violently. (He hurled it, flung it, heaved it, pitched it.)

4. Use specific instead of general verbs. Study the following examples. Notice that some verbs are general; they name the action, but they do not describe the manner of the action. Other verbs are descriptive.

He moved toward the door. (He crept, crawled, strolled, sidled, inched, drifted, flitted toward the door.)
He spoke several words. (He whispered, roared, shouted, hissed, mumbled, muttered several words.)

We put it on the wagon. (We tossed, lifted, pitched, threw it on the wagon.)

He got on the horse. (He scrambled, leaped, jumped, vaulted on the horse.)

5. Use figures of speech more often than you do.

Similes and metaphors will help you present your facts and ideas with the aid of pictures. Every figure of speech uses a picture, an image. Hence it is concrete. Try to get a few figures of speech into everything that you write. Disregard the old warning, so often directed at students, not to force figures when figures will not come of their own accord. It is true that effective figures are natural and spontaneous—at least they must seem so, no matter what creative pains their author went through in producing them. But you will never learn how to use figures unless you wheedle and coax and even bully them into life while you are learning to write. After a time, when you are more sure of yourself, you will be able to create a natural, unforced, spontaneous, and appropriate figure of speech in a half hour of grim mental struggle. Whatever you do, be not tempted to use a worn or trite figure. Forced or spontaneous, let it be your own.

WORDINESS

41. Avoid wordiness.

If you are curious about the prolix hierarchy of wordiness, investigate the following words in an unabridged dictionary: *pleonasm*, *redundancy*, *tautology*, *verbosity*, *verbiage*, *prolixity*, *diffuseness*, *circumlocution*, and *periphrasis*. The inquiry may be illuminating—if not too helpful.

But what advice can be given the student who is more

interested in good writing than in classifications of bad writing? To say, "Do not write in circles," is not enough. To say, "Write simply and directly," may be very misleading. When are words unnecessary? What is meant by writing simply and directly? A style rich in concrete detail is not wordy. Mere length is not wordiness. A short story is not better than a novel merely because it is shorter. A good essay might possibly be compressed to a few sentences, but in the process all life would be squeezed out of it. The first, and perhaps the final, bit of advice, then, must be: "Use as many words as you need, but be sure that every word is doing its work, carrying its proper load of meaning, and helping its neighbors with their loads. Keep the workers. Throw out the loafers."

An obvious type of wordiness is illustrated in the following sentences. Study these and indicate the corrections. Does compression weaken any of these sentences?

1. We met up with him at the concert.
2. Jane is the sort of girl with whom a boy likes to be with.
3. Your suggestion is equally as good as his.
4. Professor Jackson is writing his own autobiography.
5. Have you the necessary prerequisites?
6. A man came to connect up the telephone.
7. Scholarship alone is not the only thing that counts.
8. My grandmother she didn't think I should ought to study English.
9. My friend is large as to size.
10. Please refer back to the rules.
11. Let us return back to the office.
12. The teacher asked me to repeat my words again.
13. Is it perfectly all right to endorse this check on the back?
14. Jones pursued his studies along the line of mathematics.
15. We listened to lectures on college traditions, the choice of a vocation, registration, methods of study, and etc.

A type of wordiness which is illustrated in the paragraph given below is much harder to correct. In this kind of writing, wordiness is the result of fuzzy, confused thinking. Like the knight in the story, the student has leaped on his horse and galloped off in all directions. If you are guilty of confused and obscure writing like this, do not try to revise by crossing out words. Make a fresh start. Outline what you intend to say. Jot down your main ideas. Arrange them in a satisfactory order. Then express them as simply and directly as you can.

The Unknown

To be kind, intelligent, fair, cheerful, tolerant, patient, and be endowed with the technique, are those qualities, which made compact, will make an ideal English professor. When he stands before us on his feet for almost an hour, we form our certain opinions. While he is standing there looking at us he has a very kind expression on his face and is also very neat and clean. Those things we only know by looking at him but we must come to class many times, in order that we may know the real English professor. When he first speaks to us so that we may understand clearly what he is talking about and knows his subject well, we may quickly form an opinion on his intellectual powers. And, when the day comes before leaving for a game, and everyone is excited and conducting themselves so, the professor will grin and bear it.

TRITENESS

42. Avoid trite expressions.

A trite phrase is one that has been rubbed smooth and thin through long use. Trite phrases are also called hackneyed phrases or clichés. When they were new they were effective. Some of them were apt, witty, felicitous. Some began life as figures of speech. They suffered because they were good. Now they are used only for humor or irony.

The following list will put you on your guard:

aching void
acid test
after all has been said
all in all
all work and no play
a long-felt want
among those present
ardent admirers
arms of Morpheus
as luck would have it
at a loss for words
at one fell swoop
beat a hasty retreat
beggars description
better half
better late than never
blissfully ignorant
blushing bride
bolt from the blue
bountiful repast
breathless silence
briny deep
budding genius
busy as a bee
by leaps and bounds
caught like rats in a trap
checkered career
cheered to the echo
clear as crystal
conspicuous by his absence
course of true love
devouring element
discreet silence
doomed to disappointment
downy couch
drastic action

dull, sickening thud
each and every
easier said than done
equal to the occasion
fair sex
familiar landmark
favor with a selection
festive occasion
few and far between
filthy lucre
goes without saying
great open spaces
grim reaper
gridiron warriors
hands across the sea
holy bonds of matrimony
in all its glory
in the last analysis
irony of fate
justice to the occasion
last but not least
long-felt want
lonely sentinel
mantle of snow
meets the eye
method in his madness
monarch of all he surveys
mother nature
motley crowd
nipped in the bud
none the worse for his experience
none the worse for wear
no sooner said than done
partake of refreshments
pleasing prospect
powers that be

presided at the piano
proud possessor
psychological moment
reigns supreme
riot of color
replete with interest
rendered a selection
ripe old age
sadder but wiser
shadow of the goal posts
silence reigned supreme
single blessedness
specimen of humanity
sweat of his brow

sumptuous repast
sweet girl graduate
table groaned
tired but happy
vale of tears
venture a suggestion
watery grave
wends his way
wee small hours
where ignorance is bliss
with bated breath
words fail to express
worked like a Trojan
wrought havoc

EXERCISES

Exercise 1. Hand in a list of trite expressions found in your college newspaper.

Exercise 2. Hand in a list of trite expressions which you have overheard in the conversation of your friends and acquaintances.

Exercise 3. Write a paragraph in which you try to use as many trite expressions as you can. Use the list in this section. Then rewrite the paragraph in a more fresh and effective style.

FINE WRITING

43. Avoid the pompous and inflated style which is known as "fine writing."

Fine writing is not, as you might think, good writing. It is flowery, artificial, overdone writing. In an effort to be literary, the writer loads his style with too many adjectives, with big words, trite figures of speech, and tags from foreign languages.

A certain type of "fine writing" called "jargon" consists of the use of vague, high-sounding words in place of the more exact words which the writer was unwilling to find.   The jargon of newspaper writers also goes under the name of "journalese." Here are a few examples:

factor	the professional world
proposition	the business world
beg to reply	a new angle on
wish to state	element
along the line of	in the field of

EUPHONY

44. Avoid harsh and unpleasant combinations of sounds.

Euphony means "pleasing or sweet sound." The opposite of "euphony" is "cacophony," which means "harsh or discordant sound."   Good prose should be pleasant to the ear; it should not offend by harsh, jarring, or disagreeable sounds. The best prose has a rhythm, a melody, which, although it must avoid the regular patterns of poetic rhythm, is easily detected by the trained ear.   But the beginner must usually be satisfied with a negative virtue—the avoidance of unpleasant sounds.   For a further discussion of this subject, refer to the section on "Euphony and Rhythm."

45

LOGICAL COMPLETENESS

SENTENCE UNITY

45a. Write complete, unified sentences.

Unity in a sentence means singleness of thought. A sentence should express one complete thought. What is meant by "one complete thought" is difficult to explain, since there are various degrees of completeness. In most sentences nothing but your own good sense can tell you when "not enough" becomes "complete," and when "complete" becomes "too much." You can, however, learn much by analyzing mistakes which destroy sentence unity.

Obviously, sentence unity is violated in a sentence that is not grammatically complete. For a discussion of the grammatically incomplete sentence see "Period Fault." The following sentence fragments illustrate this fault:

Wrong: Roger walks with a noticeable limp. Probably a result of carelessness in setting a broken bone.

The laws of this peculiar community were made by officers of the church. The president of the church presiding over the law-making assemblies.

The noisy crowd was on its feet. Shouting encouragement and advice to the men on the field. Men who neither heard nor saw them, who were playing the game as if their lives depended on their efforts.

As I sit here in my room, looking out with windowless eyes, I can hear a variety of sounds. Sounds which convey to me the realization that others, more fortunate than I, are finding life a pleasant experience.

45b. Do not include in a simple sentence any words or phrases which have no direct bearing on the principal thought of the sentence.

Wrong: My uncle, short of temper and of breath, eighty years old at this time and weighing two hundred pounds, swore angrily at the tramp.

Better: My uncle, a short-tempered man, swore angrily at the tramp.

45c. Do not include in a complex sentence any clauses which do not have a direct bearing on the principal thought of the sentence.

Wrong: Three years ago my family moved to Corvallis, which is the home of Oregon State College and which has a population of seven thousand.

Better: Three years ago my family moved to Corvallis, the home of Oregon State College.

or: Three years ago my family, wishing to live in a small college-town, moved to Corvallis, the home of Oregon State College.

EXERCISE

Exercise 1. Determine which of the following groups of words are sentence fragments. Correct them by supplying the missing elements.

1. Allison's playing illustrates one principle that is often forgotten, that every rule of the game may be broken by a resourceful quarterback.
2. The rest of the herd preferring to go in the opposite direction, except one venerable old cow to whom stampedes are no longer a thrilling adventure.
3. Having arranged your books and papers on your desk, you must immediately, before your courage fails you, make your-

self a good student but a vile host by asking your guests to leave the room.

4. Being as yet a stranger in Hollywood and curious to observe the manners of its rural classes.

5. The prisoner refusing to eat, drink, or give his name, although the sheriff repeatedly tried to explain to him that suicide was one crime for which a person cannot be punished after the crime has been committed.

6. The foreman invariably wore a snug-fitting leather jacket. The pockets of which held almost every object that could possibly be used in the care of his cows.

7. In any case, a college student will not get out of his studies any more than he puts into them, and it seems that freshmen do not put much into them. Thus accounting for some of their failures.

8. Some freshmen get nothing done by putting off studying until a future day. Because when this day comes they have something else to do.

9. The first thing that poor liars find out is that their faces reveal the fact that they are lying. Like the pages of an open book telling the story.

10. His keen dark eyes sparkling as he greets his customers with a broad smile.

FAULTY CO–ORDINATION

46a. Do not unite unrelated ideas in a single compound sentence.

Wrong: I worked in the Cascade National Forest all summer, and I returned home on the nineteenth of September, the day before school opened.

Better: I worked in the Cascade National Forest all summer. Having finished my work, I returned home on the nineteenth of September, the day before school opened.

46b. Do not join a series of loose, straggling sentences. Break them up into compact units.

Wrong: We journeyed for an hour and reached the Wallowa River and began fishing down the stream, taking our time and wondering whether we should start eating our lunches, but neither of us was a proficient fisherman, so we soon tired of the sport and sat down to eat our sandwiches.

Better: Having reached the Wallowa River after an hour's journey, we began fishing down stream, taking our time and wondering whether we should start eating our lunches. Since neither of us was a proficient fisherman, we soon tired of the sport and sat down to eat our sandwiches.

46c. Do not co-ordinate elements which are subordinate in thought.

Wrong: The real show came later in the evening, and it was one of those wild western pictures, with a great deal of fighting and shooting.

Better: The real show, which came later in the evening, was one of those wild western pictures with a great deal of fighting and shooting.

or: The real show, one of those wild western pictures with a great deal of fighting and shooting, came later in the evening.

Wrong: The Stanford game is our hardest game, and it will be played at Eugene next Saturday.

Better: Our hardest game, the one with Stanford, will be played at Eugene next Saturday.

Wrong: Aunt Mary is our housemother, and she has been with us for twenty years.

Better: Aunt Mary, our housemother, has been with us for twenty years.

Wrong: The morning air was cool and crisp, and we made the climb
to the lookout station in three hours.

Better: In the cool and crisp morning air we were able to climb to
the lookout station in three hours.

46d. Do not destroy the unity of a compound sentence by using the wrong connective.

Poor: I went to work in a lumber mill, and my brother decided to
stay on the ranch.

Better: I went to work in a lumber mill, but my brother decided to
stay on the ranch.

Poor: Susan is never out of trouble and she is always happy.

Better: Susan is never out of trouble and yet she is always happy.

Poor: Oswald is always borrowing my clothes and he never remembers to return them.

Better: Oswald is always borrowing my clothes, only he never
remembers to return them.

If your instructor refers you to this section, read also the
sections on the "Period Fault," the "Comma Fault," and the
"Run-together Sentence." A study of the section on "Conjunctions" may help you, too. A reference to this section may
be the equivalent of saying, "You are too fond of *and*, *but*, and
so. You are too fond of co-ordination. Subordinate more."

EXERCISE

Exercise 1. Point out the fault in each of the following sentences. Rewrite the sentences.

1. He is a total abstainer from alcohol, and his marriage he calls
   a success, and he dedicates his books to his wife.
2. He is only nineteen years old, and he is a junior in the school
   of forestry.

3. Heavy breathing announces that someone is sleeping, and my brother has come home at last.
4. His programs are always interesting, and consist of selections of his own choice.
5. The furniture was painted silver gray, and consisted of a table, a desk, a bench, and four chairs.
6. One of my presents was a model lamp post, it stood about six inches high and was made of cast iron.
7. The string was securely tied to the post, it was about three feet long and had a knot in it.
8. The lake was very large and every week a group of girls would take a canoe and paddle around it.
9. Mrs. Hall was about six feet tall and she outran a few of the men in a footrace.
10. Some thoughts are like birds, they fly south in winter but return again, this would be helpful in examinations.

FAULTY SUBORDINATION

47a. Do not subordinate the principal thought of the sentence.

Wrong: One day I was pulling weeds in our garden when I saw two timber wolves near the corral.

Right: One day, as I was pulling weeds in the garden, I saw two timber wolves near the corral. (The important idea is certainly that he saw the wolves, not that he was weeding the garden.)

Wrong: We were nearing the dock when our boat overturned.

Right: Just as we were nearing the dock our boat overturned.

47b. Avoid writing sentences with overlapping dependence.

A series of phrases or clauses so written that each depends upon the preceding usually produces an awkward sentence. Rewrite the sentence.

Poor: I had heard the warning so often that I was so used to hearing it that I failed to realize that it was important.
Better: Repeated warnings had dulled my appreciation of their importance.
or: The warnings had been repeated so often that I failed to realize their importance.

47c. Do not use the wrong subordinating connective.

The following list of subordinating connectives may help you in your writing: *although, as if, as, as long as, as often as, as soon as, as though, because, before, but that, even if, every time that, except, for, how, however, if, in that, inasmuch as, in case that, in order that, just as, no matter how, now that, on condition that, provided that, seeing that, since, so that, that, though, till, until, unless, when, whence, whenever, whereas, where, wherever, wherefore, whether, while, why.* This list should suggest possibilities in sentence structure of which you have been unaware.

The following sentences illustrate the most common errors in the use of connectives:

Wrong: Let us sing like the birds sing.
Right: Let us sing as the birds sing.

Wrong: They write like they knew something.
Right: They write as if they knew something.

Wrong: I don't know as I deserve a reward.
Right: I do not know whether I deserve a reward.
I do not know that I deserve a reward.

Wrong: Because he made one mistake is no proof that he will always fail.
Right: That (The fact that) he made one mistake is no proof that he will always fail.

Wrong: While I do not dislike literature, I prefer the sciences.
Right: Although I do not dislike literature, I prefer the sciences.

Wrong: I saw in the morning paper where Mrs. Mooney has been granted a divorce.

Right: I saw in the morning paper that Mrs. Mooney has been granted a divorce.

EXERCISE

Exercise 1. Point out the errors in the following sentences. Revise the sentences.

1. Cunningham runs like he was tired.
2. One of the reasons why this picture impresses me is because it follows the plot of the novel very closely.
3. I am not sure as I want to hear the rest of the story.
4. I see by the paper where a strike has broken out in the coal mining district.
5. Gretchen dances like a professional.
6. I was talking to Mr. Jones this morning, and he said that he thought every boy should take courses in the appreciation of music and art.
7. It seemed like the truck would not travel fast enough.
8. I had no one to tell me what to do, like my mother did when I lived at home.
9. Because he talks about music is no reason he appreciates it.
10. We had the ball on their three-yard line when the game ended.
11. The man was a habitual drunkard while his wife was a splendid woman.
12. I felt like I was in a world by myself.

OVERLOADED SENTENCES

48. Do not destroy the unity, as well as the order and clearness, of your sentences by overloading them with details.

Analyze the following sentences. What is the writer trying to say? How many thoughts is he trying to express at one time?

Confused:

Military training teaches a person to stand up straight and walk with his head up; this helps in future life because it becomes a habit and so many people have the bad habit of walking stooped and this leads to poor health and poor appearance.

Military science teaches also common courtesies, not only to your superior officers but to everyone to whom courtesy is due; for instance when you enter offices, or the courtesies you should use when you are using firearms while hunting or shooting in the presence of another person.

The feed mixture usually contains rolled wheat, rolled barley, ground corn, and oil meal, mixed according to the time and age of the calf; the amount of corn meal does not vary in proportion, but rolled wheat and barley are very good body and fat builders and they are fed to a great extent at first.

If you write sentences like these, your only remedy is to go back to the first principles of thought communication: say one thing at a time; say it as simply and clearly as you can; say it so that it cannot be misunderstood.

Let us try to dissect these sentences in order to discover what the writer tried to say.

Revised:

Military training teaches a person to stand erect and to walk with his head up. (That is enough for one sentence.) Good posture (Is that what the writer meant by "this" and "it"?) becomes habitual. It leads directly to better health and a better appearance.

Military science also teaches common courtesy, not only to officers superior in rank but also to everyone. (Are there some persons to whom "courtesy is not due"?) For instance, it teaches one how to enter an office (Did the writer mean "good manners," "social propriety," or what?), or how to handle firearms with safety to others. (The two examples are so badly chosen that no sentence can make them apt or congruous.)

The feed mixture usually contains rolled wheat, rolled barley, ground corn, and oil meal, the proportions of the mixture depending on the age of the calf. (By "time" did the writer mean the time of the year?) The proportion of corn meal remains constant, but since rolled wheat and barley are good body and fat builders (This is still an awkward expression.) they are used in larger proportions than oil meal when the calf is young.

EXERCISE

Exercise 1. Reorganize and rewrite the following sentences. Discard details that do not belong here. Simplify the sentences; make them absolutely clear.

1. Such things as the vast amount of people and the way they dress is the first thing the freshman notices, then he compares other places where he has been, and starts to feel a gratifying relief coming to him, for he realizes he has seen this many people before at the little county fair.
2. The average country boy that comes to college is quite familiar with what college life will be like, for he has read all the literature he could acquire upon the matter, although it is always joked and talked about his surprises and disillusionments which arrive in his awkward path of acquiring his education.
3. My future will lead me into every type of condition, and I must be able to adapt myself to each of them.
4. My tendency to waste time inspires the professor to give threatening advice or criticism to this cause, but when I am scolded my opinions become hard toward him just as any other boy in the class.
5. We improve our reckoning by understanding all phases or sides of every subject dealt with; whether it be amusements, business, studies, or social life; thereby making the most logical decisions.

CHOPPY STYLE

49. Avoid expressing in short, choppy, co-ordinate sentences a group of ideas subordinately related to each other.

Correct the fault by combining related ideas and subordinating those that are of secondary importance.

Poor: The performance was over. I arose to go out. I was so nervous that I had to sit down on a chair. Soon I grew calm again.

Better: After the performance was over, I arose to go out, but I was so nervous that I had to sit on a chair until I became calmer.

Poor: Back of the grandstand are the stables. The stables are long, rambling, one-story barns. Each barn is divided up into box stalls. Each stall is large enough to accommodate one horse.

Better: The stables, situated behind the grandstand, are long, rambling, one-story barns, each barn being divided into stalls large enough to accommodate one horse apiece.

EXERCISE

Exercise 1. Improve the following groups of sentences by combining related ideas and subordinating where subordination will express the thought more accurately.

1. Fortunately I was able to work last summer on the Skyline Trail. The Skyline Trail of Oregon extends from Mount Hood to Crater Lake. The Three Sisters are located about sixty miles south of Mount Hood. The trail passes near them.
2. One of the boys had an old car. We went to Waldport in it. There we stayed at a cottage. The cottage belonged to the father of one of the boys.
3. Everyone should see Multnomah Falls. If he is driving along the Columbia River Highway, he will never regret stopping to see the falls. It is a sight one could never forget. There are many

charming and beautiful falls along the highway. I truly believe none exceeds Multnomah in beauty.

4. Then we were on our way. I felt very important. I was going on my first vacation alone. Our first stop was Portland. We stayed there over night. Early next morning we started for Pendleton.

COMPARISONS

50. Make your comparisons logical and complete. Use enough words to make your statement compare the things you intend to compare.

The various common errors made in comparisons may be seen by analyzing the following examples:

1. Do not omit *than* or *as* in a double comparison.

Wrong: My father is as tall, if not taller than I am.
Right: My father is as tall as, if not taller than, I am.
or: My father is as tall as I am, if not taller.

Wrong: Bob is a better dancer and quite as interesting as Henry.
Right: Bob is a better dancer than Henry and quite as interesting.

2. Do not omit one term of a comparison.

Misleading: I admire Hoover more than Landon.
Clear: I admire Hoover more than I admire Landon.
or: I admire Hoover more than Landon admires him.

3. Do not omit *other* after *than* or *as* in comparing two members of the same class.

Wrong: Buckley is heavier than any man on the team.
Right: Buckley is heavier than any other man on the team.

Wrong: Carol is as clever as any girl in her sorority house.
Right: Carol is as clever as any other girl in her sorority house.

4. In pointing out the superlative member of a class **or** group, do not use *any* or *other;* use *all.*

Wrong: I like *Gone with the Wind* the best of any novel I have read this year.

Right: I like *Gone with the Wind* the best of all the novels I have read this year.

or: I like *Gone with the Wind* better (comparative, not superlative) than any other novel I have read this year.

Wrong: E. E. Cummings is the most interesting of all the other American poets.

Right: E. E. Cummings is the most interesting of all American poets.

or: E. E. Cummings is the most interesting American poet.

or: E. E. Cummings is more interesting than any other American poet.

5. Do not omit *that of* or *those of* from the second member of the comparison when those words are necessary to make the comparison logical and complete.

Wrong: The salary of an English teacher is lower than a lawyer.

Right: The salary of an English teacher is lower than that of a lawyer.

Wrong: The duties and responsibilities of a traffic officer are more complex than a game warden.

Right: The duties and responsibilities of a traffic officer are more complex than those of a game warden.

EXERCISE

Exercise 1. Revise the following sentences. Make the comparisons complete and logical.

1. Girls are probably better at flattering their teachers than the best of the male efforts.
2. I like *You Can't Take It with You* better than any play I have read this year.

3. His step was as light as many middle-aged men.
4. Gray is the best passer of any quarterback on the Pacific Coast.
5. My theme is as good if not better than the theme which the teacher read to us.
6. Browning is more intellectual than any poet of the Victorian era.
7. The methods used in college English courses are very different from high school.
8. Alexander, our halfback, is a better blocker than any man on the team.
9. I admire a business leader more than a college professor.
10. Although he was not thirty when he died, his poems were better known than many older writers.

WORDS LEFT OUT

51a. Do not leave out words which are necessary for clearness.

Wrong: The food of hawks is different from robins.
Right: The food of hawks is different from that of robins.

Wrong: The day when honors are announced there is much suspense.
Right: There is much suspense on the day when honors are announced.

Wrong: Evenings we usually go for a swim.
Right: During the evening we usually go for a swim.

51b. In formal writing avoid the exclamatory *so, such,* or *too.* Complete the thought, or use some intensifier like *very, certainly, surely, exceedingly, extremely,* and so forth, in place of *so, such,* or *too.*

Poor: It was such a thrilling game.
Better: It was a very thrilling game.

Poor: I am so hungry.
Better: I am extremely (very) hungry.

Poor: Bob's excuse was just too weak.
Better: Bob's excuse was too weak to be credible.

51c. Do not use a noun or verb in a double capacity.

Wrong: *Winterset* is one of the best, if not the best, play I have ever seen.
Right: *Winterset* is one of the best plays I have ever seen, if not the best.

Wrong: I never have and never will like chess.
Right: I never have liked and never will like chess.
or: I never have liked chess and I never will like it.

51d. Do not leave out any part of an idiomatic expression.

Wrong: This is a good time to show your faith and devotion to your country.
Right: This is a good time to show your faith in and your devotion to your country.

Wrong: Customers have neither respect nor faith in a merchant who cheats.
Right: Customers have neither respect for nor faith in a merchant who cheats.

EXERCISE

Exercise 1. Supply the missing words in the following sentences. Rearrange the wording wherever it is necessary.

1. A fraternity house or a dormitory is a question which many freshmen have had to answer.
2. Debating has definitely made me more self-reliant, more friends, and more wrinkles in my gray matter.
3. One incident, an army officer, disguised as a traveler, had written a message in invisible ink on his white tie.

4. Old Dad, who has often told me that it is just as easy to be clean as dirty, may be seen washing not only his clothes but other men as well.

5. To an outsider this little town would not be called an exciting place to spend the winter months.

6. For these reasons, lumbering has and is contributing greatly to our economic stability.

7. The poor girl was so confused.

8. We enjoyed the concert so much.

9. Her sense of humor is just too delightful.

10. The old man was such a tiresome talker.

CLEARNESS AND ORDER

AWKWARDNESS AND OBSCURITY

52. Do not write sentences which are confused, awkward, illogical, or obscure.

An awkward and confused sentence may occasionally be a sign of slovenly thinking, but it is probably more often a result of haste and carelessness in writing. A confused sentence may have several faults: the central thought may be lost in a tangle of modifiers; the thoughts may not be arranged properly; the words used may be inexact, ambiguous, or inappropriate; several constructions may be telescoped into one. Correct the fault by rewriting the sentence. Express your thoughts as simply and directly as you can.

Bad: My belief is that if more emphasis was stressed in college on extemporary speaking, the graduating student would be better prepared to face people of social prominence and college professors.

Why he chose this occupation is for the reason he was offered good money to rid the sound of the devilfish, because he is very dangerous for bathers as well as other people in small boats.

The fact that it is a gigantic crater formed suddenly by an eruption of volcanic nature has been determined.

In high school not much need for correct punctuation and principles is stressed, but in college punctuation and correct forms are closely criticized.

Muskrats work on the dikes before we get to them by burrowing through between two ponds and thus connect them when their contents are supposed to be kept separate.

Better: I believe that colleges should stress courses in extemporary speaking in order to give college graduates more confidence and social ease.

He chose this occupation because he was offered a large sum of money for ridding the sound of devilfish. Devilfish are very dangerous to bathers and to people in small boats.

Scientists have determined the fact that a volcanic eruption had formed the gigantic crater.

Correct punctuation and the principles of good writing are stressed more in college courses than in high-school courses.

Muskrats burrow tunnels through the dikes between the ponds. Through these openings the water flows from one pond to another.

EXERCISE

Exercise 1. Reconstruct the following sentences.

1. The position at the throttle of a huge steam locomotive has struck many a boy's fancy to become an engineer on just such a locomotive.
2. All around the hall were benches, but most of the old women sat on the ground, for there was no floor, smoking long pipes filled with a mixture made of bark which gave off a peculiar yet pleasant odor.
3. When some question which seemed silly to him but was asked in earnestness by the questioner, his square chin became perceptibly more square, and his voice, which for all ordinary conversation had a slight lisp, suddenly became a harsh growl like that of a lion as he squelched the boy who was seeking for knowledge.
4. The causes of my present difficulties in English is not because of poor teachers in high-school years, but of the fact partly because I have been out of school so long that I have forgotten most of the rules, and partly because of lack of attention and interest to explanations by my high-school teachers.

5. In swimming one must move fairly rapidly his feet in a down and up position in order to keep balance in the water.
6. One must move hands in various positions depending upon style of swimming one wishes to perform.
7. My trouble in college English seems to be my inability to pick out the proper places for commas, quotation marks, and semi-colons, where should be placed, and where used, although it has become more simple for me all the time due to constant effort.
8. One may be completely worn out, and the world may seem a place of shrunk souls, and having risen in the morning the future and coming tasks may be slain with the least resistance to man's efforts.
9. Memorizing of poems, great authors, and most important works of each, the remaining two years literature was a main topic, although theme writing played quite a major part also.
10. The music consisted of an odd-shaped drum and wooden horns, which in comparison to music of today the rhythm was very poor.

PROPER ARRANGEMENT

53. Do not destroy the clearness of a sentence by improper arrangement of sentence elements.

Since the English language is not a highly inflected language, the meaning of an English sentence depends to a large extent on the arrangement of words in the sentence. The reader naturally assumes that the parts of a sentence which are placed next to each other are logically related to each other. You must therefore be careful to arrange words in a sentence in such a way that the meaning of the sentence will be clear on the first reading. The rule which will guide you may be stated in two parts: (1) place all modifiers, whether words, phrases, or clauses, as close as possible to the words they modify; (2) avoid placing these elements near other words they might be taken to modify.

1. Adverbs, such as *almost, ever, nearly, merely, only, scarcely.*

Wrong: He merely said it because he did not stop to think.
Right: He said it merely because he did not stop to think.

Wrong: The canteen only contained about two cups of water.
Right: The canteen contained only about two cups of water.

Wrong: Harry almost weeded the whole garden this morning.
Right: Harry weeded almost the whole garden this morning.

2. Phrases.

Wrong: He began to lose his desire to reach the summit after a time.
Right: After a time he began to lose his desire to reach the summit.

Wrong: I was dressed and ready to start climbing within an hour.
Right: Within an hour I was dressed and ready to start climbing.

Wrong: Every girl was really sorry to have the trip end for more reasons than one.
Right: For more reasons than one, every girl was really sorry to have the trip end.

3. Clauses.

Wrong: When you were a child do you remember all the interesting toys you had?
Right: Do you remember all the interesting toys you had when you were a child?

4. Squinting modifiers.

Modifiers so placed in a sentence that they may be understood with either the preceding or the following words are called squinting modifiers.

Wrong: Because we covered more ground with a tractor in six days we finished plowing the field.
Right: Because we covered more ground with a tractor, we finished plowing the field in six days.

Wrong: As we pulled into the service station with the help of a lady attendant we found our position on the map.

Right: As we pulled into the service station, a lady attendant helped us to locate our position on the map.

Wrong: As we drove westward every now and then the blinding rays of the sun shone into our eyes.

Right: As we drove westward, the blinding rays of the sun frequently shone into our eyes.

Wrong: As I said before each of the passengers was required to wear a life belt.

Right: As I said before, each of the passengers was required to wear a life belt. (Corrected by proper punctuation.)

5. The split infinitive.

The split infinitive is no longer considered one of the seven deadly sins of college composition. It is not true that the parts of an infinitive are inseparable. But since a split infinitive still causes many persons discomfort, if not actual suffering, it is better for the student not to split his infinitives too rashly or promiscuously.

Poor: A writer should remember to not carelessly split his infinitives.

Better: A writer should remember not to split his infinitives carelessly.

A good rule to follow is this: place the adverbial modifier between the *to* and the verb of an infinitive only when such an arrangement is necessary to avoid an awkward phrase. For a more complete discussion of this subject see: Arthur G. Kennedy, *Current English*, Ginn and Company, Boston, 1935, p. 506; Stuart Robertson, *The Development of Modern English*, Prentice-Hall, Inc., New York, 1934, pp. 504–507; George O. Curme, *Syntax*, D. C. Heath and Company, Boston, 1931, pp. 458–467. The whole subject is probably not worth the space it has been given.

6. In general, do not separate words that normally belong near each other, such as subject and verb, verb and object, the parts of a verb phrase, substantives and adjective modifiers, and substantives and appositives.

Poor: The explorers had, after many adventures and much suffering, reached the headwaters of the Salmon River.
Better: After many adventures and much suffering, the explorers had reached the headwaters of the Salmon River.
Poor: Before it became dark, the stragglers caught up with the main party, tired, wet, and discouraged.
Better: Before it became dark, the tired, wet, and discouraged stragglers caught up with the main party.

EXERCISE

Exercise 1. Point out the error or errors in each of the following sentences, and then reconstruct the sentences.

1. I shall attempt to explain the function of the least known, to one who does not play the game, section of the football team.
2. At one time I remember that she had three engagement rings.
3. We were finally settled in seats that cost twice as much as we had paid for our tickets when the play began.
4. If you should disturb her by coming in late, you will hear that she was awakened for the next two months.
5. Freshman English courses are taught by instructors who are required to have at least a master's degree in most colleges.
6. A crowd gathers to sorrowfully gaze upon the destruction of the magnificent structure.
7. If spring is early harvest is usually early.
8. They were caught in the act of eloping by Colonel Musgrave.
9. He finally had to prove that his rival was a coward in order to hold his wife.

10. Wood can be kept for a long time without danger of rotting in the woodshed or the basement.
11. As I watch Ann, my roommate, struggling with her accounting problem for tomorrow from my reclining position on the bed, I wonder what it is about her that everyone likes.
12. The forked lightning illuminates for a brief instant the otherwise grey world.
13. Our food was the best we have had since we came to Madison with the exception of certain turkey dinners.
14. The freshmen only have to wear their green caps one year.
15. Every girl will admit that an attractive hat is an essential article of apparel to a well-dressed person.

DANGLING MODIFIERS

54a. Avoid dangling verbal phrases.

The careless use of verbal phrases results in an error which goes under the name of "the dangling modifier." A phrase is said to be dangling if it is not tied to something it modifies.

Correct the error by supplying the word to which the phrase should refer or by changing the phrase to a clause with a subject and predicate.

Wrong: Being in a hurry to finish my English exercise, several dangling modifiers were left uncorrected in my theme. (The reader associates *being* with *modifiers*. Who was in a hurry? Certainly not the modifiers. Correct the sentence by supplying the word to which *being* refers.)

Right: Being in a hurry to finish my English exercise, I left several dangling modifiers uncorrected in my theme.

Wrong: Last year, after graduating from high school, my father put me to work in his office. (Who graduated from high school? Father? Correct the sentence by supplying the word to which *graduating* may refer.)

Right: Last year, after graduating from high school, I went to work in my father's office.

Right: Last year, after I had graduated from high school, my father put me to work in his office. (Correct the error by changing the phrase to a clause with a subject and predicate.)

Wrong: To appreciate this poem, it must be read aloud.
Right: To appreciate this poem, you must read it aloud.
Right: If you wish to appreciate this poem, you must read it aloud.

Wrong: I helped my mother wash clothes this morning, thus causing me to miss my English class.
Right: I missed my English class this morning because I had to stay at home to help my mother wash clothes.
Right: I helped my mother wash clothes this morning. That is the cause of my absence from my English class.

Wrong: I sold my automobile for three hundred dollars, thereby giving me enough money to pay my debts.
Right: I sold my automobile for three hundred dollars—enough to pay my debts.
Right: The sale of my automobile for three hundred dollars brought me enough money to pay my debts.

54b. Do not begin a sentence with a dangling elliptical clause.

A clause is said to dangle when its understood subject is different from that of the main clause, or when the subject is not understood at all. Correct the error by supplying the missing words in the clause.

Wrong: When cooked till tender, remove the meat from the oven.
Right: When the meat has been cooked until it is tender, remove it from the oven.

Be careful to distinguish between an absolute phrase and a dangling verbal phrase. An absolute phrase consists of a noun and its modifying participle. It is a complete and independent unit of speech, related to the rest of the sentence in thought but not in structure. An absolute phrase does not dangle.

Absolute phrases:

Right: The day's work being over, we returned to town.
The guests having arrived, Mother went to the door.

Verbal phrases:

Right: Having finished the day's work, we returned to town.
Opening the door, Mother welcomed the guests.

Certain idiomatic phrases, especially those that express a general action and those that serve as directive and transitional links, are exceptions to the rule. These are phrases like: *generally speaking, taking everything into consideration, providing, looking at,* and so forth.

EXERCISE

Exercise 1. Reconstruct the following sentences.

1. Being unaccustomed to rowing, my arms ached and my heart raced violently.
2. When conversing with her teachers, her remarks were modest and dignified.
3. While on the rocks, a small stone was dislodged and started to roll toward us.
4. After much fumbling in my pockets, a coin was finally produced.
5. Vacationing at the seaside, many opportunities to meet interesting people were offered me.
6. Not having had a profound event in my life, it is rather difficult for me to find a subject on which I could write a profound English theme.

7. While coming home from Independence one night, the starter switch on the car went out of order.
8. We ate our lunch sitting on a big, mossy log.
9. After becoming interested in the sport of fishing, all the tackle except line, hooks, and spinners can easily be made at home.
10. Meals must be taken regularly, allowing no eating between meals.
11. Since I knew she was an expert stenographer, my mind would seem to be a blank when taking dictation from her.
12. The dawn came just as we reached the snow, and looking up the steep slope of Mount Hood, the white snow glistened in the rays of the sun.
13. Being the first time I was to ride on a surf board, I was trembling with excitement.
14. While lathering his upper lip, Bob's nervousness will often lead him to insert a portion of the soap into his mouth.
15. While going to high school, my parents often accused me of spending too much time at the college gymnasium.

REFERENCE OF PRONOUNS

As a rule, pronouns should have definite antecedents, and should be placed as near their antecedents as possible. The meaning of the sentence should be unmistakable on the first reading. If the reader has to hesitate, if he has to look back to find the substantive to which a pronoun refers, the sentence is a poor one.

55a. Do not let a pronoun refer to an antecedent that is vague, or remote, or implied.

Wrong: I can remember that we met many people, but I did not enjoy it very much.

Right: I can remember that we met many people, but I did not enjoy the reception very much.

Wrong: My mother was a school teacher; therefore it is no wonder that I have chosen that as my profession.

Right: My mother was a school teacher; therefore it is no wonder that I have chosen teaching as my profession.

Wrong: Each damaged article is marked in such a way that it cannot be erased.

Right: Each damaged article is marked in such a way that the mark cannot be erased.

Wrong: We enjoyed our stay in France. They know how to live pleasantly.

Right: We enjoyed our stay in France. The French know how to live pleasantly.

It is usually awkward to have a pronoun refer to an antecedent in a subordinate position. The reader will instinctively associate a pronoun with the most prominent substantive in the clause he has just read. The result is confusion—possibly a momentary confusion but still an undesirable one.

Poor: Men have lounged and crouched around their fires; they have been the companions of their dreams and meditations. (The reader will hesitate when he comes to "they have," because he will assume that the subject of the sentence is still "men.")

Better: Men have lounged and crouched around their fires—the companions of their dreams and meditations.

or: Men have lounged and crouched around their fires, since fires have been the companions of their dreams and meditations.

55b. Do not write a sentence in which the pronoun might be understood to refer to more than one antecedent.

Wrong: Almost all of the merchants know their customers and they are in the habit of calling them by name.

Right: In a small town everyone knows everyone else so well that even the merchants usually address their customers by name.

Wrong: The crabs follow the channels when they come in from the ocean and live in them while in the bay.

Right: When the crabs come in from the ocean, they follow the channels, and they live in these channels while they are in the bay.

Wrong: At the breakfast table, Dorothy told Mary that she had committed a bad social error. (Who had committed the error? Dorothy or Mary?)

Right: At the breakfast table, Dorothy accused Mary of committing a bad social error.

55c. In formal and serious writing, do not use the pronouns *you, they,* and *it* in the indefinite sense.

Wrong: They do not have fraternities in many colleges in the East.
Right: Fraternities are not permitted in many colleges in the East.

Wrong: It says on the scoreboard that only three minutes of the second half have been played.
Right: The scoreboard indicates that only three minutes of the second half have been played.

Wrong: They say that Mrs. Dill has applied for a divorce.
Right: There is a rumor that Mrs. Dill has applied for a divorce.

Wrong: When saluting, you must stand straight and bring your right hand up smartly to the visor of your cap.
Right: When a soldier salutes, he must stand erect, and bring his right hand up smartly to the visor of his cap.

55d. Do not use *this, that, which,* or *it* to refer vaguely to an idea implied or suggested but not clearly expressed in the preceding clause or sentence.

A pronoun may have a clause or a sentence for its antecedent; it may even refer to a thought expressed by a part of the preceding sentence. As long as the reference is unmistakable, the sentence is clear. But the careless writer may fall into the habit of stringing together a series of "this," "that," and "which" clauses, without troubling himself about either clearness or exactness. Whenever the writer suspects the clearness or definiteness of an antecedent, he should try to summarize the general idea of the clause referred to by using some expression like *this fact, this condition, a fact which,* and so forth. If the result is still unsatisfactory, the sentence should be entirely rewritten.

Notice that the references are entirely clear in the following sentences.

Right: I have given up smoking. That should please my mother.

So you have decided to support my candidate. This is indeed a surprise.

Father suggested that I keep the money, which I did without a protest.

Now notice the vague references in the following.

Poor: If a girl suspects that her roommate needs help or a friendly word of encouragement, she should do it before it is too late.

Better: If a girl suspects that her roommate needs help or a friendly word of encouragement, she should offer assistance before it is too late.

Poor: The fish are kept alive and fresh in glass tanks, and it also attracts people, which helps the business considerably.

Better: The fish are kept alive and fresh in glass tanks. The display of live fish helps business by attracting people to the place.

Poor: After locking the beasts in the barn, I went to bed and slept soundly, which is one of the effects of hunting cows.

Better: After locking the beasts in the barn, I went to bed and slept soundly, for sound sleep is one of the effects of hunting cows.

55e. Avoid the awkward use of *same, such, above,* and *said* as reference words.

These words are used as reference words in legal or technical writing; in ordinary writing they should be avoided, not because they are incorrect but because they usually lead to awkwardness of expression.

Poor: I stood there holding the monkey wrench and oil can in my hands. The foreman ordered me to return the same to the engine room.

Better: I stood there holding the monkey wrench and oil can in my hands. The foreman ordered me to return the tools to the engine room.

Poor: The significance of said decision is not yet fully comprehended.

Better: The significance of the decision referred to is not yet fully comprehended.

Poor: Please return same to me by bearer.

Better: Please return it (or name the object) to me by the bearer of this note (or *letter, communication*).

Poor: The above is a complete refutation of their arguments.

Better: These facts completely refute their arguments.

Poor: The person who has the best car and is most generous with same is Bob's friend.

Better: Bob's friend is always the person who has the best car and is most generous with it.

55f. Make a pronoun agree with its antecedent in number, gender, and person.

For a discussion of the agreement of pronouns and antecedents, see "Pronouns," section 5 in the handbook.

Wrong: I advise every beginner to purchase the best instruments they can afford.

Right: I advise every beginner to purchase the best instruments he can afford.

Wrong: When an orchestra becomes successful, their success reflects upon the type of leadership they have had.

Right: When an orchestra becomes successful, its success reflects the kind of leadership it has had.

EXERCISE

Exercise 1. Reconstruct the following sentences. If you find the sentences wordy, clumsy, or confused, improve the wording.

1. Our love of a fireplace is inherited from the time when they were the best and only source of heat.
2. More than anything else I want to be able to impress people. Perhaps in itself it is an unworthy ambition.
3. These badges were the ornaments of his trade, and he was inordinately proud of it.
4. This type of girl must be popular, for they may be seen everywhere in the company of boys.
5. If you have this material ready, you will not waste any time looking for them when you start to write your theme.
6. The map showed a complicated network of roads, which wound its way through the mountains.
7. Many persons will look at a man, and because they are not attractive they will say, "That fellow will never amount to much."
8. A window display must draw attention to the merchandise. This is done by a neat and attractive arrangement, by cleverly worded cards, and by the use of suitable fixtures.
9. The trolling arms are the long poles they use to fish with.
10. A person's enjoyment of music depends entirely on the mood they are in.

PARALLELISM AND CORRELATIVES

56a. Use parallel structure for sentence elements that are co-ordinate in rank.

It is not true that every series of words, phrases, or clauses, or any combination of these elements, must always be expressed in parallel form. Occasionally an attempt to produce complete parallelism in structure results in a stilted and artificial writing which some critics refer to as "schoolmarm" English. The student writer, however, will seldom be guilty of too much structure. Any rule which helps him to design and build good sentences is a good rule. The rule may be restated in this form: a noun should be followed by another noun, an infinitive by an infinitive, a phrase by a phrase, and a clause by a clause.

A particular form of error in parallel structure—an error in grammar, too, for that matter—is the use of an "and which" or "and who" clause in a sentence which contains no other "which" or "who" clause.

Wrong: Our English instructor asked us to close our books, to take pen and paper, and that we were to write a short theme.

Right: Our English instructor asked us to close our books, to take pen and paper, and to write a short theme.

Wrong: Few of the leaders anticipated the bitterness of the strike or how long it would last.

Right: Few of the leaders anticipated the bitterness or the duration of the strike.

Wrong: It had never occurred to me before to thank God for the blessings I already had and that there were worse afflictions in this world than broken friendships.

Right: It had never occurred to me before that I should thank God for the blessings that I already had and that there were worse afflictions in this world than broken friendships.

Wrong: Dennis is honest, likable, but he has no sense of responsibility.

Right: Dennis is honest and likable, but irresponsible.

56b. Use correlatives (both . . . and, either . . . or, neither . . . nor, not only . . . but also, whether . . . or) only before sentence elements that are parallel in form.

Wrong: You are either mistaken or I am.
Right: Either you are mistaken or I am.

Wrong: Unselfish people not only are happier but they are more successful.

Right: Unselfish people are not only happier but also more successful.

Wrong: Our guide was undecided whether to continue on the trail or if we should return to our camp.

Right: Our guide was undecided whether to continue or to return to the camp.

EXERCISE

Exercise 1. Reconstruct the following sentences. Use parallel structure where it is appropriate.

1. Personality to me means the habits of a person and how these habits work together.
2. Not only my table manners, but my manners of talking with other people, and how to act when entertaining, have been improved.
3. The merchandise must be in season, it must be attractively displayed, the price signs must be visible, and descriptive cards telling about the merchandise help.
4. The fact that my vocabulary is limited and neglect of practicing in public may be good cause for my stage fright.
5. A clear, strong voice not only helps the teacher to hold the attention of the class, but a student will better understand the discussion if he can hear everything that is being said.

SHIFT IN POINT OF VIEW

57. Avoid an unnecessary and illogical shift in point of view.

One of the most common faults committed by inexperienced writers is shifting from active to passive voice, from past to present tense, from *one* to *you*, from indirect to direct discourse, or from formal to colloquial style. A point of view once chosen should be kept until there is a logical reason for changing to another.

Wrong: You must make yourself interesting to the group that listens to you and are constantly trying to detect your mistakes. (Shift from singular to plural.)
If one's mouth is dry, eat a lump of sugar or chew gum. (Shift from *one* to *you*.)
Elsie asked the doctor about her mother but receives an evasive reply. (Shift in tense.)

57a. Avoid an illogical shift in subject, voice, or tense.

Wrong: Miller was a great athlete, but studying was not his strong point. (Shift in subject.)
Right: Miller was a great athlete but a poor student.

Wrong: I am taking a course in forestry, although life in the woods does not greatly appeal to me. (Shift in subject.)
Right: I am taking a course in forestry, although I am not especially fond of a life in the woods.

Wrong: A roommate is a person who shares your joys and sorrows; shirts and neckties are also shared. (Shift in voice.)
Right: A roommate is a person who shares one's shirts and neckties as well as one's joys and sorrows.

57b. Avoid an illogical shift in number or person.

Wrong: When we examined the sand, it was found to be white and almost pure. (Shift from *we* to *it.*)
Right: When we examined the sand, we found it to be white and almost pure.

Wrong: If one is careful about their appearance, you may even win a quick promotion. (Shift from *one* to *their* to *you.*)
Right: If you are careful about your appearance, you may even win a quick promotion.
or: If a person is careful about his appearance, he may even win a quick promotion.

57c. Avoid a shift from one style of composition to another.

In expository writing, which as a rule is serious, avoid the use of slang or colloquialisms, even when you apologize for them by the use of quotation marks. Quotation marks do not justify slang; at best they merely indicate that you know you are using slang.

Wrong: Personality may put you over in social life, but charm endears you to your friends.
Better: Personality may promote (or *advance, hasten, aid*) your social success, but charm endears you to your friends.

Wrong: The Russian authorities seemed to be steamed up about another attack upon their merchant ships in the Mediterranean.
Better: The Russian authorities seemed to be angered (*provoked*) by another attack upon their merchant ships in the Mediterranean.

EXERCISE

Exercise 1. Correct the illogical shifts in point of view.

1. No matter what one may be discussing with her, she always argues with you.
2. This type of program gives a person a chance to find out if they really have any talent.
3. Not all of your time is spent with your roommate, but since a large portion of it is, a roommate that will help one become a better man is almost a necessity in college.
4. There is little enthusiasm shown by the students. However, why should they?
5. When a system of forest management will be worked out whereby irresponsible hunters will be kept out of our forests, the problem of conservation of game is near its solution.
6. Somehow, when I read the story, it gave me a feeling of admiration for all football players.
7. Christmas to me is a day to be celebrated because of the very fact that you are alive and well.
8. Holidays are valuable for the mental change one gets. During the days you can rest your mind, and during the night your body is refreshed.
9. If we would try to help other persons instead of worrying about ourselves, we would be much happier. Give the best that is in you and do not hold it back because you think that it is not good enough.
10. We must see ourselves as others see us, and ponder the question, "Do I represent my ideal of the perfect man?" If you do not, can you visualize your shortcomings? If we admit the possession of certain faults, how can you excuse your not overcoming them?
11. I wonder what is the power of salt that causes many to believe that when it is spilled it will bring you bad luck, or that when it is thrown over one's shoulder, the future holds something promising for them.

MIXED CONSTRUCTIONS

58a. Avoid an illogical shift from one construction to another.

Wrong: In our basement we found a small wood stove, which upon removing the front, made it resemble a fireplace.

Right: In our basement we found a small wood stove, which we made into a fireplace by removing its front.

or: In our basement we found a small wood stove. By removing its front we made it resemble a fireplace.

Wrong: She didn't say a word, but took me to the back yard in what seemed to me a bit hurriedly.

Right: She did not say a word, but took me to the back yard in what seemed to me a hurried manner.

Wrong: It took us an hour and a half to motor from Portland to Troutdale, a distance, as I said before, was only fifteen miles.

Right: It took us an hour and a half to travel the distance of fifteen miles between Portland and Troutdale.

or: It took us an hour and a half to motor from Portland to Troutdale, a distance, as I said before, of only fifteen miles.

Wrong: Nobody could help but admire his courage.
Right: Nobody could help admiring his courage.

58b. Avoid unintentional humor or absurdity in serious writing.

Bad: Pete has also saved several lives; both victims were in the hold of a devilfish.

I saw a spout of water and I thought it was a whale, but I don't know what kind of fish it was.

In my case I apply golf to myself as others apply stamps or antiques to themselves.

Exercise 1. Revise the following sentences.

1. You may notice an old hound lying on the ground and looks as if he were asleep.
2. The ladies of a century ago thought it necessary to lead a life of leisure and a disgrace to work.
3. Is it true what they are saying about her?
4. The more advanced one goes into a subject, the more interesting it becomes.
5. If you will remember a few years ago, of an account of a young German who crossed the Atlantic Ocean in a sixteen-foot boat.
6. I think I am walking very fast, and then to see those tall boys passing me with long, even strides.
7. Our first impression being it was something like candy, it tasted sweet but a great deal stronger.
8. Just because one has a college education does not mean that he is sure to succeed.
9. After a house has quieted down for study is the best time for planning an English theme.
10. The happiest time is being able to sit before a fireplace on a davenport, watching the fire play merrily or reading a book and just feeling comfortable.

MIXED IMAGERY

59. Do not combine incongruous figures of speech.

In the teaching of writing, warnings against scrambled metaphors may have been given an undeserved and an unfortunate prominence. A mixed metaphor is often a sign of mental vitality. It is surely a lesser literary crime than page after page of dull and uninspired prose. If you scramble two incongruous images, you probably need little more than a hint to show you that your metaphors are inappropriate. It is manifestly absurd to speak of "watering the spark of originality," or "blazing a trail over the sea of knowledge," or of "being blinded by a thirst for revenge." Even Shakespeare spoke of taking arms against a sea of troubles. If your instructor points out a mixed figure of speech in your writing, laugh over it. He will laugh with you and then "encourage the spark of imagination which the mixed metaphor foreshadows, water it with drops of kindness and fertilize it with encouragement, so that the springs of originality may blossom forth like a tree and shed their light over many arid pages of prose writing!"

Study the following figures of speech. What are your comments on each one?

1. The village lay pasted flat on the marsh.
2. Slender poplar trees, evenly spaced, rule off the distance with inky lines.
3. She wore a hat as nondescript as a last-year's bird's nest.
4. Her voice was the thin cry of a quail.
5. The lurid twilight was lanced everywhere with leaping tongues of flame.
6. Its powerful headlight fingered rails and telegraph wires.
7. He played the King in *Hamlet* as if he momentarily expected somebody to play the ace.
8. She clings like a long hair to a wet hand.
9. A witty writer is like a porcupine; his quill makes no distinction between friend and foe.
10. He had an eye like a loose button on an ulster.
11. He was a man of high principle and no interest.
12. Long sentences in a short composition are like large rooms in a little house.
13. He had a face like a smoked herring.
14. His conversation puts a terrific strain on the eyebrows.
15. Lightning stabbed earth's breast with a brilliant blade.
16. I fanned through camp like a prairie fire shot in the sirloin with a hot wind.
17. He disappeared like a palmed coin.

18. He would boil awhile to himself, and then overflow and scald me again.
19. He raised his loose eyebrows abruptly so that his eyeglass fell on the problem.
20. He clipped out three icy words.

EXERCISES

Exercise 1. Get a volume of O. Henry's stories from the library. Find ten unusual figures of speech and bring them to class for comment.

Exercise 2. Use five figures of speech in your next theme.

TRANSITIONS

60. Use the connective that most exactly expresses the relation between the thoughts in a sentence or between sentences.

If your instructor refers you to this section, read the discussion of "Conjunctions," section 8. Then look over the following list of transitional expressions to see if one of these will help you to show the reader that you have finished talking about one idea and are proceeding to another.

on the other hand	in particular
in the second place	in addition
conversely	next
on the contrary	in spite of this
at the same time	similarly
of course	again
finally	in like manner
in conclusion	and so again
to sum up	furthermore
after all	accordingly
I mean	and truly
indeed	I repeat

You must not think that the list given here is complete; neither should you assume that the natural, spontaneous phrases of transition that occur to you as you write are either incorrect or unliterary. They are usually better than these formal expressions. You will learn most about transitions by analyzing some good essay that your instructor selects for you. Make a list of the transitional expressions used, and notice, as you collect your list, those phrases which seem to grow naturally out of the subject discussed.

EFFECTIVENESS

EMPHASIS BY POSITION

61. Make your sentences more effective by placing the important words in the important positions in the sentence.

The most conspicuous places in the sentence are the beginning and the end. Use these positions for ideas which deserve attention and emphasis. Put your important ideas where they will stand out.

No writer can consistently rearrange his sentences so as to begin and end them with important ideas. Many sentences are so short that the reader's mind comprehends them as units. In many others the word order is determined by the nature of the English language. For example, we write: "He is a good man. Her son was killed in France. The day's work is done. The President saluted the flag." In sentences like these the question of emphatic position cannot arise.

"Emphasis by position," as a rhetorical device leading to more effective sentences, is best studied in connection with three types of constructions: (1) sentences containing explanatory or parenthetical phrases; (2) sentences ending with a preposition; (3) periodic sentences.

1. Whenever possible without sacrificing clearness, place explanatory phrases or minor details within the sentence.

Weak: My father is the most gullible man in the state of Oregon I really believe.

Better: My father, I really believe, is the most gullible man in the state of Oregon.

Weak: The student who cheats in an examination is cheating only himself in the final analysis.

Better: The student who cheats in an examination is, in the final analysis, cheating only himself.

Weak: Public speaking should be taught in the freshman English course I think.

Better: Public speaking, I think, should be taught in the freshman English course.

Weak: However, the author failed to end his story logically.

Better: The author failed, however, to end his story logically.

   2. Avoid an awkward placing of a preposition at the end of a sentence.

If you have been taught that it is always wrong to end a sentence with a preposition, read what some of the recognized students of the language have to say on the subject:

George Philip Krapp, *The Knowledge of English*, pp. 153–154.
H. W. Fowler, *Modern English Usage*, pp. 457–459.
Stuart Robertson, *The Development of Modern English*, p. 527.
Arthur G. Kennedy, *Current English*, pp. 507–508.

Then you will probably continue to write and speak good idiomatic sentences like the following:

What are you waiting for?
What are you crying about?
I do not know what you are talking about.
Now he has something to live for.
Where did you come from?

   3. Occasionally you may express a thought more effectively by changing your sentence from the loose to the periodic form.

A sentence in which the thought is not complete until the end is called a periodic sentence. The effect of the periodic sentence is one of suspense. Your reader, in other words, is forced to wait for the main idea until after he has comprehended the subordinate details upon which the main idea is based. Not all sentences in English are periodic; a large majority of them, in fact, are loose. It is precisely because of this that an occasional periodic sentence is emphatic.

Study the difference in the effect produced by the following:

Loose: Stop talking if you have nothing more to say.
Periodic: If you have nothing more to say, stop talking.

Loose: It is of course impractical to legislate for those who will behave themselves while completely ignoring those who will not.
Periodic: To legislate for those who will behave themselves while completely ignoring those who will not is, of course, impractical.

Loose: The catalytic agents of college life are athletics, forensics, musical organizations, journalism, parties, and dances.
Periodic: Athletics, forensics, musical organizations, journalism, parties, dances—these are the catalytic agents of college life.

In your reading find a number of sentences like the following and bring them to class for comment:

In the almost unique intimacy and good-fellowship of Oxford life, where for the moment men from every nation and every class are living together and surveying the nations of the earth in human and humorous companionship, the Rhodes Scholar, if he has in him the capacity for wisdom, learns the difference between an abstract formula and a living point of view.—Frank Aydelotte.

To transfer admiration from the thing possessed to its possessor; to conceive that the mere possession of material wealth makes of its possessor a proper object of worship; to feel abject before another who is wealthier—such emotions do not so much as enter the American mind.—Hilaire Belloc.

—333—

61 · EFFECTIVENESS

EXERCISES

Exercise 1. Examine some good modern essay. Find five sentences which have transitional or explanatory words and phrases hidden within the sentence. Copy them and bring them to class for discussion.

Find five other sentences which begin or end with transitional or explanatory words or phrases. Try to explain and justify the fact that important positions are given to words of minor importance.

Exercise 2. Make a summary of the discussions of the subject illustrated by the following sentence: "A preposition should not be used to end a sentence with." Be prepared to report your findings to the class.

Write five short sentences ending with prepositions. Rewrite these sentences so as to avoid placing the preposition at the end. Which sentences do you think are more effective?

Exercise 3. Using the principle of "emphasis by position," improve the following sentences:

1. College offers two kinds of culture, intellectual and social, in my opinion.
2. We may do some things that are wrong, but we are quite able to take care of ourselves, generally speaking.
3. College students are able to arrange their lives in a satisfactory manner if they are given the chance, in the writer's opinion.
4. The metamorphosis of the plastic material that makes up a college freshman into a fully developed man or woman can be considered a chemical change in a sense.
5. The morning newspaper devotes a whole column to the story, I perceive.
6. Her reputation is all that saves her, one might say.

REPETITION

62a. Make your sentence more effective by repeating the important word for emphasis.

Note the skillful use of repetition in the following sentences:

Wycliffe was, no doubt, a *learned* man. But the *learning* of his day would have *burned* him, had it dared, as it did *burn* his dead body afterwards.—Wendell Phillips.

The nation has been deeply *stirred, stirred* by a solemn passion, *stirred* by the knowledge of wrong, of ideals lost, of government too often debauched and made an instrument of evil.

—Woodrow Wilson.

It was as *scholars* that you were here; it is to the feeling and life of *scholars* that you return.—George William Curtis.

The effectiveness of a sentence, or of a series of sentences, may be strengthened by repeating the same form of construction:

To differ is grotesque and eccentric. To protest is preposterous. To defy is incendiary and revolutionary.—George William Curtis.

Fly from such sights and scents and sounds, for fear lest terror for your fate should visit you; fly to the streets; fly to your neighbors' houses; talk, and be brave.—John Galsworthy.

Made drunk with the freedom of ideas, college students should charge destructively against all the institutions of a faulty world and all the conventions of a silly one.—Bernard DeVoto.

The life of Man is a long march through the night, surrounded by invisible foes, tortured by weariness and pain, towards a goal that few can hope to reach, and where none may tarry long.

—Bertrand Russell.

An elementary and obvious form of repetition is illustrated in the following examples. If used infrequently it may be made effective.

I blew out the light, and presently the only sound that broke the stillness of the night was the drip-drip-drip of the water in the kitchen.

"Boom! Boom! Boom!" replied the guns hidden in the ravine below us.

Soon we heard the steady put-put of his outboard motor.

62b. Avoid awkward repetition.

A word carelessly repeated weakens the effectiveness of a sentence. Correct the fault by using synonyms, by using pronouns, or by completely rewriting the sentence.

Poor: I have been asked to write on a subject that has been the subject of controversy among sports commentators for years. That subject, as you have probably guessed, is none other than the question of which is the most interesting, basketball or football.

Better: Which is more interesting to watch—basketball or football? Is basketball more interesting than football?

Poor: A person who has seen each game for the first time would probably prefer the basketball game to the football game because this game is easy to comprehend and can be understood much more quickly.

Better: A person seeing each game for the first time might prefer basketball to football because of its greater simplicity.

EXERCISES

Exercise 1. Find five sentences in which words or constructions are repeated for emphasis. Copy and bring them to your class.

Write five sentences in imitation of the five which you have found in your reading.

Exercise 2. Reconstruct the following sentences. Avoid the awkward repetition of words.

1. Naturally, the amount of time and money that is virtually wasted by college students amounts to a great deal.
2. Since we never had a net for a goal, we used our skates in making a line across the ice, and this line meant the same as a goal to us.
3. The door slammed twice for every person that entered, and its close proximity and the vibrations caused by the slamming caused me to take a firmer hold on my tilting bed.
4. My ambition to become a musician was created with the creating of a grade-school band.
5. There are many reasons for failure in college. Many students are intelligent, but still they do not make high grades for several good reasons. The three most important reasons are as follows.
6. The Spaniards built a large wall, complete with redans, completely around the city to protect it from the fierce Moro pirates.

BALANCE

63. Place similar or contrasted thoughts in balanced constructions.

Balance, like parallelism, uses similarity of structure to show similarity or contrast of ideas. The following examples will make the principle clear:

Gush is bad taste, the parade of emotion. Prudery is bad taste, the parade of modesty. Fine writing is bad taste, the parade of elegance. Slang is bad taste, the parade of smartness or knowingness.—Oscar W. Firkins.

Education ought to foster the wish for truth, not the conviction that some particular creed is the truth.—Bertrand Russell.

If they [the Puritans] were unacquainted with the works of philosophers and poets, they were deeply read in the oracles of God. If their names were not found in the registers of heralds, they felt assured that they were recorded in the Book of Life. If their steps were not accompanied by a splendid train of menials, legions of ministering angels had charge over them. Their palaces were houses not made with hands; their diadems crowns of glory which should never fade away!—Macaulay.

EXERCISES

Exercise 1. Find in your reading five examples of balanced sentences, copy them, and bring them to class.

Exercise 2. Write a paragraph on one of the following topics. Use a number of balanced sentences to show the contrast between the topics.

> Freedom and anarchy
> The liberal and the conservative
> High-school teachers and college teachers
> Sentiment and sentimentality
> Good and bad sportsmanship
> The good teacher and the poor teacher

CLIMAX

64. **Whenever you write a sentence which contains a series of elements of varying importance, try to arrange these elements in the order of climax.**

As a device for increasing the impact of a sentence, climax has lost favor among modern writers. It is still used, especially in oratorical prose, but few writers now strive for it as consciously as did Macaulay, from whose essay on Milton the following examples are quoted. And yet who among us can resist an involuntary turning of his face toward the east when he reads sentences like these?

The very meanest of them [the Puritans] was a being to whose fate a mysterious and terrible importance belonged—on whose slightest actions the spirit of light and darkness looked with anxious interest—who had been destined, before heaven and earth were created, to enjoy a felicity which should continue when heaven and earth should have passed away. . . . For his sake empires had risen, and flourished, and decayed. For his sake the Almighty had proclaimed his will by the pen of the evangelist and the harp of the prophet. He had been rescued by no common deliverer from the grasp of no common foe. He had been ransomed by the sweat of no vulgar agony, by the blood of no earthly sacrifice. It was for him that the sun had been darkened, that the rocks had been rent, that the dead had arisen, that all nature had shuddered at the sufferings of her expiring God!

EXERCISE

Exercise 1. Read several good modern essays and bring to class a copy of every sentence in which the device of climax is used.

WEAK PASSIVE VOICE

65. Avoid the use of the passive voice whenever the active voice is more natural and direct.

The passive voice is properly used when the receiver of the action is more important than the doer of the action or the action itself.

Right: Several priceless old manuscripts were destroyed.
The wounded prisoner was dragged into the trench.

But notice the difference in the following sentences when the active replaces the passive.

Weak: Other games are also played by the guests.
Better: The guests also play other games.

Weak: As the top of the stairs is approached, a quickening of the steps of the person is announced by the trembling of the floor.
Better: As the intruder approaches the top of the stairs, the trembling of the floor announces the quickening of his steps.

Weak: The Sunday dinner is a meal at which everyone is present and is enjoyed immensely by all.
Better: Sunday dinner is a meal at which everyone is present and which everyone enjoys.

Weak: Many agonizing minutes are spent by the student in deciding on a subject for a speech.
Better: The student spends many agonizing minutes deciding upon a subject for a speech.

EXERCISE

Exercise 1. Improve the following sentences by changing the verbs from the passive to the active.

1. A last puff is taken, which momentarily illuminates the boy's face, and a glowing arc is noticed when the cigarette is flicked across the lawn.
2. Here and there are heard whispered explanations and giggles.
3. Three women came in, and the question "Are you relatives of the groom?" was asked.
4. A daily trip is made to the attic to wipe the dust from her keepsakes, and then she sheds a tear or two over them.
5. In the laboratory all available information is studied by chemists. After this extensive study, experiments are performed. The data are recorded in detail. If no satisfactory results are obtained, another study is carried out, but this time the data obtained from the first trial are included. These trials are carried on until satisfactory results are gained.

CONCISENESS

66. Do not use more words than are necessary for the adequate expression of your thought.

If you are referred to this section, read also "Wordiness," section 41. Then rewrite the sentence to which your instructor objects. It may be that you cannot understand why your instructor thinks your sentence is wordy. If that is true, you must be content to accept his judgment for the present. But continue to study good modern essays. What do you observe? Do modern writers of prose use more words or fewer words than you do to express an idea? Are they wordy—or do they have more to say?

Do not mistake brevity for conciseness. A sentence is not concise if it lacks the words necessary not only for the adequate expression of the idea but also for the effective communication of the idea to the reader. Cutting out words will not always result in conciseness. You may summarize *Anthony Adverse* or *Gone with the Wind* in five hundred words, but can you persuade three million persons to read your five-hundred word summary? Cutting out words in a good essay might also cut out of it those qualities which make it good—strength, variety, maturity, grace, cleverness, even accuracy.

Study the difference in the effect produced by the following pairs of sentences:

1. Objects, on our first acquaintance with them, have that singleness and integrity of impression that it seems as if nothing could destroy or obliterate them, so firmly are they stamped and riveted on the brain.
2. Our first impressions of objects are the most lasting.

1. The ant and the moth have cells for each of their young, but our little ones lie in festering heaps, in homes that consume them like graves; and night by night, from the corners of our streets, rises up the cry of the homeless—"I was a stranger, and ye took me not in."
2. Insects are more careful about their young than are human beings.

1. When we had done all this, there fell upon us the beneficent and deliberate evening; so that as we sat a little while together near the rakes, we saw the valley more solemn and dim around us and all the trees and hedgerows quite still, and held by a complete silence.
2. When we had finished, it was evening; so that we sat a little while near the rakes and looked out upon the quiet valley.

Now study this set of sentences. Do you see what is meant by conciseness?

1. Whenever anyone called for someone to help him do some certain thing, Jim was always the first to volunteer and lend his help for the cause.
2. Whenever anyone called for help, Jim was always the first to volunteer.

1. This spirit of co-operation is essential and necessary for anyone to have in order to get along with other people and this is a quality that Jim had what it took.
2. Jim had the spirit of co-operation which is necessary if one wishes to get along with people.

1. Jim was one of those people of whom there are few in this world like him.
2. There are few people like Jim.

1. Lumbering is placed in the upper ten industries in the United States from the standpoint of importance.
2. Lumbering is one of the ten most important industries in the United States.

Exercise 1. Express the ideas in the following sentences more concisely.

1. The ringing of the alarm clock startled me from the deep depths of slumber.
2. To illustrate this, a large country loves its adjoining country so long as they have a knowledge of the circumstances existing in that adjoining country.
3. In order to broaden the mind on the outlook of life one must mingle with other students and take an interest in social life as well as in studies.
4. In the college of today a teacher must be the best in his profession.
5. From my point of view English ranks first in line with other college subjects in importance and interest.
6. In my opinion the perfect teacher is one who has a pleasing personality combined with a genuine interest in each and every member of the class, an interest which is entirely impartial in nature.
7. I should want a teacher to be able to put himself on the same level of mentality as his class in order that the class would be able to understand what he is talking about.
8. He has all the basic fundamentals which make a good teacher.
9. I believe that a good teacher should have an unprejudiced view point of all subjects that might be discussed in his class.
10. Home means to me the idea of finding there an atmosphere which makes me feel at ease and carefree.

Exercise 2. Rewrite the following selection. Compress it without sacrificing any of the thought.

As students there are many problems which we will have to contend with all through the four years of college life that it will be an endless task to name and describe each personal characteristic that one must have. We meet up with a new angle of things each day that we tread along the walks of our college campus. There are many things which have helped each and every one of us in our way and yet there are many things which will detract from these certain standards set down by each individual person.

My job, which I believe will contain all the important human characteristics, is being a worthy student. The first and most important, as a student, will be intelligence, because after all that is the main reason that we are here as students. We may become more intelligent in every way, just as study day by day we add more knowledge. Because of the keen competition of so many students at college it makes it necessary to develop our ability to gain knowledge to the fullest extent. College may also be harmful to some students when it comes to getting an education. The reason some do give up is that they are not used to having such keen competition and too they will probably be required to take many subjects which they are not adapted in and will consequently become discouraged because of the low grades. This may also result in the fact that their scholastic rating was much higher in high school and if and when they were going to school somewhere else.

Honesty, of course, will be another important factor and it can make or break a person in college. It may be developed more by the lectures the teachers use and the method used at examination time. In some it will be developed more by the fact that they are left alone in examinations to do the correct thing or not to do the thing which is correct. It may also be detrimental if all begin to cheat because you will not be honest in order to stay up with the rest of the class in order to get as high a grade. You are conscious of the fact that your grade will go down and of course their average will become higher and yours lower; consequently you will not be honest.

VARIETY

67. Make your writing more effective by varying the structure of your sentences.

You may avoid monotony of sentence structure by: (1) not beginning a number of successive sentences with the same word; (2) not beginning a series of sentences with subordinate clauses; (3) not beginning a series of sentences with participial phrases; (4) avoiding the same general sentence pattern throughout a selection. The principle may be expressed in positive form: mix simple sentences with complex or compound sentences; put a short sentence in the midst of several long ones; occasionally begin a sentence with modifiers instead of with the subject.

Notice the monotonous sentence structure in the following paragraph:

My Roommate

My roommate has some very good traits. She spends most of her study time in the library. She always has her work done, for she is quite studious. She is very good at giving good advice. She keeps me well informed as to the college rules and regulations. She, being a sophomore, knows the students and the professors quite well. She knows each member of the football team personally. She is what is termed a campus "big shot." She is very much interested in all competitive sports. She is minoring in physical education and is playing volley ball. She is a very ardent football fan. She knows the technical name for every move that is made on the football field. She is looking forward to the next game this week end at Madison with enthusiasm. She loves to dance and is a very good dancer. She never misses the Wednesday rally dances and very rarely misses any other school dance. She is quite a socialite. She is able to carry on all she undertakes with an air of sophistication. She knows each of the sorority and fraternity houses and their rating on the campus.

EXERCISES

Exercise 1. Try to rewrite the paragraph about the roommate. Use the same topic sentence and the same details, but vary the sentence structure.

Exercise 2. Analyze the following paragraph for variety of sentence structure.

Do not allow yourself to be misled by the common notion that an hypothesis is untrustworthy simply because it is an hypothesis. It is often urged, in respect to some scientific conclusion, that, after all, it is only an hypothesis. But what more have we to guide us in nine-tenths of the most important affairs of daily life than hypotheses, and often very ill-based ones? So that in science, where the evidence of an hypothesis is subjected to the most rigid examination, we may rightly pursue the same course. You may have hypotheses, and hypotheses. A man may say, if he likes, that the moon is made of green cheese: that is an hypothesis. But another man, who has devoted a great deal of time and attention to the subject, and availed himself of the most powerful telescopes and the results of the observation of others, declares that in his opinion it is probably composed of materials very similar to those of which our own earth is made up: and that is also only an hypothesis. But I need not tell you that there is an enormous difference in the value of the two hypotheses. That one which is based on sound scientific knowledge is sure to have a corresponding value; and that which is a mere hasty random guess is likely to have but little value. Every great step in our progress in discovering causes has been made in exactly the same way as that which I have detailed to you. A person observing the occurrence of certain facts and phenomena asks, naturally enough, what process, what kind of operation known to occur in Nature applied to the particular case, will unravel and explain the mystery. Hence you have the scientific hypothesis; and its value will be proportionate to the care and completeness with which its basis has been tested and verified. It is in these matters as in the commonest affairs of practical life: the guess of the fool will be folly, while the guess of the wise man will contain wisdom. In all cases, you see that the value of the result depends on the patience and faithfulness with which the investigator applies to his hypothesis every possible kind of verification.

—Thomas Henry Huxley.

THE PARAGRAPH

The numbered rules and the brief discussions in this section are for the convenience of both teacher and student in the process of grading and revising themes. A reference to any of these rules should be an invitation to reread the chapter on paragraph writing, and to study the examples of various types of paragraphs which may be found in it.

THE TOPIC SENTENCE

68. Construct each expository paragraph either with a definite, expressed topic sentence, or with a topic sentence so clearly implied that you could state it without hesitation.

A succession of paragraphs each beginning with a topic sentence may become monotonous. But monotony of structure is not an adjunct of clearness of thought, and even monotony is better than fuzziness of thought or a hopeless fog. Remember that the position of the topic sentence may easily be varied. It usually comes first, or immediately after the necessary transitional phrases. Frequently the transitional elements are combined with the topic sentence. But the topic sentence may also come last in the paragraph, or it may even be placed anywhere in the paragraph.

If your instructor refers you to this section, underline the topic sentence of your paragraph in red or write a topic sentence if it is implied in your paragraph.

Exercise 1. If your class is using a book of readings in this course, ask your instructor to select for you an essay in which most of the topic sentences are actually expressed. Then underline each topic sentence. Put parentheses around transitional elements found in the topic sentences.

LENGTH

69. Write paragraphs of suitable length.

Rarely do college freshmen write paragraphs that are too long. An occasional long paragraph is not a literary crime. Neither is an occasional short paragraph, for that matter.

If you have three or four paragraphs for every page of your theme paper, your paragraphs are too short. If you split up a five-hundred-word theme into ten or twelve paragraphs, your paragraphs are too short. It follows that the thoughts in your theme are undeveloped, that they are not expressed with the detail necessary to make them clear or impressive or interesting.

If your instructor refers you to this section, rewrite your theme. Start with a plan, or an outline, which calls for a limited number of main facts or ideas. Your trouble may be too ambitious a subject. Cut it down to fit your space. Then write a topic sentence for each paragraph. Develop each topic sentence adequately. Be specific. Use concrete details, examples, and instances.

Exercise 1. Select a typical serious essay in the current issue of *Harper's Magazine*, count the number of words in each paragraph, and then group your figures to show the paragraph length most frequently used in that essay. Do not compute averages, since a few short transitional paragraphs, or a very long paragraph, may make your averages very misleading.

UNITY

70. Do not violate the principle of unity in paragraph structure.

A paragraph is a unit of structure. It deals with one idea, or with one phase of a larger idea. Its unity is destroyed by digressions from the main thought, by the addition of irrelevant details, or by afterthoughts that should have been disposed of earlier in the composition.

Analyze the following paragraph written in a course in English composition. The second sentence is meant to be the topic sentence. The paragraph should confine itself to this one idea. Does it? What do "pride and hope," a "good tutor," and "personality" have to do with the amount of practice it takes to develop a dancer?

Dancing as a career must be started early in life. Dancing takes years of tiring and endless practice. Dancing should be started in the home when the child is young. A tutor who has the confidence of the child is a great benefactor. The student should invariably be praised to establish pride and hope. Pride and hope when established are two great elements in gaining a career. There are other elements that enter into dancing as a career such as personal appearance and personality. A good personal appearance on the stage may detract attention from a mistake in the step. Personality off the stage may determine whether a dancing career will be fruitful or not. People will notice an individual quicker by their personality. They may go as far as to inquire about a person; hence, a chance for a step up in a career.

If your instructor refers you to this section, cross out the material which is not related to the topic idea of the paragraph. If you feel that it is important to your theme, put it where it belongs.

ARRANGEMENT

71. Arrange the details in your paragraph in the most effective manner.

Study the section on "The Paragraph" for an understanding of the various ways in which material may be arranged in expository writing. If your instructor refers you to this section, he may wish to suggest one of the following methods as being better than the one you have used. Rewrite the paragraph in conformity with his suggestion.

1. Try the "order of enumeration." In your topic sentence state that your idea may be seen from two points of view, that it has three important aspects, that you are going to use four illustrations, that you have two excellent reasons for believing it, and so on. You can see the various uses of this method. You should also see that this order may help you to write a clear, compact, and well-organized paragraph.

2. Try the "inductive order." It may be that your paragraph idea should not be stated bluntly in the first sentence. The reader may not be ready for it. Prepare him for it by using your details, your examples and instances, to guide his thoughts, so that when you are ready to use your summarizing topic sentence he will also be ready to accept it.

3. Try the "order of climax." If you are using a number of examples, you may possibly arrange them in a series of increasing importance.

4. Try the "order of known to unknown." If your idea is new to the reader, build up to it by giving him first what he will most readily accept. Lead him gradually to those ideas before which he might hesitate.

5. Try the "time order." If details can be arranged in the order of happening, there is no particular advantage to be gained by trying any other arrangement. The order of time, or happening, produces a clear and orderly paragraph. It is inherently simple, perhaps elementary—but it has the unquestioned virtue of being almost foolproof. It may be used with material that at first glance does not arrange itself in the order of time. For instance, "How to Train a Horse" can become "How I Trained My Horse"; "Academic Freedom" can become "The Historical Development of the Concept of Academic Freedom"; "The Right to Work" can become "How the Notion Grew Up That a Job Is Property."

USE OF DETAILS

72. Use an adequate amount of concrete details in developing a paragraph.

The tendency of beginners is to write in generalities and abstractions. In criticism—"I like this poem." Why do you like it? Because it makes you think, or because it repeats what you have always believed? Because it irritates you? or because it soothes you? In presentation of character—"My father is an honest man." How is he honest? What does he do that shows honesty? Bring him on the stage and let us see him being honest. In discussion of college problems— "College women are more conservative and conventional than college men." Give us examples—many of them. Let us see these college men and women in situations that require choice; let us see how they act and what they think in relation to political questions, to books, to art, to social morality. Give the reader proof. Give him the evidence you have observed.

TRANSITIONS

73. Use transitional words and phrases to help your reader pass from one part of your thought to another.

Do not leave awkward gaps in your paragraph. Let the reader know when you have finished talking about one subject and are beginning to talk about another. Let him also know how each thought is related to the preceding thoughts.

If your instructor refers you to this section, first read pages 74–77 in the section on paragraph writing. Study the models analyzed there. Then read section 8, "Conjunctions," and section 60, "Transitions." With the necessary information at your command, revise the paragraph by inserting transitional words and phrases where they will insure a smooth flow of thought in your paragraph.

In the first selection given below notice that the enumeration of subtopics given in the first sentence is one of the most effective means of tying together the different parts of the discussion. The obvious transitional elements—including repetition of key words—are underlined for your convenience.

Dramatic conventions are of three kinds: the permanent, which are found in all periods of the drama; the temporary, which belong to special periods; and the individual, for all authors tend to fall into conventional ways of doing things. The permanent and the temporary conventions need to be clearly distinguished, for they are easily confused. Professor Baker calls our attention to the fact that "almost everything which leading play-placers, managers, and actors have in the past twenty-five years declared the public would unwillingly accept or would not accept at all has become not only acceptable but often popular."

Every art rests upon the acceptance of certain implied conventions. In fact, the drama, like other arts, is of convention all compact. We cannot have opera without the convention that there exists a race of men and women who express themselves not in speech but in song. We cannot have painting without an agreement on the part of the painter and spectators that an object of three dimensions may be represented on a flat surface. Even the sculptor, who works in three dimensions, asks us to believe that the motionless, hard, white marble represents the soft, moving flesh of human beings.

The dramatist likewise asks us to believe a number of things which are to the senses obviously false. In the first place, we must, when we witness a play, accept the convention that the actors are really the persons they pretend to be. In other words, we must play the game in the spirit of make-believe. When the dramatist asks us to believe that we are—while actually sitting in a New York theater—looking into a ranch-house in Arizona, we must co-operate with him; otherwise the play is no play for us. The audience has a tacit agreement with playwright, producer, and actors; it says to them in effect: "If you will give us an interesting story, show us interesting persons, we will accept the story as real and witness sympathetically what you show us; and we will accept as real your painted scenery, your imitation lightning and thunder, your stage banknotes, and your paste jewelry."

In its eagerness for a story, an audience is always willing to accept the convention that all foreigners speak English. In Shakespeare's "Julius Caesar" or Shaw's "Caesar and Cleopatra" we are not disturbed by the obvious absurdity that Caesar speaks

English instead of Latin. In opera we are not disturbed by the fact that the characters in "Lucia di Lammermoor," which is based on Scott's "The Bride of Lammermoor," speak Italian rather than English. Stranger things than these have happened upon the stage. In one performance of "Othello" Salvini, in the role of Othello, spoke Italian while Edwin Booth, who took the part of Iago, and the remainder of the cast spoke English. In another performance of the same play a similar thing occurred: Devrient as Othello spoke German while Booth and others in the cast spoke English. In this second performance one actress, who spoke English with a foreign accent, alternated between German and English, using German only in addressing Devrient.

> —Jay B. Hubbell and John O. Beaty, *An Introduction to Drama*, pp. 16-17. By permission of The Macmillan Company, publishers.

STYLE

You know, of course, that no handbook of writing can give you "rules" by which you can acquire an individual style. It can, however, help you materially in one way—by making it easy for your instructor to warn you against those faults that usually plague the writing of beginners.

TONE

74. Give your style the tone which the subject calls for.

1. Do not incorporate facetious remarks in a discussion which is essentially serious and formal.

2. Avoid the use of collegiate slang in a serious discussion.

3. Avoid the use of colloquial abbreviations in writing, even in fairly informal writing. Some of the abbreviations that students are apt to carry over from their conversation to their themes are: *prof* for *professor, exam* for *examination, libe* for *library, chem* for *chemistry, gym* for *gymnasium, frosh* for *freshman, soph* for *sophomore, dorm* for *dormitory, lab* for *laboratory, math* for *mathematics, psych* for *psychology.*

4. Avoid a tone of stiff formality in informal discussions. If the subject calls for informal treatment, try to give your writing an air of ease and naturalness, but remember that writing, on any level, is always just a little more formal than conversation.

5. Avoid the use of technical terms in an article written for popular reading. If technical terms cannot be avoided, translate them into a language understood by everyone.

MATURITY

75. Do not write in a juvenile style.

If you naturally express your thoughts in childish language, it is true that you cannot grow up over night. But you can try to increase your vocabulary, and to vary the structure of your sentences. You can avoid writing a long series of short, simple sentences. You can occasionally begin with a phrase or with a clause. You can learn to subordinate the less important thoughts. It may be that your juvenile style is just a defense reaction: you use a childish style because you are afraid of making mistakes if you attempt a more complex mode of expression. Then let a reference to this section be a warning to you. Goodness in writing is not negative; it does not consist of avoiding mistakes. Mistakes must be avoided, it is true, but before writing can appeal to mature readers it must have positive virtues—strength, vividness, ease, fluency, honesty, clearness, dignity, authority.

CONCRETENESS

76. Write concretely.

The best single bit of advice to the student of writing still remains: say it with pictures!

If your instructor refers you to this section, it is a sign that you have not heeded the counsels and admonitions scattered throughout this little book.

If you honestly cannot understand why your instructor considers your theme vague and general, take it to him for a thorough analysis in conference. Ask him to show you how vague statements can be made definite and concrete.

A GLOSSARY OF FAULTY EXPRESSIONS

The following list of miscellaneous faulty expressions has been prepared for your convenience. You must not look upon it as a comprehensive dictionary of errors in usage. No such comprehensive list is possible. Nor would it be desirable were it possible. This list will serve you in two ways: as a quick check list when you are writing themes, and as a starting point for excursions to the more complete and scholarly discussions of the questions which are mentioned here.

1. Barfield, Owen, *History in English Words*, George H. Doran Company, New York, 1924.
2. Fowler, H. W., *A Dictionary of Modern English Usage*, Oxford, the Clarendon Press, 1926.
3. Greenough, James B., and Kittredge, George Lyman, *Words and Their Ways in English Speech*, The Macmillan Company, New York, 1901, 1923.
4. Kennedy, Arthur G., *Current English*, Ginn and Company, Boston, 1935.
5. Krapp, George Philip, *The Knowledge of English*, Henry Holt and Company, New York, 1927.
6. Krapp, George Philip, *A Comprehensive Guide to Good English*, Rand McNally and Company, Chicago, 1927.
7. McKnight, George H., *English Words and Their Background*, D. Appleton and Company, New York, 1923.
8. Robertson, Stuart, *The Development of Modern English*, Prentice-Hall, Inc., New York, 1934.
9. Smith, Logan Pearsall, *Words and Idioms*, Houghton Mifflin Company, Boston, 1925.
10. Smith, S. Stephenson, *The Command of Words*, Thomas Y. Crowell Company, New York, 1935.

And, of course, you should constantly refer to *Webster's New International Dictionary*, second edition, or at least to your own desk-size dictionary.

Accept, except. These two words are often confused because of a slight resemblance in sound. *Accept* means *to receive something offered, to agree to.* *Except* means *to exclude, to make an exception.*

We must accept (not *except*) his apology.
We agreed to except (not *accept*) the third problem.

A.D. *Anno Domini* means *in the year of the Lord.* It is used with dates in the Christian era only when necessary for clearness. When so used, it precedes the date.

He was born 36 B.C. and died A.D. 22.

Ad. This abbreviation for *advertisement* is acceptable in informal conversation, but it is still considered too new for use in writing or in formal speech.

Advise, inform, apprise, acquaint. *Advise* in the sense of *inform* has been one of the sins of the business-letter writer. In ordinary writing it should be avoided as an error in taste. See *Webster's New International Dictionary.*

Affect, effect. These two words may be confused because of a similarity in sound. *Affect* means *to influence.* *Effect* means *to bring about, to accomplish.*

The strike will affect the lumber industry.
The labor board will attempt to effect a compromise.

Both words have noun uses, for which you may consult a dictionary.

Aggravate. *Aggravate*, in the sense of *provoke, irritate, annoy, exasperate*, is still considered an error although good writers have so used the word. It is better to say *annoy* when you mean *annoy*, and to save *aggravate* for its true meaning, *to increase, to make worse*.

Her complaints annoyed (not *aggravated*) me.
The terrible heat aggravated her headache.

Ain't, an't. Illiterate for *are not, am not, is not, have not*. If you want to use a contraction, say *aren't, isn't, haven't*, but not *ain't, an't*, or *amn't*. The English language has no convenient contraction for *am not*.

Allow. Do not use for *assert, say, think*, or *believe*.

All-around. The correct idiomatic form is *all-round. Webster's New International Dictionary* labels the latter form *colloq.*

All the farther, all the faster, etc. Do not use for *as far as, as fast as*, etc.

This is as far as (not *all the farther*) we can go today.
Is this as fast as (not *all the faster*) your car will go?

Allude, refer. *Allude* means refer to a person or thing indirectly or by suggestion. To *refer* to something means to mention it specifically.

I shall now take time to refer (not *allude*) to the question of smoking on the campus.
I shall now take time to speak of (or to discuss) the question of smoking on the campus.
When the teacher spoke of "budding Swifts," every student wondered to whom he was alluding.

Alright. The correct form is *all right*. There are no such forms as *all-right, allright*, or *alright*. Used in the sense of *satisfactory*, or *certainly* or *very well*, the expression should be avoided in formal writing. See Fowler, *A Dictionary of Modern English Usage*, p. 16, and Krapp, *A Comprehensive Guide to Good English*, pp. 32–33.

Altogether, all together. *Altogether*, an adverb, means *entirely, completely, on the whole.*

After a long separation, we were all together again.
It was altogether too much to expect of so young a child.

And etc. *Etc.* means *and so forth.* *And etc.* would mean *and and so forth.*

A.M., P.M. Do not use for *in the morning* or *in the afternoon.*

This afternoon (not *this P.M.*) we shall see a football game.

Among, between. Use *among* when referring to more than two things or persons. Use *between* when referring to two things or persons.

The members of the team discussed the play among themselves.
James and Henry divided the provisions between them.

Anyplace. A colloquial form. *Anywhere* is preferred. Similar colloquial forms are *no place* for *nowhere, everyhow* for *in every way, every place* for *everywhere, some place* for *somewhere.*

Anywheres. Incorrect for *anywhere.*

Apt, likely, liable. *Apt* suggests a habitual or inherent tendency. *Likely* suggests a probable happening, usually pleasant in nature. *Liable* suggests a probability regarded as unfortunate or unfavorable.

Mrs. Jones did not mean what she said. She is apt to be irritable because she is not well.

A cheerful boy is likely to succeed in that occupation.

You are liable to break your neck if you try to climb that rock.

As . . . as, so . . . as. In negative statements some careful writers prefer *so . . . as* to *as . . . as.*

Tom is as old as I am.

I am not so sure of it as I was yesterday.

As. Do not use in place of *that* or *whether.*

I do not know whether (not *as*) I shall vote this year.

I cannot say that (not *as*) I care much for his verses.

At. Do not use, either in speech or in writing, in such sentences as: Where were you at? Where are we at now?

At about. You may use either one but not both.

We reached Pasadena at (not *at about*) seven o'clock.

Auto. Both the noun and the verb forms are marked colloquial in *Webster's New International Dictionary.*

Awful, awfully. *Awful* in the sense of *ugly, very bad, very great,* and *awfully* as a "vague intensive" are labeled slang in *Webster's New International Dictionary.* That is just too frightfully awful, one might exclaim, since cultured and educated women—and men, too—will continue to speak sentences like these: We are *terribly* grateful! Thanks *awfully.* I was *frightfully* bored. That is just *too, too* precious! I am *so* happy. The use of "vague intensives" in formal and serious writing is, of course, a different matter. But see Krapp, *A Comprehensive Guide to Good English,* p. 63.

Back of, in back of. *Back of* is colloquial for *behind*. *Back of* is defensible in informal writing, but *in back of*, probably suggested by *in front of*, is considered undesirable in both speech and writing.

Badly. Used colloquially for *very much* or *very greatly* with words signifying *to want* or *to need*.

> *Colloquial:* He needs a haircut very badly.
> I want to go badly.

Balance. Colloquial when used for *the remainder, the rest*.

> *Colloquial:* The balance of the team is stronger than it was last year.
> *Literary:* The rest of the team is stronger than it was last year.
> *Colloquial:* We played cards the balance of the evening.
> *Literary:* We played cards the rest of the evening.

Bank on. In the sense of *rely upon* it is a colloquial idiom. Do not use in formal writing.

Because of. See *reason is*.

Beside, besides. According to present usage, *beside* is employed as a preposition meaning *at the side of*, as in *Please sit down beside me*. *Besides* is ordinarily used as an adverb, meaning *in addition to*. For other uses of *beside* and *besides*, some of them obsolete, consult *Webster's New International Dictionary*.

Between, among. See *among*. For a discussion of other faulty uses, see Fowler, *A Dictionary of Modern English Usage*, p. 50.

Blame on. Do not use for *blame* or *put the blame on.*

> *Wrong:* He blamed the mistake on me.
> *Right:* He blamed me for the mistake.
> He put the blame for the mistake on me.

Boughten. Dialectal for *bought.*

> I prefer bought (not *boughten*) bread to homemade bread.

Broadcast, broadcasted. *Broadcasted* seems to have been accepted as a correct form when used in connection with the radio.

Burst, bust, busted, bursted. *Bust, bursted,* and *busted* are considered dialectal, inelegant, and slangy. But he who has occasion to say that he is *going on a bust* should not make matters worse by saying he is *going on a burst!* See Fowler, *A Dictionary of Modern English Usage,* p. 59.

But what, but that. Both should be avoided when a simple *that* is meant.

> I have no doubt that (not *but that*) they will come.

Calculate, reckon. Colloquial for *plan, think, expect.*

Can, may. *Can* implies ability. *May* implies permission or possibility.

> Mother, may (not *can*) I go now?
> Howard can speak three languages.
> If it does not rain, we may go for a walk.

Can't hardly. To be avoided as a double negative. Say *can hardly.*

Can't seem to. A colloquial expression for *seem unable to.*

Cannot help but admire. You may avoid difficulties if you say *cannot help admiring*, but see what Mr. Curme has to say about this form in *Syntax*, pp. 252–253.

Cause of. It is illogical to say that the *cause of* something was *on account of*. Complete the sentence with a substantive. For a discussion of this subject, see Fowler, *A Dictionary of Modern English Usage*, p. 71.

The cause of my late theme was my having (not *on account of having*) too much work to do.
The cause of my late theme was the fact that I had too much work to do.

Caused by, due to, owing to. Grammarians are still fighting over these three forms. *Owing to* seems to be generally recognized as a compound preposition. *Caused by* and *due to* are still used by careful writers with proper regard for their adjectival function. A simple means of avoiding error is to use *caused by* and *due to* only after a verb.

Wrong: Due to the accident, I came late.
Right: My lateness was due to the accident.
Wrong: Caused by a rainy season, the crop was a failure.
Right: The failure of the crop was caused by the rainy season.

Consult also: Curme, *Syntax*, pp. 560–561; Fowler, *A Dictionary of Modern English Usage*, p. 123; Krapp, *A Comprehensive Guide to Good English*, p. 210.

Claim. Do not use for *say, assert, declare, maintain.*

He says (not *claims*) that he came in before ten o'clock.

Combine. *Webster's New International Dictionary* states that it is an American colloquialism for "a combination of persons or organizations to effect some commercial, industrial, or political object." You might say *a trust, a ring, a cabal, a conspiracy, a gang, a junto*, but none of these means exactly the same thing as *combine*.

Company. Colloquial for *guests, visitors, escort.*

Complected. Do not use for *complexioned.*

I met a dark-complexioned (not *dark-complected*) man.

Considerable. Colloquial when used as a noun. For the British usage, see Fowler, *A Dictionary of Modern English Usage*, p. 92. See also Krapp, *A Comprehensive Guide to Good English*, pp. 160–161.

Colloquial: He lost considerable by gambling.
Formal: He lost a considerable amount by gambling.

Continual, continuous. If a difference exists between the meanings of *continual* and *continuous*, it is that *continual* implies a continued succession or recurrence, and *continuous* implies unbroken continuity.

He wrote his play in spite of continual interruptions.
The men advanced toward the continuous roar of distant artillery.

Contractions. In formal and serious writing avoid such contractions as *I'm, I'd, he'll, don't, doesn't, can't*, and so forth. These are correct in speech and in informal writing.

Could of. Illiterate for *could have.*

Couldn't seem to. See *can't seem to.*

Couple. Colloquial for *two, a few.*

Colloquial: A couple of men left the theater.
Formal: Two (or *several*) men left the theater.

Criticize. May mean *to find fault with* but may also mean *to judge, to review.*

Crowd. Colloquial for *a set, clique.*

Data, strata, phenomena. These are plural, not singular forms. The singular forms are *datum, stratum, phenomenon.*

Date. A blanket colloquialism for everything from a casual meeting to an assignation. It seems a pity that the English language is so poor that it does not have an acceptable word for a concept so important in the life of an undergraduate. After all, a *date* is not exactly an *appointment,* nor an *engagement*—certainly not an *assignation.* Nor could a college girl who brought her "date" to her mother's home find time to speak of him as "the male person with whom I have made a social engagement."

Deal. Used figuratively in "a square deal" or "a new deal," but still considered colloquial when used for "a political bargain."

Different than. The correct American idiom is *different from.* But see the note on *different than* in *Webster's New International Dictionary.*

She is different from (not *different than*) other girls.

Doesn't, don't. The accepted contraction of *does not* is *doesn't.* The contraction of *do not* is *don't.*

Harry doesn't (not *don't*) care for golf.

Dove. Colloquial for *dived.*

He dived (not *dove*) into the pool.

Drownded. The correct form is *drowned.*

Due to. See *caused by.*

Effect. See *affect.*

Elegant. Should not be used to mean *excellent, beautiful, good.*
That was a delicious (not *elegant*) salad.

Elegant means *characterized by elegance, fastidious, refined.*
It is correct to speak of elegant furnishings, an elegant
style, an elegant gentleman.

Enthuse. The correct form is *to be enthusiastic.*
Who could become enthusiastic (not *could enthuse*) about this
game?

Equally as. The *as* is unnecessary. Say *equally good* or *just as
good.* See Fowler, *A Dictionary of Modern English Usage,*
p. 145.

Wrong: My theme is equally as good as his.
Right: My theme is just as good as his.

Etc. *Et cetera,* meaning *and so forth, and others, and the rest,*
should never be used in literary or artistic writing. If you
use it in informal writing, never write *and etc.*

Everyplace, everywheres. See *anyplace.*

Exam. An abbreviation, like *prof., lab., soph., frosh., chem.,
libe.,* never correct in writing and to be avoided in formal
speech.

Except. Not at present used for *unless.*

Wrong: I will not go except you go too.
Right: I will not go unless you go too.

Expect. Do not use for *suspect* or *suppose*.

> *Wrong:* I expect that he will be late.
> *Right:* I suspect (or *suppose*) that he will be late.

Extra. Do not use for *very* or *unusually*.

> She served an unusually (not *extra*) good dinner.

Favor. Do not use for *letter* in business correspondence.

Fellow. Colloquial for *a person, a boy, a man, a beau, a sweet-heart*. Do not use in ordinary writing.

> *Colloquial:* One of the fellows borrowed my shirt.
> *Formal:*　　One of the boys (or *men*) borrowed my shirt.

> *Colloquial:* My sister has a fellow.
> *Formal:*　　My sister has a sweetheart.

Fewer, less. Use *fewer* when referring to numbers. Use *less* when referring to quantity or degree. See *less*.

Fix. In the sense of *a predicament, to arrange, to repair*, it is colloquial. But read Mr. Krapp's defense of this word in *A Comprehensive Guide to Good English*, pp. 248–249.

> The boys were in a bad predicament (not *fix*).
> Wait until I arrange (not *fix*) my hair.
> Can you repair (not *fix*) this alarm clock?

Flunk. College slang for *a failure* or *to fail*.

For to. Now archaic or illiterate. Omit *for* in such expressions as: He went for to buy a new hat.

Funny. Colloquial for *strange, queer, odd*.

Gent. Vulgar for *gentleman*.

Get. *Get to go* for *manage* or *contrive* is dialectal. *Have got* for *have* or *possess* is colloquial. Study the list of idioms, some of them colloquial or slang, under *get* in *Webster's New International Dictionary*. See also Krapp, *A Comprehensive Guide to Good English*, p. 270.

Gotten. *Got* is preferred to *gotten* as the past participle. See Fowler, *A Dictionary of Modern English Usage*, p. 217.

Had of. Illiterate for *had*.

I wish I had (not *had of*) written my theme yesterday.

Had better, had best, had rather. Just as correct as *would better, would best, would rather*.

Had ought. Illiterate for *ought*.

I ought (not *had ought*) to go home.

Hanged, hung. Use *hanged* with reference to the death penalty.

Carter was hanged (not *hung*) for murdering his wife.
Her wet clothes were hung (not *hanged*) on a stick before the fire.

Hardly, scarcely, only, but. Do not use with another negative.

I was so tired that I could (not *couldn't*) hardly move.
The little animal ventures out (not *does not venture out*) only at night.
He could (not *couldn't*) scarcely see the man on the dock.

Have got. See *get*.

Healthful, healthy. *Webster's New International Dictionary* states that *healthy* and *healthful* "are interchangeable within certain limits." But in a strict sense, *healthy* means *being in a state of health; healthful* means *serving to promote health*.

In back of. The American colloquial idiom is *back of*. The literary form is *behind*.

Inside of. The *of* is unnecessary. In reference to time, meaning *within, in less than*, the expression is colloquial.

You are safe inside the (not *inside of the*) corral.
Within (not *inside of*) an hour, every servant had left.

Invite. Do not use for *an invitation*.

We sent her an invitation (not *an invite*) to the dance.

Is when, is where. Do not use as subjective complements. Do not say: A sonnet is when a poem has fourteen lines. A touchdown is where a man carries the ball over the goal line. Use a noun or a noun clause to complete the sentence.

A sonnet is a poem of fourteen lines.
A touchdown is carrying the ball over the goal line.
A touchdown is made when a player carries the ball over the goal line.

Its, it's. *Its* is the possessive form of it. *It's* is the contraction of *it is*. Do not confuse the two forms.

Job. Commercial slang when used for *model, design, color*.

Just. See *awfully*.

Kind, sort. The words are singular and therefore should be modified by singular modifiers.

I do not like this (not *these*) sort of apples.

Kind of, sort of. Colloquial when used to modify a verb or an adjective. Use *somewhat, somehow, rather, in some degree, for some reason*.

It is still early, but I feel somewhat (not *sort of*) tired.

When used correctly, to express a class, *kind of* and *sort of* should not be followed by *a* or *an*.

He is that kind of (not *kind of a*) doctor.

Lay, lie. Learn the principal parts of these two verbs. Do not confuse them.

The dog was lying (not *laying*) in the road.
It had lain (not *laid*) there all morning.
He had laid (not *lain*) his bundle on the table.

Leave, let. *Leave* means *to abandon* or *to go away*. *Let* means *to allow*.

Please let (not *leave*) me go with you.
Please leave me; I wish to be alone.

Less, fewer. *Less* refers to quantity; *fewer* refers to numbers.

There are fewer (not *less*) boys than girls in the room.

Liable, apt, likely. See *apt*.

Like, as, as if. *Like* is a preposition. It is followed by the objective case. It should not be used to introduce a clause. See Curme, *Syntax*, pp. 281–282.

I am like her in my love of music.
I felt like telling him to go home.
Let us sing as (not *like*) the birds sing.
They write as if (not *like*) they knew something.

Line. Use with extreme care or not at all. See *field* in Fowler, *A Dictionary of Modern English Usage*, p. 179.

Poor: We bought a few things in the line of groceries.
Right: We bought some groceries.

Poor: Have you any interesting books in the line of fiction?
Right: Have you any interesting novels?

Poor: He wrote epics and other poems along that line.
Right: He wrote epics and other narrative poems.

Literally. Use accurately. Do not use when you mean *figuratively, practically,* or *virtually.*

Literature. Do not use *literature* when you mean *advertising, handbills, circulars,* or *printed folders.*

Locate. A colloquialism for *settle.*

He settled (not *located*) in Oregon.

Lot, lots of. Colloquial for *many, much, a large number, a large amount.*

There is much (not *a lot*) still to be done.
Many (not *lots of*) freshmen did not buy green caps.

Mad. *Mad* means *insane.* It is colloquial for *angry.*

My mother was angry (not *mad*) because I went fishing.

Might of. Illiterate for *might have.*

Messrs. Pronounced *mĕs′rz.* Plural of *Mr.,* and (like *Mr.*) not to be used without names following it.

Most. Illiterate for *almost.*

Almost (not *most*) any kind of answer will do.
She is almost (not *most*) as tall as I am.

No good. Colloquial when used for *worthless, useless, of no value.*

The check is worthless (not *no good*).

Noplace. See *anyplace.*

Nowhere near. Colloquial for *not nearly*.

This is not nearly (not *nowhere near*) as much as I expected.

Off of. The *of* is unnecessary.

He jumped off (not *off of*) the dock.

Onto. *Onto,* as one word, is a colloquial preposition for *upon.* As two words, it is correct when *on* is an adverb.

He climbed upon (not *onto*) a chair.
We went on to the end of the road.

Other times. Use *at other times*.

Out loud. Colloquial for *aloud, loud, loudly, audibly*.

He pronounced the words loudly (not *out loud*) so everyone could hear.
He called aloud (not *out loud*) for help.

Outside of. Colloquial for *except, besides*.

No one saw him except (not *outside of*) three small boys who were playing ball in the street.

Party. Do not use for *person*.

Do you know the person (not *party*) in the next seat?

Pep. Juvenile slang for *energy, high spirits, liveliness, activity*.

Per. Except in technical writing, should be used only with Latin words, such as *diem, annum*. Do not use *as per* for *according to*.

He received five thousand dollars a year (not *per year*).
We sold the horses according to (not *as per*) your instructions.

Per cent. Not strictly correct as a synonym for *percentage.* Correct after numerals. Do not use the sign % except after figures in technical writing or in tabulations.

A small percentage (not *per cent*) of them refused to join.
Over eighty per cent (not *eighty %,* or *80%*) of them were either killed or wounded.

Phenomena. A plural form. The singular is *phenomenon.*

Piece. Incorrect for *a short distance.*

Will you walk a short distance (not *a piece*) with me?

Plan on. The *on* is unnecessary.

We planned (not *planned on*) a fishing trip.
We planned to go (not *on going*) fishing.

Plenty. Colloquial in such expressions as *plenty hot enough, plenty good enough.*

He was very (not *plenty*) rich.
There is enough (not *plenty*) wood for another fire.

Poorly. Colloquial for *in poor health, not well, unwell.*

Aunt Sarah has been in poor health (not *poorly*) all year.

Proposition. Avoid using *proposition* for *project, task, a commercial enterprise, proposal, objective, problem, undertaking, prospect.* See Fowler, *A Dictionary of Modern English Usage,* pp. 469–470.

Proven. The correct form is *proved. Proven,* according to *Webster's New International Dictionary,* is archaic and dialectal, but it seems to be holding its own in American speech and writing.

We have proved (not *proven*) that the plan is unsound.

Quite. Means *entirely, completely,* as in *The theme is not quite ready.* Used colloquially, it means also *to a considerable extent, rather.*

Colloquial: Your theme is quite good.

Quite a few, quite a number, quite a little. All colloquial expressions.

Raise, rise. Two verbs often confused. Learn the principal parts.

Real. Do not use for *really* or *very.*

It was a very (not *a real*) exciting game.

Reason is because, reason is due to, reason is on account of. All incorrect. Complete a *reason is* clause with a noun or a noun clause.

The reason he was late was that (not *because*) the roads were blocked.
The reason for my poor work in English was my poor high-school preparation (not *due to my poor high-school* preparation).

Remember of. The *of* is unnecessary.

I do not remember (not *remember of*) his taking the package when he left.

Right. *Right,* in the sense of *very,* is dialectal.

He was a very (not *right*) good speaker.

Rise. See *raise.*

The water has risen (not *raised*) two feet since morning.

Same, such. Do not use as a substitute for a pronoun.

Please repair the camera and ship it (not *same*) to me tomorrow.

Seldom ever, seldom or ever. The correct expressions are *seldom, very seldom, hardly ever, seldom if ever.*

Set, sit. Two verbs often confused. Learn the principal parts.

Please sit (not *set*) down.
He set the parcel on a shelf and sat down.

Shape. Colloquial for *condition.*

The equipment was in good condition (not *good shape*).

Show. Colloquial for *play, concert, opera, chance, opportunity.*

We enjoyed the performance (not *show*).
He tried hard but he had no chance (not *show*) of winning against Louis.

Sign up, sign up with. Colloquial for *engage, enroll, join.*

The foreman hired (not *signed up*) three new men.
Harry joined (not *signed up with*) the navy.

Some. Do not use for *somewhat, a little.*

He is somewhat (not *some*) better this morning.
I worked a little (not *some*) last month.

Sort of. See *kind of.*

So. In writing avoid the use of *so* as the "feminine intensive." See *awful, awfully.*

She was very (not *so*) kind.

So. As a conjunction, in the sense of *with the result that, so* is colloquial. In writing do not use it to join co-ordinate clauses.

Weak: The men were tired and discouraged, so they went home.
Better: Since the men were tired and discouraged, they went home.

Specie, species. Consult the dictionary. *Species,* meaning *kind, class,* has the same form in the singular and plural.

Such. See *so, awfully.*

Sure. Do not use for *surely, certainly, indeed.*

This is certainly (not *sure*) an interesting story.

Suspicion. Do not use as a verb. The correct form is *to suspect.*

We suspected (not *suspicioned*) that something was wrong.

Swell. Colloquial for *stylish, fashionable, smartly clothed.* Slang for *excellent, very good, interesting, enjoyable,* and a host of other words expressing approval or commendation.

We had an enjoyable (not *a swell*) evening.
It is a thrilling (not *a swell*) game.

Take stock in. Colloquial for *accept, to believe, to put faith in.*

Can we believe (not *take stock in*) his promises?

That there, this here, etc. Illiterate forms. Use *that, this, these, those.*

Wait on. Correct in the sense of *attend, perform services for.* Colloquial when used to mean *wait for* or *stay for.*

Are you the girl who waited on us?
Will you wait for (not *wait on*) me if I hurry?

Want in, want off, want out, etc. Dialectal forms for *want to come in, want to go out, want to get off.*

Open the door. I think Rover wants to get in (not *wants in*).
I want to get off (not *want off*) at the corner of Sixth and Washington.

Ways. Dialectal and colloquial for *distance, way*.

We walked a long distance (not *ways*) before we rested.

Where at. Do not use for *where*.

Where (not *where at*) is he now?

Without. Illiterate for *unless*.

I will not go unless (not *without*) you go too.

Part III: Appendix

DIAGRAMS

A diagram is a picture showing the relation between the different elements of the sentence.

Diagraming is useful in teaching grammar and sentence structure to the visual-minded students, to those who grasp an idea more quickly if they see it pictured than if they hear it explained. Diagrams should be used principally in the early stages of the study of grammar. Beyond a certain point they begin to lose their usefulness rapidly. Diagram forms should themselves be simple, and they should be used with comparatively simple sentences. Once the student has mastered the basic patterns of sentence structure, he will be able to build the more complex patterns with greater sureness and ease. The construction of architectural monstrosities in the name of diagraming should be avoided as a waste of time.

Any system of diagraming may be used, so long as it is simple and logical.

SUBJECT AND VERB

In a diagram, the simple subject and verb are placed on a horizontal line, which is cut by a vertical line separating the subject from the verb.

Time flies.

Time	flies

Games are won.

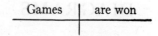

Potatoes should have been planted.

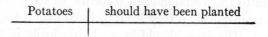

Men, women, and children shouted and screamed.

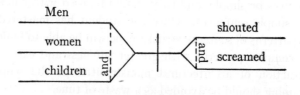

EXERCISE

Exercise 1. Diagram the following sentences.

1. Birds sing.
2. Harry and I quarreled.
3. Spring has come.
4. Sally and Jim laughed and shouted.

SUBJECT, VERB, AND COMPLEMENTS

The direct object is placed on the principal line, after the verb, and separated from it by a vertical line which does not cut the horizontal line.

She will believe anything.

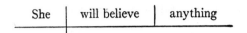

Remove your cap.

```
(You) | remove | cap
```

The subjective complement and the objective complement are placed on the main horizontal line. The direction of the dividing line indicates the grammatical relationship of the complement to either the subject or the predicate.

The milk tastes sour.

```
milk | tastes \ sour
```

He is an officer.

```
He | is \ officer
```

They elected him their chairman.

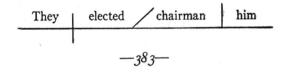

DIAGRAMS

The indirect object is placed on a horizontal line below the principal line. A slanting line is used to connect this line with the main line at a point directly under the verb.

Father gave me a dollar.

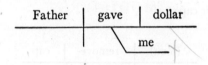

Mr. White taught us mathematics and chemistry.

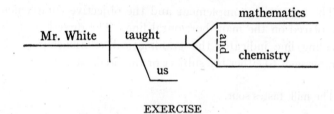

EXERCISE

Exercise 1. Diagram the subject, verb, and complement (if any) in each of the following sentences.

1. Will you do me a favor?

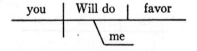

2. All of his wealth was invested in a Mexican mine.
3. Every afternoon at four o'clock, a cool breeze comes from the west.
4. His last days were spent in poverty and distress.
5. For his evening meal he heated a can of beans.
6. His inability to speak Chinese was a handicap to him.

—*384*—

7. In spite of the rain the men fished until dark.
8. According to their code, honest poverty was not a disgrace.
9. The other three boys removed the body from the tracks.
10. Disgraced and friendless, the culprit boarded a freight train for the West.

MODIFIERS

Modifiers are placed on slanting lines under the words they modify.

The little old lady smiled sweetly.

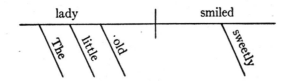

The little boy gave his mother a red rose.

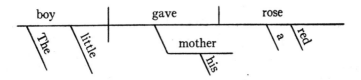

The diagram of a prepositional phrase is placed under the word it modifies.

The father of the child watched from the window.

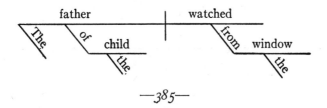

DIAGRAMS

Under the bridge two tramps had built a fire.

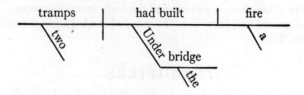

A participle is placed on a broken line under the line of the word it modifies.

Having given him the required amount, I left the store.

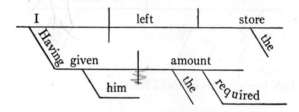

EXERCISE

Exercise 1. Diagram each of the following sentences.

1. Having shut off the radio, George picked up his hat and went out.

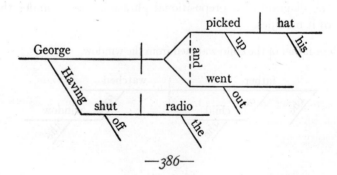

2. The torn and tattered flag hung on the wire, flapping gently in the breeze.

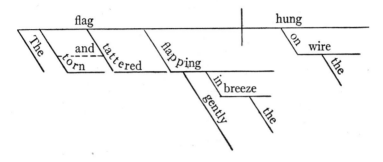

3. On the upper shelf are two broken dishes.
4. Being a woman, she could not reply properly.
5. The sound of his voice reached us clearly.
6. He looked under the bed and found a whimpering puppy.
7. He cast his line into the rippling waters.
8. In spite of his warning, I knocked on the closed door.
9. Having finished his breakfast, he went into the garden.
10. A closed door barred his progress.
11. Smiling faces greeted him.
12. The frightened horse galloped off.
13. Picking up his book, the boy walked out.
14. A barking dog stood at the gate.
15. He hung his torn coat on the nail.
16. She gave an apple to the crying child.
17. Protesting tearfully, the boy removed his shoes.

GERUND AND INFINITIVE

The gerund is placed on a stepped line. The position of this line must depend on the function of the gerund. Since a gerund may have modifiers and complements, you must raise its diagram on stilts in order to give yourself sufficient room.

Working in a garden is his recreation.

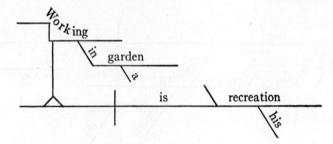

Hearing that song brings back sad memories to me.

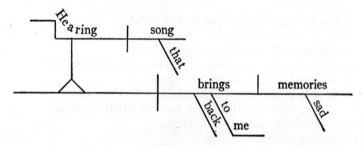

Mary objected to my telling the story.

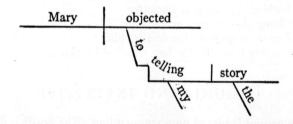

The infinitive phrase is diagramed like a prepositional phrase, but the diagram is raised on stilts to allow room for modifiers.

GERUND AND INFINITIVE

She wanted me to drive the car.

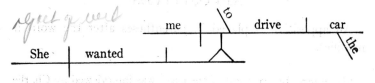

My orders were to deliver the guns.

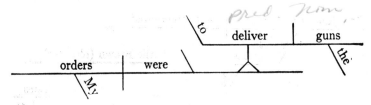

I am happy to see you again.

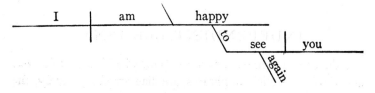

EXERCISE

Exercise 1. Diagram the following sentences.

1. Collecting old books is his hobby.
2. To work is to pray.
3. After removing my cap, I politely addressed the dean.
4. The day is sure to be pleasant.
5. Susan promised to buy a new dress.
6. It is easy to laugh at his plight.
7. The committee asked to see the dean.
8. The food is ready to be served.
9. Crying will do no good.
10. He had a right to be offended.

APPOSITIVES

An appositive is placed in parentheses after the word it modifies.

Mr. Jones, the president of the class, was interviewed by Charlie Brown, a reporter from the *News*.

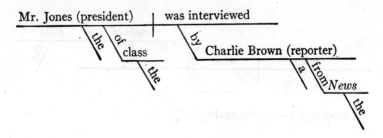

INDEPENDENT ELEMENTS

Independent elements, such as nouns of address, expletives, and absolute participial phrases, are diagramed separately, the diagram being placed above the main diagram.

Howard, bring me that book.

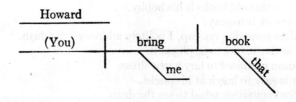

INDEPENDENT ELEMENTS

To tell the truth, he never promised to take it.

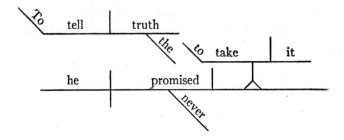

The game being won, they smiled happily.

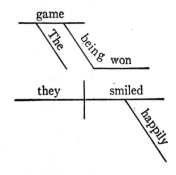

EXERCISE

Exercise 1. Diagram the following sentences.

1. Mrs. Blake, the housemother, greeted us at the door.
2. The rain having stopped, we continued our game.
3. The rest of the boys went to the game.
4. He gave the package to Jones, the janitor of the building.
5. The men abandoned their position, all their ammunition having been exhausted.
6. Mother, have you seen the flying kite?
7. The doors being locked, we tried to open a window.
8. Give the story to Mr. Sanders, the night editor.

COMPLEX SENTENCES

Diagram a noun clause as you would diagram a separate sentence. Raise the diagram on stilts and place it in proper relation to the main diagram.

What he told the officers was never revealed.

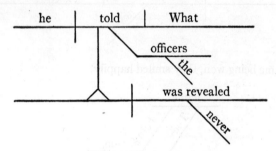

The teacher said that the answer was correct.

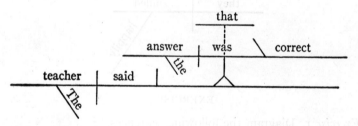

Give it to whoever calls for it.

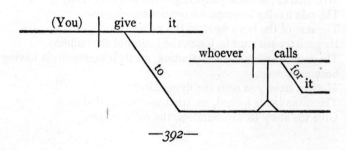

COMPLEX SENTENCES

Diagram an adjective clause as if it were a separate sentence. Use a dotted line to connect the clause with the word it modifies.

This is the boy who brought the papers.

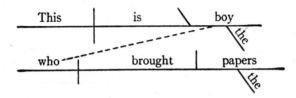

We visited the place where the first battle of the war was fought.

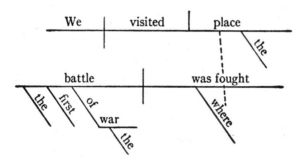

We visited the field on which the first battle of the war was fought.

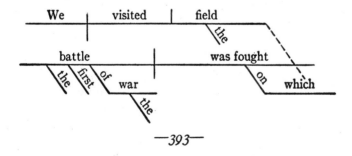

Diagram an adverbial clause as if it were a separate sentence. Use a dotted line to connect the verb of the adverbial clause with the word which the clause modifies. Write the subordinating connective along the dotted line.

The whistle blew before the ball was fumbled.

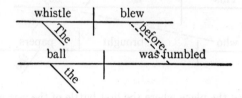

He ran as fast as he could.

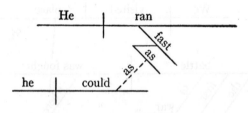

Carol is prettier than I am.

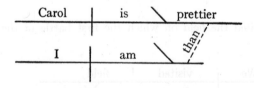

EXERCISE

Exercise 1. Diagram the following sentences.

1. Whoever answers my question will receive a prize.
2. Send home whoever is playing in the garden.
3. He said that he could not understand me.

4. This is the boy who took your flowers.
5. The dean is a woman whom everyone respects.
6. He found the place where he had left his baggage.
7. She wanted to learn how she could become popular.
8. If I go, will you go?
9. We ate whatever she brought us.
10. Warbuck is heavier than his brother.

THE COMPOUND SENTENCE

Diagram the compound sentence as you would two simple sentences, one above the other. Connect the verbs of the two clauses by a stepped line, on the horizontal part of which you place the conjunction.

The performance was poor, but the audience was enthusiastic.

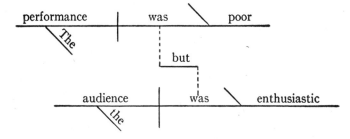

In the diagram of a compound-complex sentence, the diagrams of subordinate clauses are connected with the words they modify as in the diagrams of complex sentences.

EXERCISE

Exercise 1. Diagram the following sentences.

1. Spring is here, and the days are filled with activity.
2. The boys were discouraged over the tied score, but they smiled as if the game had been won.

3. The reception was scheduled for eight, but no one came until ten.
4. The night was stormy, but a large crowd came in spite of the weather.
5. You speak as if he were your friend.
6. Wisdom is better than rubies.
7. Every dog has his day, but the night belongs to the cats.
8. He knew the right time to say nothing.
9. Mere ideals are the cheapest things in life.
10. All is well that ends well.

PREPARATION OF MANUSCRIPT

A manuscript (either in handwriting or in typewriting) intended to be set into type by a printer is called *copy*. The person who revises a manuscript for publication is called a *copyreader*. It is the duty of the author to prepare his manuscript in such a way that the printer will be able to set it up with the fewest possible changes or corrections. The author, not the copyreader, should be responsible for grammatical correctness, for sentence structure, for correct punctuation, capitalization, and word division. The business of the copyreader, often called the "copy preparer," is to make the copy ready for the printer. It is true that he will check the uniformity of spelling, capitalization, punctuation, and word division, and that he will correct obvious errors in grammar, but his chief function is to indicate to the typesetter the kind of type to be used, the arrangement on the page, the spacing, and such matters. The real responsibility, however, for "clean" copy rests with the author. He must not shirk it or delegate it to others.

For information on the preparation of manuscript, see the chapters on mechanics, punctuation, and spelling in this book. If you have frequent occasions to prepare manuscripts for publication, get a copy of the *United States Government Printing Office Style Manual*, which may be purchased for a dollar from the Superintendent of Documents, Washington, D. C. Among other manuals you should seriously consider two: *A Manual of Style of the University of Chicago Press* and *The Secretary's Handbook* (published by The Macmillan Company).

PROOFREADING

A proof, or a proof sheet, is a trial impression from type, taken for the purpose of correcting errors made by the type-setter. Any errors made by the author which have escaped his or the copyreader's eyes will also be corrected in the process of proofreading.

A complete set of proofreader's marks may be found in any good dictionary or in the style manual issued by the United States Government Printing Office.

℘	Dele, or delete; take out.
◡	Close up; no space.
⊙	Insert period.
, or **,/** or ⋏	Insert comma.
; or **;/**	Insert semicolon.
: or **:/**	Insert colon.
∜ or ∜	Insert quotation marks.
∜	Insert apostrophe.
⊦=⊦ or **=/** or **-/**	Insert hyphen.
#	Space; more space.
✓	Less space.
eq. #	Equalize spacing.
↓	Push down a space.
[	Move to the left.
]	Move to the right.

⌐⌐	Elevate letter or word.
⌐⌐	Lower a letter or word.
‖	Align; straighten ends of lines.
/// or ≡	Straighten a crooked line.
ට	Turn to proper position; invert.
☐	Space with em quad; indent one em.
✗ or ⊗	Change broken letter; imperfect type.
¶	Paragraph.
𝑛𝑜 ¶	No paragraph.
l.c. or *lc*	Lower case; use small letter.
≡ or *cap.*	Use capital letter.
═ or *sc* or *s.c.*	Use small capital.
bf.	Use bold-face type.
ital.	Use italic type.
rom.	Use roman type.
tr.	Transpose.
w.f. or *wf.*	Wrong font.
ⓢⓟ	Spell out.
ld. or *lds.*	Insert lead or leads.
stet	Let it stand; restore words crossed out.
Out s.c.	Refer to copy; insert matter omitted.

A LETTER

EXECUTIVE MANSION, WASHINGTON
November 21, 1864 ☐ ☐

Mrs. Bixby, Boston, Massachusetts.

DEAR MADAME: I have been shown in the
files of the War department a statement of the
Adjutant General of Massachusetts that you are
the mother of five sons who have died gloriously
on the field of battle. I feel how weak and fruitless
must be any words of min which should attempt
to beguile you from the grief of a loss so over-
whelming. But I cannot refrain from tendering
to you the consolation that may be found in the
thanks of the Republic the died to save. I pray
that our Heavenly Father may assuage the
anguish of your bereavement and leave you only
the cherished memory of the loved and lost, and
the solemn pride that must be yours to have laid
so costly a sacrifice upon the altar of freedom
Yours very sincerely and respectfully,

ABRAHAM LINCOLN. ☐ ☐ ☐

Corrections on proof sheets should be made in the margins
directly opposite the indicated errors, usually in the nearer
margin. For every mark in the text there should be a corresponding mark or explanation in the margin. These marks
must be kept in the order in which the errors occur in the text,
and separated from each other by a vertical or diagonal line.

PRÉCIS WRITING

A précis is a condensed version of a longer composition. Its essential qualities are clearness, simplicity, good English, and absolute accuracy in thought and emphasis. The précis is said to differ from the abstract and the summary, but the distinction, if it exists except in theory, need not concern the student who is primarily concerned with the training in accurate thinking and expression which précis writing will give him. Précis writing is invaluable training in intelligent reading, straight thinking, and accurate expression. To write a good précis, a student must first master the thought of the original. He must train himself to get at the heart of the selection he is reading. No lazy, half-awake reading will do. And then he must express the essential thought of the original in clear, well-ordered, and attractive language. All this is intellectual discipline of the most useful sort.

The length of the précis will depend to a certain extent on the thought content of the original. Some writing is pithy and compact; it may be cut down but it can scarcely be boiled down. Other writing is diffuse. It will bear a loss in words without a corresponding loss in content. But as a practical guide for the beginner in précis writing, it is safe to say that a précis is usually from a fourth to a third of the length of the original.

Original

My next thought concerned the choice of an impression, or effect, to be conveyed; and here I may as well observe that, throughout the construction, I kept steadily in view the design of rendering the work universally appreciable. I should be carried too far out of my immediate topic were I to demonstrate a point upon which I have repeatedly insisted, and which, with the poetical, stands not in the slightest need of demonstration—the point, I mean, that Beauty is the sole legitimate province of the poem. A few words, however, in elucidation of my real meaning, which some of my friends have evinced a disposition to misrepresent. That pleasure which is at once the most intense, the most elevating, and the most pure is, I believe, found in the contemplation of the beautiful. When, indeed, men speak of Beauty, they mean, precisely, not a quality, as is supposed, but an effect—they refer, in short, just to that intense and pure elevation of the soul—not of intellect, or of heart—upon which I have commented, and which is experienced in consequence of contemplating the "beautiful." Now I designate Beauty as the province of the poem, merely because it is an obvious rule of art that effects should be made to spring from direct causes—that objects should be attained through means best adapted for their attainment—no one as yet having been weak enough to deny that the peculiar elevation alluded to is most readily attained in the poem. Now the object Truth, or the satisfaction of the intellect, and the object Passion, or the excitement of the heart, are, although attainable to a certain extent in poetry, far more readily attainable in prose. Truth, in fact, demands a precision, and Passion a homeliness (the truly passionate will comprehend me), which are absolutely antagonistic to that Beauty which, I maintain, is the excitement, or pleasurable elevation of the soul. It by no means follows from anything here said that passion, or even truth, may not be introduced, or even profitably introduced, into a poem—for they may serve in elucidation, or aid the general effect, as do discords in music, by contrast—but the true artist will always contrive, first, to tone them into proper subservience to the predominant aim, and secondly, to enveil them, as far as possible, in that Beauty which is the atmosphere and the essence of the poem.

—Edgar Allan Poe, *The Philosophy of Composition*.

Précis I

In considering the choice of the effect to be conveyed by the poem, I kept in mind my purpose of making the poem generally appreciable. As I have always insisted, the sole province of poetry is beauty. A pure, intense, and elevating pleasure—an elevation of the soul, not of the intellect or the heart—is to be found in the contemplation of beauty. Truth, or the satisfaction of the mind, and passion, or excitement of the emotions, are best attainable in prose, since truth requires a precision and passion a homeliness, both of which are antagonistic to beauty. Truth and passion may, however, be used as contributory effects in a poem, for either clearness or contrast.

Précis 2

I next concerned myself with the selection of an effect that would render my work universally appreciable. I have always maintained that Beauty is the sole legitimate province of the poem and is the excitement or pleasurable elevation of the soul. Truth, or the satisfaction of the intellect, and Passion, or the excitement of the heart, may be introduced into a poem, but the true artist should, first, tone them into proper subservience to the predominant aim, and, secondly, enveil them, as much as possible, in that beauty which is the atmosphere and essence of the poem.

EXERCISES

Exercise 1. Study the following précis. Judge them by these standards:

1. Has the essential thought of the original been conveyed?
2. Has any important part of the thought been omitted?
3. Have the author's ideas been given the same relative importance, or emphasis, as in the original?
4. Does the précis preserve the point of view of the original?
5. Is the précis expressed in good English?

Be specific in your criticisms of each précis. Do not say merely that the thought of the original has not been adequately reproduced; tell what ideas have been left out or slighted, what ideas have been given a prominence not found in the original. Which of the following précis is the most successful?

PRÉCIS WRITING

Précis 1

In making a choice of an impression or effect which would be universally appreciable I designated Beauty as the legitimate province of a poem. Beauty was chosen as it is the most readily attained in the poem, whereas such objects as Truth or Passion are far more readily attainable in prose. The true artist will make beauty the predominant aim but will add other objects for contrast to the general effect. They will be toned in subservience to the aim and will be enveiled, for beauty will be the atmosphere and essence of the poem.

Précis 2

Keeping the design of rendering the work universally appreciable in view, I next sought a single impression or effect. Beauty, that pleasurable effect which is at once the most intense, the most elevating, and the most pure, is the sole legitimate province of the poem. I chose it as the effect best fitted to and most readily attained in poetry. Truth and Passion may be worked into a poem as contrast but only when kept in proper subservience to the real aim and enveiled in the atmosphere of beauty.

Précis 3

My thoughts seemed to follow Poe's, that Beauty was the essential factor of a poem, for Beauty is the province of a poem. I seemed to see the fact that truth is also essential, for it infers a thought of homeliness. A combination of both of these allows a passion to steal forth and endow itself upon the poem. Yes, I believe beauty is the essence of this poem.

Précis 4

Beauty more than passion or truth should be the dominant effect of a poem. The elevation of the soul which beauty brings can only reach its greatest height in a poem, while passion and truth, which excite the heart and satisfy the intellect, are best attained in prose. The two objects, when used in a poem, should be subordinate and made as beautiful as possible.

Exercise 2. Write précis of each of the following selections:

It is a great point then to enlarge the range of studies which a University professes, even for the sake of the students; and, though they cannot pursue every subject which is open to them, they will be the gainers by living among those and under those who represent the whole circle. This I conceive to be the advantage of a seat of universal learning, considered as a place of education. An assemblage of learned men, zealous for their own sciences, and rivals of each other, are brought, by familiar intercourse and for the sake of intellectual peace, to adjust together the claims and relations of their respective subjects of investigation. They learn to respect, to consult, to aid each other. Thus is created a pure and clear atmosphere of thought, which the student also breathes, though in his own case he only pursues a few sciences out of the multitude. He profits by an intellectual tradition, which is independent of particular teachers, which guides him in his choice of subjects, and duly interprets for him those which he chooses. He apprehends the great outlines of knowledge, the principles on which it rests, the scale of its parts, its lights and its shades, its great points and its little, as he otherwise cannot apprehend them. Hence it is that his education is called "Liberal." A habit of mind is formed which lasts through life, of which the attributes are freedom, equitableness, calmness, moderation, and wisdom; or what in a former Discourse I have ventured to call a philosophical habit. This then I would assign as the special fruit of the education furnished at a University, as contrasted with other places of teaching or modes of teaching. This is the main purpose of a University in its treatment of its students.—Cardinal Newman.

Before it is very long, I am of opinion that you will both think and speak more favorably of woman than you do now. You seem to think that from Eve downwards, they have done a great deal of mischief. As for that lady, I give her up to you: but since her time, history will inform you that men have done much more mischief in the world than women; and, to say the truth, I would not advise you to trust either, more than is absolutely necessary. But this I will advise you to, which is, never to attack whole bodies of any kind; for, besides that all general rules have their exceptions, you must unnecessarily make yourself a great number of enemies, by attacking a corps collectively. Among women, as among men, there are good as well as bad; and it may be full as many, or more, good than among men. This rule holds as to lawyers, soldiers, parsons, courtiers, citizens, etc. They are all men, subject to the same passions and sentiments, differing only in the manner, according to their several educations; and it would be as imprudent as unjust to attack any of them by the lump. Individuals forgive sometimes; but bodies and societies never do. Many young people think it very genteel and witty to abuse the clergy; in which they are extremely mistaken: since in my opinion, parsons are very like men, and neither the better nor the worse for wearing a black gown. All general reflections, upon nations and societies, are the trite, threadbare jokes of those who set up for wit without having any, and so have recourse to commonplace. Judge of individuals from your own knowledge of them, and not from their sex, profession, or denomination.—Lord Chesterfield, *Letters to His Son.*

I must now beg to ask, Sir, Whence is this supposed right of the states derived? Where do they find the power to interfere with the laws of the Union? Sir, the opinion which the honorable gentleman maintains is a notion founded in a total misapprehension, in my judgment, of the origin of this government, and of the foundation on which it stands. I hold it to be a popular government, erected by the people; those who administer it, responsible to the people; and itself capable of being amended and modified, just as the people may choose it should be. It is as popular, just as truly emanating from the people, as the state governments. It is created for one purpose; the state governments for another. It has its own powers; they have theirs. There is no more authority with them to arrest the operation of a law of Congress, than with Congress to arrest the operation of their laws. We are here to administer a Constitution emanating immediately from the people, and trusted by them to our administration. It is not the creature of the state governments. It is of no moment to the argument, that certain acts of the state legislatures are necessary to fill our seats in this body. That is not one of their original state powers, a part of the sovereignty of the state. It is a duty which the people, by the Constitution itself, have imposed on the state legislatures; and which they might have left to be performed elsewhere, if they had seen fit. So they have left the choice of President with electors; but all this does not affect the proposition that the whole government, President, Senate, and House of Representatives, is a popular government. It leaves it still all its popular character. The governor of a state (in some of the states) is chosen, not directly by the people, but by those who are chosen by the people, for the purpose of performing, among other duties, that of electing a governor. Is the government of a state, on that account, not a popular government? This government, Sir, is the independent offspring of the popular will. It is not the creature of state legislatures; nay, more, if the whole truth must be told, the people brought it into existence, established it, and have hitherto supported it, for the very purpose, amongst others, of imposing certain salutary restraints on state sovereignties. The states cannot now make war; they cannot contract alliances; they cannot make, each for itself, separate regulations of commerce; they cannot lay imposts; they cannot coin money. If this Constitution, Sir, be the creature of state legislatures, it must be admitted that it has obtained a strange control over the volitions of its creators.—Daniel Webster, *Reply to Hayne.*

The regulation of streams by storage reservoirs is really an imitation of what nature is able to accomplish by the forests. Forests at the sources of the streams are veritable storage reservoirs, and without them no artificial remedy can be either adequate or permanent. Erosion destroys reservoirs, and must be controlled if reservoirs are to succeed. This can be done only by conserving or restoring the forests. The forest cover alone can reduce the amount of sediment carried by water, and make possible the permanent improvement of inland waterways. To check erosion by reforestation, work must begin in the highlands, because there the slopes are the steepest, the rainfall greatest, and the action of frost most considerable, and therefore the process of erosion is most rapid and the results most destructive.—Gifford Pinchot.

The only difference between organisms which annually produce eggs or seeds by the thousand, and those which produce extremely few, is, that the slow-breeders would require a few more years to people, under favorable conditions, a whole district, let it be ever so large. The condor lays a couple of eggs and the ostrich a score, and yet in the same country the condor may be the more numerous of the two; the Fulmar petrel lays but one egg, yet it is believed to be the most numerous bird in the world. One fly deposits hundreds of eggs, and another, like the hippobosca, a single one; but this difference does not determine how many individuals of the two species can be supported in a district. A large number of eggs is of some importance to those species which depend on a fluctuating amount of food, for it allows them rapidly to increase in number. But the real importance of a large number of eggs or seeds is to make up for much destruction at some period of life; and this period in a great majority of cases is an early one. If an animal can in any way protect its own eggs or young, a small number may be produced, and yet the average stock be fully kept up; but if many eggs or young are destroyed, many must be produced, or the species will become extinct. It would suffice to keep up the full number of a tree, which lived on an average for a thousand years, if a single seed were produced once in a thousand years, supposing that this seed were never destroyed, and could be insured to germinate in a fitting place. So that, in all cases, the average number of any animal or plant depends only indirectly on the number of its eggs or seeds.

—Charles Darwin.

The increased momentum of American life, both in its particles and its mass, unquestionably has a considerable moral and social value. It is the beginning, the only possible beginning, of a better life for the people as individuals and for society. So long as the great majority of the poor in any country are inert and are laboring without any hope of substantial rewards in this world, the whole associated life of that community rests on an equivocal foundation. Its moral and social order is tied to an economic system which starves and mutilates the great majority of the population, and under such conditions its religion necessarily becomes a spiritual drug, administered for the purpose of subduing the popular discontent and relieving the popular misery. The only way the associated life of such a community can be radically improved is by the leavening of the inert popular mass. Their wants must be satisfied and increased with the habit of satisfaction. During the past hundred years every European state has made a great stride in the direction of arousing its poorer citizens to be more wholesomely active, discontented, and expectant; but our own country has succeeded in traveling farther in this direction than has any other, and it may well be proud of its achievement. That the American political and economic system has accomplished so much on behalf of the ordinary man does constitute the fairer hope that men have been justified in entertaining of a better worldly order; and any higher social achievement, which America may hereafter reach, must depend upon an improved perpetuation of this process. The mass of mankind must be aroused to still greater activity by a still more abundant satisfaction of their needs, and by a consequent increase of their aggressive discontent.

—Herbert Croly, *The Promise of American Life*. Published by The Macmillan Company.

LETTER WRITING

A letter is, in a sense, a theme, governed by the same laws of writing that govern every other kind of composition. It must be clear, well organized, coherent. It must be correct in spelling, grammar, and punctuation. And it should be interesting. Interest in a letter, as in other forms of composition, can be created by concreteness, by originality, by vitality. But a letter is also governed by certain other laws, or conventions, of usage, which the letter writer cannot ignore without serious penalty. Since everyone has occasion to write letters—personal letters, business letters, informal or formal social notes—the college student should know the correct usage in the different types of letters.

These are the parts of a letter:
1. The heading.
2. The inside address.
3. The salutation or greeting.
4. The body of the letter.
5. The complimentary close.
6. The signature.

For each of these parts usage has prescribed certain set forms. These forms must not be ignored or altered, especially in business letters. Conformity is a virtue here, not originality.

THE HEADING

The parts of a heading, written in the following order, are the street address, the name of city or town, the name of the state, the date. A letterhead takes the place of a typed address.

On paper with letterheads, the writer types the date, either directly under the letterhead or flush with the right-hand margin of the letter.

[*Letterhead*]

March 20, 1938

(or)   March 20
1938

(or)   20th
March
1938

On paper that does not have a letterhead, the writer types the heading at the right according to one of the following forms:

327 East Walnut Street
Glendale, California
March 20, 1938

327 East Walnut Street,
Glendale, Calif.,
March 20, 1938.

Department of English
Oregon State College
Corvallis, Oregon
February 24, 1938

Philomath, Oregon
July 5, 1938

The first and third examples show the block form with open punctuation. The second example shows the indented form with closed punctuation. The last example shows the indented form with open punctuation.

THE INSIDE ADDRESS

In a business letter the inside address is the address of the person written to. In a personal letter the inside address is usually omitted. It may, however, be written at the bottom of a personal letter, in the lower left-hand corner. The first line of the inside address should be flush with the left-hand margin of the letter. One of the following forms may be used, but the style should be the same as in the heading. Either the block form or the indented form should be used throughout the letter.

Dr. Claudius Pochelu
235 East Hortense Street
New Ulm, Minnesota

Miss Dorothy L. Anderson,
   1740 University Avenue,
      Glendale, California.

In a business letter it is always correct to use a personal title with the name of the person addressed. The use of a personal title is correct even when a business title follows the name. A business title should not precede the name. Correct personal titles are: Mr., Mrs., Miss, Dr., Professor, Messrs. The business title may follow the name of the person addressed if the title is short, or it may be placed on the line below it if the title is long.

Professor Henry M. Jones, Secretary
Shattuck Alumni Association

Dr. Howard Olson
Superintendent of Schools

Mrs. Cornelius Blank, Chairman
Finance Committee, Woman's Club

Miss Helen Throckmorton
Chairman, Council of Teachers of English

SALUTATION

The following forms are correct for business and professional letters:

Dear Sir:
Dear Madam:
Gentlemen:
Mesdames:
My dear Sir:
My dear Madam:
Dear Mr. Jackson:
My dear Miss Blank:
Ladies and Gentlemen:
Dear Professor Potts:

In personal letters the use of *Sir, Madam, Gentlemen,* and *Mesdames* suggests an inappropriate formality. Correct forms which may be used are:

Dear Mr. Howard:
Dear Miss Brown:
My dear Chambers:
Dear Jack,

For correct usage in addressing government officials and other dignitaries, see *The Secretary's Handbook,* pp. 271–306.

In personal letters either a colon or a comma is correct after the salutation. The comma is probably more generally used than the colon. In both business and personal letters, *My dear Mr. Howard* is more formal than *Dear Mr. Howard; My dear Sir,* than *Dear Sir.*

BODY OF THE LETTER

The composition of business letters is a subject much too complex to be discussed here. A good letter obeys the principles of good writing. It should be clear, direct, coherent, dignified, and courteous. A student who can write a good theme should be able to write a good business letter. The following are good guides to the various types of business letters:

Hotchkiss, George Burton, and Kilduff, Edward Jones, *Advanced Business Correspondence*, Harper & Brothers, New York, 1935.

Saunders, Alta Gwinn, *Effective Business English*, The Macmillan Company, New York, 1936.

Taintor, Sarah Augusta, and Monro, Kate M., *The Secretary's Handbook*, The Macmillan Company, New York, 1937.

COMPLIMENTARY CLOSE

Correct forms for business letters are:

> Yours truly,
> Very truly yours,
> Respectfully yours,
> Yours very truly,
> Sincerely yours,
> Yours sincerely,
> Cordially yours,

It is now considered bad taste in business letters to use a participial phrase, such as, *Hoping for an early answer*, with the complimentary close. A comma after the complimentary close is the usual punctuation, but if punctuation is omitted after the salutation it may also be omitted after the complimentary close. In ordinary formal business letters *Yours truly*, or *Yours very truly*, is the accepted form; in business letters between persons who know each other more or less intimately *Yours sincerely* and *Cordially yours* are often used.

THE SIGNATURE

The form of the signature may depend upon certain special conditions which will be discussed later, but for the ordinary person it is correct to sign a letter as he would sign a check. If possible, he should write his name legibly. Since a legible signature is impossible for many persons, it may occasionally be desirable—and strictly correct—to type the name under the signature.

Some of the conventions which govern the form of a signature are:

1. Neither professional titles, such as *Professor, Dr., Rev.*, nor academic degrees, such as *Ph.D., LL.D., M.A.*, should be used with a signature.
2. An unmarried woman should not sign herself as Miss Laura Blank, but she may place *Miss* in parentheses before her name if she feels that it is necessary for proper identification.
3. A married woman or a widow signs her own name, not her married name. For example, *Diana Holoday Brown* is her own name; *Mrs. George Brown* is her married name. She may place *Mrs.* in parentheses before her signature, or her married name in parentheses under it.
4. When a secretary signs her chief's name to a letter, she may add her own initials below the signature.

INVITATIONS, ACCEPTANCES, REGRETS

INFORMAL

An informal invitation should be written in an easy, natural, and cordial manner.

1520 East 34th Street
May the fifth

My dear Mrs. Fowler,

Will you and Mr. Fowler dine with us on Saturday, May the fourteenth, at seven o'clock? We shall probably drive out to the Oasis to dance afterwards. We shall be very glad if you are able to come.

Sincerely yours,
Beatrice W. Scott

Dear Mrs. Fowler,

Mr. Scott and I shall be greatly pleased if you and Mr. Fowler can come to an informal dinner at our apartments on Saturday, May the fourteenth, at seven o'clock. If you feel like dancing afterwards, we shall drive out to the Oasis for an hour or two.

Sincerely yours,
Beatrice W. Scott

1520 East 34th Street
May fifth

My dear Mrs. Scott,

Mr. Fowler and I are delighted to accept your very kind invitation to dine and dance with you on Saturday, May the fourteenth, at seven o'clock. We are looking forward to seeing you again.

Sincerely yours,
Marion Fowler

46 West Clinton Avenue
May sixth

My dear Mrs. Scott,

Mr. Fowler and I regret exceedingly that we are unable to accept your invitation for dinner on Saturday, May the fourteenth, as unfortunately we have another engagement for that evening.

Sincerely yours,
Marion Fowler

46 West Clinton Avenue
May sixth

FORMAL

Formal social notes are written in the third person. No abbreviations are used. Dates and hours are written in full. The following examples will serve for ordinary invitations, acceptances, and regrets. For correct forms in engraved invitations and announcements it is usually better to depend upon the stationer.

Mrs. Prentiss requests the pleasure of Miss Roxbury's company at dinner on Friday evening, May the thirteenth, at seven o'clock.
620 Monroe Street,
    May the fifth.

Miss Roxbury accepts with pleasure the kind invitation of Mrs. Prentiss to dinner on Friday evening, May the thirteenth, at seven o'clock.
1224 Franklin Road,
    May the sixth.

Miss Roxbury regrets that she is unable to accept the kind invitation of Mrs. Prentiss to dinner on Friday evening, May the thirteenth, at seven o'clock.
1224 Franklin Road,
    May the sixth.

FAULTS TO AVOID

1. Do not omit pronouns, prepositions, and articles where they are grammatically necessary. If your letter should begin with *I* or *we*, begin with *I* or *we*.

    Bad: Received your letter yesterday.
           Am writing to you in reply . . .
           Have not heard from you . . .
    Right: I received your letter yesterday.
           I am writing to you . . .
           I have not heard from you . . .

2. Do not close a letter with a sentence or a phrase introduced by a participle.

> *Bad:* Hoping to hear from you soon . . .
> Hoping for an early answer . . .
> Thanking you again for your past favors . . .
> Trusting to hear from you by return mail . . .

3. Do not write *yours, your favor,* or *your esteemed favor* for *letter*.

> *Bad:* In reply to yours of the 20th . . .
> Your esteemed favor at hand, and in reply . . .
> In reply to yours of the 15th . . .

4. Avoid certain trite and stilted expressions frequently used in business letters.

> *Bad:* In reply would say . . .
> Yours of the 10th inst. received . . .
> And contents thereof noted . . .
> Your valued favor . . .
> And oblige, Yours truly . . .
> Enclosed please find . . .

EXERCISES

Exercise 1. Write a letter to a friend who lives in your home community explaining to him the value of the course you are now taking in your college.

Exercise 2. Write a letter to your college newspaper in which you correct a wrong impression produced by a news story which has appeared in the paper. Make your letter courteous, dignified, and logical.

Exercise 3. Write a letter to your dean in which you request permission to take your final examinations several days before the scheduled period. Give your reasons clearly and convincingly.

Exercise 4. As secretary of a student organization, write a letter to the members urging them to pay their dues.

Exercise 5. You plan to work at one of the national parks during the summer. Write a letter of application. Apply for some position that you could fill. Give adequate information about yourself and your qualifications.

Exercise 6. Write to a friend asking him to accompany you on a fishing and camping trip.

Exercise 7. Write to your hostess thanking her for the pleasant time you have had at her home. She is your roommate's mother.

Exercise 8. A man for whom you worked last summer owes you thirty dollars. Write him a letter that will induce him to pay what he owes you.

Exercise 9. You have been asked to tell what you think of some acquaintance who has applied for a position as teacher in the public schools. Write a letter in which you convey a favorable impression. Be specific.

Exercise 10. You forgot a conference you had scheduled with your English teacher. Write a note of apology.

Index

INDEX

(Figures in boldface refer to sections; in roman to pages.)

INDEX

And, excessive use of, **46**, 292–294; number of verb with subjects joined by, **4**, 148–149; punctuation of clauses joined by, **20**, 213–214.

And etc., 360.

And which construction, **56**, 321.

Antecedent, ambiguous, **55**, 316–317; defined, **9**, 178; vague or remote, **55**, 315–316.

Anybody, singular number, **5**, 157.

Anyplace for *anywhere*, 360.

Anywheres for *anywhere*, 360.

Apostrophe, **23**, 227–229; to form plurals of figures, letters, and words as words, **23**, 228; to indicate omission, **23**, 228; with possessive, **23**, 227.

Appear, subjective complement with, **6**, 163.

Appositives, defined, **9**, 179; diagram of, **390**; punctuation with, **20**, 217.

Apt, likely, liable, 360.

Arabic numerals, used in dates, page numbers, street and room numbers, **13**, 198; in bibliography, **17**, 205–206; in footnotes, **18**, 206–208.

Archaic words, **38**, 279.

Arrangement, sentences, 76; words in a sentence, **53**, 308–312.

Article, definite and indefinite, **9**, 179.

Articles, quotation marks with titles of, 116–117.

Art Index, 105.

As, with *so* in negative statements, 361; misuse for *that, whether*, 361.

As if, used with subjunctive, **7**, 169.

As well as, subject not made plural by, **4**, 150.

Associated meanings of words, 267–269.

At about, wrong use of, 361.

Author card, 91.

Auto for *automobile*, 361.

Auxiliary verbs, defined, **9**, 179.

Awful, awfully, misuse of, 361.

Awkwardness, caused by repetition of words, 62, 336; in sentence structure, **52**, 306–308; in reference of pronouns, **55**, 316–317; with *same, such, above, said*, **55**, 319.

Back of, in back of, for *behind*, 362.

Badly, misuse of, 362.

Balance for *the remainder, the rest*, 362.

Balance in sentence structure, **63**, 337–338.

Bank on for *rely upon*, 362.

Barbarisms, **38**, 279.

B.C., used with dates, **14**, 200.

Be, subjective complement with, 41.

Because of, correct use of, 6, 165; 362.

Beginning a theme, suggestions for, 20–23.

Beside, besides, correct use of, 362.

Between and *among*, 360.

Bibliography, cards, 114–120; correct forms, **17**, 204–206; defined, 113; final form, 121–123; for research paper, 113–123; references to book, 115–116; references to encyclopedias, 114–115; references to government bulletins, 117–119; references to magazine articles, 116–117; references to newspapers, 120.

Biographical dictionaries, 99.

Biographical information, use of dictionary for, **35**, 264.

Blame on for *blame*, 363.

Books, reference to, **17**, 205–206; **18**, 206–207; 115; titles of, italicized, **16**, 203.

Borrowed material, acknowledgment of. See *Footnotes*.

Boughten for *bought*, 363.

Brackets, section on, **27**, 237–239.

Brevity, 66, 341–344.

Broadcasted, 363.

Business letters, section on, 410–419; parts of, 410; heading of, 419–420; inside address, 412; salutation, 413; body, 414; signature, 415; faults to avoid, 417–418.

INDEX

Co-ordinating connectives, list of and punctuation with, **8,** 175; **20,** 213–214.

Co-ordination, faulty use of, **46,** 292–294.

Copulative verb, defined, **9,** 181; subjective complement with, 41; subjective complement after *become, appear, seem, prove, remain, look, smell, taste, feel,* **6,** 163–164.

Copy, preparation of, **10,** 191; 397–400.

Correction of proof, 397–400.

Correlatives, 39; **56,** 322; defined, **9,** 181.

Could of for *could have,* 365.

Couple for *two, a few,* 365.

Crabb's English Synonyms, 101.

Criticize, correct uses of, 366.

Crowd for *a set, clique,* 366.

Cyclopedia of American Agriculture, 97.

Cyclopedia of Education, 97.

Dangling modifiers, **54,** 312–315; difference between absolute phrase and dangling verbal phrase, **54,** 313–314; elliptical clauses, **54,** 313; verbal phrases, **54,** 312–313.

Dash, **25,** 234–235; for sudden break in thought, **25,** 234; for hesitation or uncertainty, **25,** 235.

Date, colloquial use of, 366.

Dates, use of figures for, **13,** 198; in letters, 410–411.

Deal, incorrect uses of, 366.

Declension defined, **9,** 181.

Definite article. See *Article.*

Definition, in paragraph development, 69–70; 77–78; theme of, 13–14.

Degree, comparative and superlative, **6,** 161.

Demonstrative pronouns, **9,** 187.

Denotation of words, **36,** 268–269.

Dependent clauses, 46–49.

Details, in development of paragraph,

67–68; use in paragraph, **72,** 351–352; use in writing, 23–24.

Determination, expressed by *shall* **and** *will,* **7,** 170.

Development of paragraphs, 65–76; by particulars and details, 67; by examples or typical instances, 68; by definition, 69; by comparison or contrast, 70; by repetition, 72; by analogy, 72; by giving causes or effects, 73.

Dewey Decimal system explained, 93–95.

Diagrams, 381–396; subject and verb, 381; complements, 382; modifiers, 385; gerund and infinitive, 387; appositives, 390; complex sentences, 392; compound sentences, 395.

Diction, appropriateness, **36, 270;** concreteness, **39,** 280–282; euphony, 44, 289; "fine writing," **43,** 288–289; good use, **38,** 277–280; idioms, **37,** 271–274; sections on, **35–44,** 253–289; specific words, **39,** 280–282; the right word, **36,** 267–269; triteness, **42,** 287–288; vividness, **40,** 282–284; wordiness, **41,** 284–286. See also *Glossary,* **77,** 357–378.

Dictionaries, listed, 99–100; recommended for desk use, 253.

Dictionary, section on, **35,** 253–267; abbreviations, **35,** 265; accent, **35,** 257–258; biographical information, **35,** 264; compounding of words, **35,** 260; etymology of a word, **35,** 256–257; exact meanings of words, **35,** 253–254; idioms, **35,** 261–262; inflectional forms, **35,** 262–263; pronunciation, **35,** 255–256; spelling, **35,** 254–255; synonyms, **35,** 260–261; syllabication, **35,** 258–259; usage, **35,** 259–260.

Dictionary of American Biography, 99.

Dictionary of National Biography, 99.

Different than for *different from,* 366.

INDEX

INDEX

Wordiness, section on, **41**, 284–286.

Words, **35–44**, 253–289; appropriate, **36**, 270; concrete, **39**, 280–282; list of books about, **38**, 279–280; similar in form, **36**, 270–271; specific, **39**, 280–282; the right word, **36**, 267–269; used in double capa-city, **51**, 304; vivid, **40**, 282–284.

World Almanac, 98.

Would and *should*. See *Shall* and *will*.

Year books, 98–99.

You, used in indefinite sense, **5**, 158–159.

Nominative absolute is an expression grammatically independent of the rest of the sentence

An infinitive is a verb form that has the
sign "to" either expressed or understood
It is used like a noun, adjective, or adverb

(Understood) Will you let me use these tools

(Subject) to be great &c is &c P.N.

(Object of verb) They wish &c

(Adverb) We shall hurry
not refuse

(Adjective) many are overpriced
houses
to be sold

HANDBOOK KEY

GRAMMAR

1 Period Fault	2 Comma Fault	3 Run-Together Sentence	4 Subject and Verb	5 Pronouns
6 Adjectives and Adverbs	7 Verb Forms	8 Conjunctions	9 Grammatical Terms	

MECHANICS

10 Manuscript	11 Titles	12 Capitals	13 Numbers	14 Abbreviations
15 Syllabication	16 Italics	17 Bibliographies	18 Footnotes	

PUNCTUATION

19 Period Question Mark Exclamation Pt.	20 Comma	21 Semicolon	22 Colon	23 Apostrophe
24 Quotation Marks	25 Dash	26 Hyphen	27 Parentheses Brackets	

SPELLING

28 Pronunciation	29 Final -E	30 Ie or Ei	31 Final Consonant	32 Final -Y
33 Similar Forms	34 Spelling List			

WORDS

35 Use of Dictionary	36 The Right Word	37 Idioms	38 Good Use	39 Concreteness
40 Vividness	41 Wordiness	42 Triteness	43 Fine Writing	44 Euphony